Desperate Visions

CW00821513

CREATION BOOKS

London • *San Francisco*

Desperate Visions 1:
Camp America
The Films Of John Waters And George & Mike Kuchar
Written by:
Jack Stevenson
ISBN 1 871592 34 8
© Jack Stevenson 1996, all rights reserved
First published 1996 by:
Creation Books
83, Clerkenwell Road, London EC1, UK
Tel: 0171-430-9878
Fax: 0171-242-5527
E-mail: creation@pussycat.demon.co.uk
Desperate Visions – a periodical publication.
Interviews with John Waters, Divine, Mary Vivian Pearce, Mink Stole, Jean Hill, George Kuchar and Mike Kuchar first appeared in *Pandemonium*.
"The Day The Bronx Invaded Earth – The Life And Cinema Of The Brothers Of Invention" was published in condensed form in issue 14 of *Bright Lights* film journal, 1995.
"In Praise Of Gorgeous Dialogue, Or What To Do When Your Wig Falls Into The Toilet (Put It Back On)" was originally translated into German and published in condensed form in issue 2 of *24* film journal, 1992.
Design/layout/typesetting:
PCP International, Bradley Davis
Photos by courtesy of Jack Stevenson and individual owners; all additional visual material from the BFI and the Jack Hunter Collection.
British Library Cataloguing in Publication Data:
A catalogue record for this book is available from the British Library

creation books are distributed by:
uk & europe: turnaround distribution, 27 horsell road, london N5 1xl
tel: 0171-609-7836 fax: 0171-700-1205
usa: subterranean company, box 160, 265 south 5th street, monroe, or 97456
tel: 503 847-5274 fax: 503-847-6018
canada: marginal, unit 102, 277 george street, n. peterborough, ontario k9j 3g9
tel/fax: 705-745-2326
australia & nz: peribo pty ltd, 58 beaumont road, mount kuring-gai, nsw 2080
tel: 02-457-0011 fax: 02-457-0022
japan: charles e tuttle co. inc., 21-13 seki 1-chome, tama-ku, kawasaki, kanagawa 214
tel: 44-833-1924 fax: 44-833-7559

other film books from creation:
deathtripping an illustrated history of the cinema of transgression
by jack sargeant: isbn 1 871592 29 1, £11.95/$16.95
inside teradome an illustrated history of freak film
by jack hunter: isbn 1 871592 41 0, £11.95/$16.95
house of horror an illustrated history of hammer films
edited by jack hunter: isbn 1 871592 40 2, £12.95/$19.95
fragments of fear an illustrated history of british horror movies
by andy boot: isbn 1 871592 35 6, £11.95/$17.95
killing for culture an illustrated history of death film
by david kerekes & david slater: isbn 1 871592 20 8, £12.95/$17.95

Desperate Visions

1

CAMP AMERICA

Interviews & Essays by
Jack Stevenson

CONTENTS

MOVIE SCREEN AS TRAP DOOR

My first encounter with the cinema of John Waters was a double-feature of PINK FLAMINGOS and FEMALE TROUBLE in 1980 at the Prytannia theatre in New Orleans. I was in a state of depression at the time and the films jolted me back to life like shock therapy – something that both spectators and participants, including Mink Stole, have likened them to.

The films, especially FEMALE TROUBLE, had an overwhelming **personal** effect on me in a way that I never knew movies could have. I was unprepared, as were many of the uninitiated at the crowded show. The effect was something like mass-rape by UFOs – and who could pass on that? It was, at the risk of dipping deeply into the bubbling purple brew of over-dramatization that the subject matter so richly deserves, a veritable religious experience.

My bloodshot eyes were opened.

Around this time I was looking for a new apartment, and I almost rented a particularly appalling, nightmarish, windowless room, hideously trashed and encrusted in countless sloppy ancient paint jobs in the back of a squalid slum house – all because I thought it looked like something out of FEMALE TROUBLE. I was trying to walk into the movie screen, but I don't think it would have been so hilarious.

I've known Waters to have this effect on others who've been pushed over the edge from aficionado or film buff to hopelessly obsessed film freak and cultist... and somewhere, as Presley might sing, another mother cries. I harassed a New York acquaintance into giving me John's address, which he did under the strict admonition that I never tell John where I got it, and I began launching a copious mass of letters in his direction. He responded. It was like getting a letter back from the Wizard of Oz. I didn't know who was behind the curtain...

Much as I intended to apply a scholarly, objective tone to this introduction, I've blown it. I can't keep the personal aspect out of it because therein lies its essence. I can also see, with some mortification, this text taking on the embarrassingly confessional feel common to the reminiscences of those who've been held in the blind grip of fanaticism at some point in their lives.

I became a rabid devotee of John Waters because of the specific films but also because he had revealed the power personal filmmaking could have. He had opened up a box full of ridiculous evil, some great hell. I know all this sounds hopelessly theoretical and figurative but that's where it **is**, in the realm of the spiritual. History is full of bizarre delusions and hysterias that swept the masses but defy straight-forward analysis. Today the movie screen serves as delivery system of a similar set of delusions and hysterias in modern wrapping. Whenever I read some writer launching into a rote recital of Waters' plot lines, I know he's missing it **completely**. I'm also at a loss to understand the value of published scripts. Nothing there.

I hitch-hiked around America continuously from 1981 to 1984, staying in cheap inner-city flophouse hotels, getting and quickly quitting jobs and going to the movies. I spent September of 1982 at the Franklin hotel in Baltimore and visited John on several occasions. During the day I aimlessly basked in the somehow familiar seediness of old Baltimore that John had celebrated in his films and his book, *Shock Value*, which I'd bought and devoured in 1981. At night I went from one bar to another, looking for... something strange. It was a pilgrimage of sorts. Years later I met a Norwegian guy from up near the arctic circle who travelled to Baltimore for similar vague purposes.

I engaged in an intermittent 15-year correspondence with John, published five interviews with him and went to some of his film openings and Christmas parties. I became friends with Mary Vivian Pearce, Jean Hill and Mink Stole whom I bombarded with letters and postcards at one point, with a frequency that today sends a shudder up my spine. I spent a sentimental December day in 1989 with Jean Hill in her ghetto flat reading pornographic love letters by the light of her beautifully twinkling Christmas tree. (Her recent spread in the skin mag, *Jumbo*, had reared a vast harvest of mail from drooling admirers of all persuasions.)

These interviews with John and his troop, originally self-published in my underground *Pandemonium* book series (1986–1989) comprise the bulk of the material here and offer background atmosphere and specific insights into the formulation of John Waters' filmmaking that superficial TV specials and recent mag puff-pieces cannot provide. And if we can consider John's films to be "songs" for another purple moment, they were glass-shattering off-key choruses composed of many voices, and some of the main voices are here to lend a depth and dimension that John alone cannot give.

In my earliest writings about Waters, I championed what I deemed to be his absolute **originality**. I had never seen anything like it. My fanaticism at that point was only equalled by my ignorance. Waters did indeed have his influences, a **lot** of them, even if the crudely synthesized end-product was like nobody else's.

His main influence, of "the underground guys", were the Kuchar Brothers, George and Mike, twins born in 1942 in New York City who would develop in the '50s a personal home-movie style of cinema driven by the same violent melodrama that would strike a chord with a young John Waters soon to be terrorizing neighbourhood children with bloody backyard puppet shows. In the early '60s the Kuchars achieved recognition in the New York Underground and would exert a strong influence on Waters who would hitch-hike or take the bus up from Baltimore.

In 1988 George came to Boston to present a retrospective of his film work at the Brattle theater and I immediately saw the connection – plus much that was **new**. In 1989 I published a raw mass of interviews and writings by Mike and George in *Pandemonium* #3. In 1990 I moved out to San Francisco. George and Mike had a flat there in the Mission District since the early '70s and I became acquainted with them on a personal basis. Whenever I stopped by the San Francisco Art Institute in North Beach, where George teaches film, he would screen for me some of his class movies and other miscellaneous filmic oddities he would dig out of a tiny crammed locker in the basement, and we'd ditch out to a Chinese restaurant afterwards. I was also an occasional visitor to their flat in the Mission where they would show me their latest video productions and we'd sometimes set up a 16mm projector and George would snap on a reel of something he pulled out of the kitchen cupboard.

In this casual fashion, over the course of several years, I was able to gain a wider perspective on their cinema and to view some of the obscurer titles from their oeuvre that had literally only been screened a couple times then stacked away and had never been put on video. The text I've written for this volume (*The Day The Bronx Invaded Earth*) benefits from this and offers a more enlightened, comprehensive and digestible examination of their life and cinema than the exploratory slabs of verbiage that appeared in *Pandemonium* #3. I was also able to obtain from George some rare, never-before-published photographs which are here included.

The chapter on Marion Eaton (*In Praise Of Gorgeous Dialogue*) serves as a companion text to the Kuchar Brothers material, focusing as it does on the adventures of one of George's leading ladies. It also functions as a more detailed and free-standing exploration of the vital but seldom written-about San Francisco Underground film scene of the 1970s – via which George, Mike and John are progenitors of a distinct and singular cinematic sensibility which had its roots in the emergence of the 1960s New York Underground movement and which continues to inspire much of what is being done today in independent American cinema. Although all three are distinctly individual personalities and have followed different career paths, their accomplishments are cut from the same cloth – leopard-skin velour no doubt – and a collective consideration, more fully explored within the various texts of this book, is natural.

I would like to thank George and John for trusting me with some of their most precious, personal photographs, and thanks also to Dale Ashmun, Joseph Casarona, Donna Kerness, Christina Lamb, Ronald Beauregard and Tiana Morris for photographic contributions. Gratitude is also due Dennis Harvey, Chuck Stephens, Jonas Mekas, Galen Young, Stefan Jaworzyn, and J. Hoberman for documentation on the Kuchar Brothers on which I've drawn to varying degrees. Thanks especially to Cindy Gold, whose unstinting – and unpaid – efforts made the original *Pandemonium* series possible. Additionally, thanks to Phil Kelly, Dennis Dermody, Johannes Schönherr, Mary Briggs and Mark Finch for help in various ways, and finally appreciation is due to all those others who supported and participated in the making of this book.

—Jack Stevenson, Copenhagen, 1995

PART ONE

Touched By Genius, Raped By A Lobster

Chapter One

JOHN WATERS
THE MAN, THE MYTH, THE MOVIES

No film director carries the cross of his past as heavily as John Waters. Upping the ante for shock effect in film after film throughout the 1970s, he was willingly, gleefully typecast as America's beastliest movie maker and his films got the kind of ink usually reserved for natural disasters and deadly plagues. Variously known as "The King Of Kink", "The Sultan Of Sleaze" and "The Prince Of Puke", he couldn't have been happier as he went about it all with the energy of the truly possessed. He tried to make his films as unforgettable as possible – and nobody's forgetting. Or forgiving.

By the time he began to develop a full-blown style around 1970, he had metamorphosed from a dance-crazed teenage J.D. "beatnik" into an acid-dropping anarchohippy whose main motivation in life was to make himself as vile and objectionable to decent townsfolk as possible. He was one of those greasy, repugnant, long-haired creatures we tend to overlook in our soft-focus nostalgia for the 1960s. He was... **trouble**.

Waters' sense of style was forged out of a mass of contradictions and unlikely syntheses which could easily blow the circuits of anyone who tried to use his films to psychoanalyse him. By the same token he could throw analytically-minded critics off the scent and get them to talk about what he wanted them to talk about. Or they could just simple **hate** a given film, and if they did so with enough vitriol that was so much the better. He never intended his films to be "reviewed" as such, they were not supposed to be "read" – they were to be reported on as sociological phenomena, as mind-fuckers. For 25 years he's been jousting with critics and interviewers and they've never been able to dismantle him or even get a grip and usually end up scribbling down his latest string of hilarious if often-to-be-repeated one liners.

EARLY INFLUENCES: ALL-AMERICAN BOY ON A MISSION

Waters' cinema, as it came into existence, was a mutant hybrid of two markedly disparate film genres: Exploitation and Underground. To any serious film artist the lines between the two were starkly drawn: The Commercial versus The Personal, Commodity versus Art Object, Job versus Vision. Waters threw all that bullshit out the window and baldly stuffed his movies full of things that excited him and that would get him **attention** – the thing he wanted most. Promotion is usually something employed to sell a film but with Waters the film and the promotion were one and the same. It was not always easy to tell whether the hype was promoting the film or the film was promoting the hype. He never saw film as an "artistic expression" even though many of the people he knocked around Baltimore with were boho artists. On the other hand he was smart enough to target his natural audience, the disaffected of his own generation, and cultivate a marketable product in a way that any exploitation filmmaker would admire. *Variety* and *Film Culture* were his twin bibles.

Addictive reader and news junkie, he was plugged into the restless politics and issues of his generation while at the same time he was appalled by the lethargic peace/love hippy conformity all around him. He was as much a product of his generation as Jerry Garcia but the flip side of the coin. And while he had fiercely-held political views, they never showed up in any direct way in his films. In an era of intense politicization, it was almost revolutionary to be apolitical.

Waters' early work was a very personal kind of filmmaking, but not in the usual confessional style of gay compatriots like Curt McDowell, who bared his soul and his sexuality before the camera's eye. Waters himself never appeared on camera in any of his early work and would go to any lengths to disguise personal concerns in bizarre costuming and grotesquerie. Waters' films appeared to be "reality-proof". His favourite approach to portraying sexuality, for example, was to have straights playing gays and gays playing straights so that all roles ended up ridiculously over-played. Like the Wicked Witch in THE WIZARD OF OZ, Waters would probably have melted to the floor screaming if anything real had splashed on him. Conversely, in ways that seem to defy analysis, Waters' films were **very** personal and **very** real. It all boils down to the intentionally cloudy relationship he has with his own films. While he cultivated the public persona of an insane, amoral hippy degenerate, he was at heart anything but: only a radical **puritan** could have made those films. He was artistically, intellectually and morally dishonest and thank God for that – it made for great movies.

These tensions, frictions and contradictions gave his films force. There was something boiling under the surface. An **on** the surface.

Stylistically, he was heavily influenced by the street-theatre actions and "happenings" of left-wing '60s radicals like the Diggers and the Yippies and their ability to create bizarre scandals and get free publicity. Dressing a rotund Divine in a sheer cocktail dress and outlandish make-up to have him promenade down a crowded mid-winter Baltimore street blowing kisses and smiling hideously at shocked pedestrians, who would start screaming and laughing, was essentially filmed street theatre provocation. But Waters was equally in the thrall of the old-fashioned red hot carney hype of his heros from Exploitation like William Castle and Russ Meyer, and he emulated their very different tactics.

Other contradictions would present themselves as Waters began to produce a body of work. Although an habitué and in many ways a product of the New York underground scene, which was militantly anti-Hollywood for the most part, Waters' films had strong (if forced) story-lines, ambitious plots and memorable (if one-dimensional) "star" performances. Like Hollywood. In bare essentials his films boil down to the domestic dramas and "coming of age" sagas that have always been the bread and butter of Hollywood. Even his most radical film, DESPERATE LIVING, "a monstrous fairy tale" as he describes it, owes a major debt to Walt Disney. "I always believed in everything Hollywood believed in", Waters would maintain many years later in the face of accusations that he had betrayed his Underground roots.

Waters was clearly dedicated to the narrative form, albeit true that some of his early films, like MONDO TRASHO, appear almost experimental in nature as a chaotic mass of music, sound, plot and image fragments hurtle willy-nilly at the viewer who might be prone to duck for cover. Waters always wanted to tell stories, it's just that in the beginning his story-telling skills were so unformed and he was so wildly over-ambitious. It's hard to tell whether MONDO TRASHO had the most complicated plot in history or has no plot at all. It wasn't until FEMALE TROUBLE that Waters managed a solid, coherent narrative with characters motivated by at least some scant degree of emotional plausibility, instead of characters jerking through his films like puppets, mouthing and pantomiming Waters' latest conglomerate of fixations and obsessions. This is not intended as criticism: this blatant unnaturalness, this exaggerated unreal quality was the essence of his early film work and was totally intentional. God forbid, we didn't **want** emotional plausibility in the typical John Waters character! Edie "the Egg Lady" is a hilarious grotesque because she blows our circuits. She is simply too much, she overloads anyone's capacity to feel genuine pity for her. And we know it's not real anyway which gives Waters wider latitude to fuck with sensitive subject matter. Had any filmmaker attempted a serious investigation into why an aged, over-weight, imbecilic woman would sit in a play-pen all day eating raw eggs, it would all quickly become hopelessly depressing. Waters' genius was to play this right to the edge so you were never in safe emotional territory. Edith Massey was disturbingly credible in the role of the Egg Lady, and her consummate inability to handle memorized dialogue gave her delivery a stiff, mechanical quality that in other circumstances might be deemed the result of genuine brain damage. She was a puppet, but her character was so all-absorbing that we forgot to look for the strings. Her scenes only work because they're so completely over the top, but it also depends on the individual viewer's capacity to set aside normal human responses to the situation, and some people could not. They were genuinely shocked and repelled. All the better as

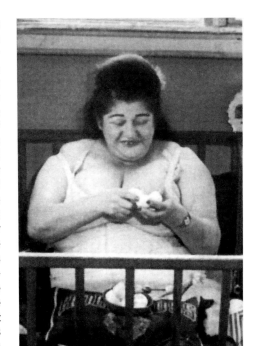

'The Egg Lady'; *Pink Flamingos*

far as Waters was concerned. It was this element that made his films truly "underground" and that separated them from the rash of parodies and imitations he would inspire. Anyone could haul out stock grotesqueries and assault audiences with bucketfuls of bad taste, but Waters had mastered a certain ambiguity of intention that was the "active ingredient" in his filmmaking. Maybe he really **was** a fucked-up sonofabitch. As with any art form or public expression, intention was key. And here you had to wonder who the hell was pulling the strings.

While attuned to the Hollywood aesthetic on many levels, Waters learned much from the Underground. He learned what you could do with the only kind of a budget available to him: a nearly non-existent one. He learned from CHELSEA GIRLS that a purely underground film could make huge profits in theatrical exhibition. He learned from Warhol that with a stable of "superstars" he could effectively mimic Hollywood's star culture and sell his movies the same way they did but with an ironic twist. (Movies without people was an alien concept to him.) He learned from Mike Kuchar's SINS OF THE FLESHAPOIDS that one could craft an exciting and luxurious visual style from out-dated film stock and junk bought in armfuls down at the local thrift shop. He saw that over-acting and non-acting was sometimes preferable to good acting, and that a raw look, a confrontational approach and a flagrant perversity could all be forged into a low-budget film style and compensate for what he couldn't afford, which was much. From all this he crafted his technique.

If Warhol, with his lethargic pacing, endless takes, non-editing and small casts had forced the viewer into a compressed, claustrophobic reality and created a cinema of limitation, Waters was the polar opposite, frenetically hurling out every imaginable influence, shred of music and fragment of idea from the gravity core of his film and creating a cinema of violent desorption.

Waters took advantage of Underground film distribution apparatus like the

New York Film Co-op and Art Theatre Guild without which he wouldn't have gotten a toe-hold. In this way he got his films seen, noticed and reviewed. This early exposure, while hardly profitable in any real commercial sense, was essential. Had he been unable to stir up any public reaction to his films, he and his actors would simply have ceased making them. They **had** to know they were offending somebody! It's the old "if-a-tree-falls-in-the-forest-and-no-one-hears-it" riddle. If a giant lobster rapes a fat transvestite (MULTIPLE MANIACS) and nobody sees it, did it really happen?

It's interesting to conjecture at this point what would happen if Waters was struggling to get known today instead of in 1970. While filmmaker-friendly '60s-rooted distributors like Canyon Cinema and The New York Film Co-op still exist, there is no public "off" theatrical circuit of consequence left any more where a young filmmaker aiming to raise a shit storm can get what he needs most: scandalous infamy and the potential monetary return so necessary with such an expensive medium. Today the young filmmaker usually shoots on video and markets his product by mail-order or rental. He/she might make a substantial profit but they lose a shot at any sort of greater impact of the kind that was absolutely critical to the establishment of people like Waters as famous provocateurs and not just filmmakers. Waters knew the art of showmanship and quickly into his career he turned himself into the main point of promotion of his films.

Admittedly these are different times, but scandals, outrages and controversy can still sell a movie in theatres. Todd Phillips proved this in the summer of 1993 when his film HATED: G.G. ALLIN & THE MURDER JUNKIES, about an infamous punk rock star, took the remnants of the American midnight movie circuit by storm.

The fact that Waters made his films in Baltimore and not in media capitals like New York or Los Angeles also contributed to the uniqueness of his cinema. He maximized local flavour in his productions in contrast, for example, to much that was happening in New York that had a hermetically-sealed feel to it. Here Baltimore starred.

Over the years loose comparisons were drawn between Waters' cinema and the exaggerated, violent black humour of the French Grand-Guignol, and the films of the Vienna Aktionist movement with its provocative, purgative radicalism, but Waters was, if anything, so very American.

CAREER ARCH – UP FROM THE UNDERGROUND

Waters scored a commercial breakthrough in 1972 with PINK FLAMINGOS which New Line Cinema picked up and parlayed into one of the hottest midnight movie attractions of the era. It drew crowds of perverse thrill-seekers who in another day and age would have been piling into the circus freakshow tent. While not a stylistic or casting departure for Waters, for many people this was their first pungent whiff of what he was offering.

In 1974 he followed up with the film that many Waters freaks still consider his best: FEMALE TROUBLE, and in 1977 he shot what was undoubtedly his strangest film, DESPERATE LIVING. By the end of the '70s he had created his own genre, built a strong cult following in America and set the foundations of an international audience – all outside the Hollywood system. But DESPERATE LIVING had also been desperate film-making – he often refers to it as his least favourite – and by the end of the decade Waters was desperate to move on.

These three films, the tarnished nuggets of his early fame which established him as an American sub-culture celebrity, unspool more like visual psychiatric reports on Waters' current mental condition – never healthy – than movies. One reviewer in fact described PINK FLAMINGOS as "rage into psychosis". These were spasms, convulsions, obsessions-set-in-motion populated with local freaks and his trash-hippy

soulmate friends who stole film for him and helped create the scandals that got him known. These films evolved out of a local scene driven by the spirit of bent, bored, rampaging youth and fused with the anger and confusion of the times.

It was not the stuff of a long, comfortable career in the movies.

Waters turned a corner in 1981 with his first quasi-mainstream film, POLYESTER. Despite a minuscule budget of $300,000, the Production boasted a glossy look and featured John's first real Hollywood star: Tab Hunter. POLYESTER would mark a clear departure from the blatantly outrageous provocations of his '70s work and foreshadow a penchant for more "viewer-friendly" satire, but with sharp edges intact.

Polyester

Hairspray

Aping his gimmick-master heros of the '50s, Waters did the film in "Odorama".

It would be another seven years of knocking around Hollywood pitching scripts and looking for money before he followed up with HAIRSPRAY. Critics loved

Crybaby

this film, in part due to Waters' creative casting, sympathy inspired by Divine's likable performance and the upbeat "socially conscious" treatment of racial integration in early-'60s Baltimore (Heretofore Waters had never been thought of as a socially-conscious filmmaker!). HAIRSPRAY was a good-spirited dance movie and the start of Waters' mainstream period, although Waters himself still refers to the "M-word" with trepidation. Shockingly for a John Waters film, HAIRSPRAY was given a PG rating and became a top rental video for children's parties. It made money, "legitimized" Waters in America and broke him in Britain and Europe.

Three years later, in 1990, Waters made CRYBABY with Johnny Depp playing a teenage J.D. from the wrong side of the tracks who falls in love with a square but beautiful society gal. It was another retro piece set in the early '60s. The casting of famous porn starlet, Traci Lords, was a natural press hook, and TV teen-throb, Depp, in a Waters' movie aroused curiosity and raised box-office potential through the roof. Yet CRYBABY failed to catch on. Its story failed to win over new audiences or interest the old fans while its period stylizations were considered by some as too slick. It appeared that classic Waters' situations and characters weren't enhanced by better production values which made them seem too pre-meditated and polished. Therein lay the essence of the Catch-22 situation Waters was in with his old fans. With CRYBABY Waters proved he could make an exciting, great-looking and even weird film in purely cinematic terms, which of course made one all the more aware that one was watching a **movie**. In his films from the '70s, no matter how preposterous the plots, something jaggedly real always glimmered through and audiences **connected**. Energy flowed back and forth from the screen. These weren't just movies and in fact they were usually referred to by other names, like "celluloid atrocities", etc. Ironically for Waters, making a great movie was weirdly counter-productive. Now a Waters' movie was more of a passive, orthodox, movie-going experience, an entertainment. Now he was making movies about teenage angst whereas before he had made movies **out of** teenage angst.

Original Waters' fans who had given HAIRSPRAY the benefit of a doubt found CRYBABY too sweet, and might have started to become uncomfortable with the

Crybaby

blatant nostalgia that informed these last two films which navigated in territory uncomfortably close to shit like GREASE and AMERICAN GRAFFITI. They also missed Divine, who had died suddenly in 1988. (It should be noted that even though Divine had been tamed and domesticated in HAIRSPRAY, his live stage act remained ultra vulgar right up to the end.) CRYBABY did especially poorly with kids from the South. "They liked Depp," figured Waters, "but they smelled a rat – me!"

Waters' last movie, SERIAL MOM (1993) did well with audiences and critics alike and stands as his most perfectly realized production to date. He shucked the nostalgia this time for an ever-so-up-to-date suburban setting that provided fertile ground for his agile, barbed satirizations of modern media culture and family life. While largely a reworking and updating of the same themes he had explored in POLYESTER, SERIAL MOM is a much more modulated, ambitious and stylish film and marks his ascent as a different kind of filmmaker.

Waters' films are such radically different finished products today, despite the treatment of a familiar cycle of themes, that it begs an answer to the riddle of what exactly is it that has changed: Waters? Us? The times? It's a more complicated issue than one might suspect, and pundits and critics who charge Waters with "selling out" are engaging in crashing superficialities.

It's an enigma that beckons us to look, once again, back into the past.

Waters was always a showman, a tireless promoter and a colourful personality in his own right. He came to dominate his films in a unique way, which clouded the fact that his early productions were full-fledged collaborations. He benefited from the creativity, energy and interactive chemistry of his amateur cast and crew friends as much as they benefited from his obsessive will-power and absolutely unstoppable determination to **make movies**. Now with the main players in his original ensemble either dead (Divine, Mueller, Massey, Lochary), drifted away or relegated to cameos (with the exception of Mink Stole) his new material is deprived of the wild, raw-edged spirit that all the money in Hollywood can't buy. Anyone looking for a jolt of the old shock therapy today is bound to be disappointed.

On the other hand, money **can** buy production values and Waters has proven himself adept at using glossiness as a subversive technique in and of itself, most notably in SERIAL MOM where visual set pieces establish atmosphere in long takes and slow pans. He can now make use of subtle textures and quiet moments instead of having everybody constantly screaming and shouting at each other, à la DESPERATE LIVING. The bigger budgets and heavier clout he wields have enabled him to utilize the talents of major Hollywood stars, often against type and to intriguing effect.

Kathleen Turner; *Serial Mom*

All that said, something **is** lost, and this cannot be analysed by looking only at the films themselves, for indeed their impact owes to a host of intangibles as much as what was actually put on celluloid. There was a little bit of voodoo involved, and hippy witch-doctor, Waters, could never be exactly sure what was going to crawl out of the pot no matter how dictatorially he tried to choreograph every scene and rehearse every line. The fact that journalists and pundits are still nailing Waters on charges of "sell out" 13 years after POLYESTER attests more than anything to the potency of those early films. It seemed there was no line he wouldn't cross, no beastly horror he wouldn't inflict on an audience. And if you have the stomach for it, of course you **will** get known, just like somebody who forces a busload of schoolchildren off the road and over a cliff will probably get some amount of press out of it. Waters made kind of a deal with the devil to get famous in the '70s and undoubtedly paid for it in various ways over the years, but he wasn't the only one who would pay for it. Mink Stole, who quickly matured into a very good actress, still has trouble getting acting roles... adored by casting agents who beg to meet her but consider her way too "underground" to cast in anything. Being typecast as a John Waters' actress turned out to be a mixed blessing for her professionally speaking, even though she is the only one of his original players who still gets major roles in **his** films.

What the movie critics, film professors and the "the uninitiated" never understood was that Waters gave "his people" more than obvious gross-outs, like Divine's fabled shit-eating scene in PINK FLAMINGOS, which were basically just marketing gimmicks. What he gave his core audience – a loose rabble of anarcho-punko-hippies, freaks, degenerates, hopeful transvestites and motley unclassifiables that could make a punk concert look like Sunday School – was something else. He gave them a cathartic outlet through laughter for their own anger and malevolence, and in effect forged a very personal link with these people in the purest "cult" tradition. And although he aimed his films at a specific audience, they were anything but calculated product. He made the films he **had** to make, and he was the only one who could make a "John Waters movie". Obvious imitations, such as the Jed Johnson-directed "Andy Warhol" film, BAD (1977), paled indeed (get that, Kim). Troma studio films offer more proof of the inability to shock when even the most offensive set-ups are not driven by some kind of genuine spirit. (Troma was at one point slated to co-finance the never-to-be-made Waters film, FLAMINGOS FOREVER.) Waters was like an undiluted base chemical: whether you found the fumes intoxicating or toxic, you knew it was pure John Waters.

He was more than just a filmmaker to his people, he was some kind of pirate leader. His films were not just films but bubonic attacks on all that was oppressively dull, conformist and suffocatingly normal in America.

Today he is just a filmmaker.

Any magazine you browse in the dentist's office has an interview with him, and he is a frequent guest on the circuit of TV talkshows. He has become accessible with a vengeance: imagine the horror to realize your small-town parents just read about him in *The New York Times* Sunday supplement magazine, and your sister casually rents MULTIPLE MANIACS down at the local combination video/gas-station mart.

Any retrospective analysis of Waters must take into account the thick tangle of pathological emotional inputs that feed into his films, and as happy as he probably is with that situation, it must be frustrating for him not to be judged solely for the movies he makes, but for all sorts of other hocus-pocus.

Positive response to Waters' new accessibility is articulated by people like *Film Threat* magazine editor, Chris Gore, who lauds Waters' launch into the mainstream as an act of even greater subversion, since like the proverbial Trojan Horse, his movies are now "corrupting" a much wider audience, and he is not merely preaching to the converted. This highly debatable rationale also conveniently doubles as an apology for *Film Threat*'s own transformation from ranting broadside to celeb-fixated glossy slick, but it is also an idea that Waters subscribes to: "If I can have a hit in mid-America", he says, "that would be the most devious thing I could do."

Some argue that Waters is still Waters, that it's the world around him that's done the changing. The Underground, out of which Waters evolved, was very much a creature of the '60s, while the Midnight Movie phenomenon of the '70s in which he established himself has been usurped by home video as America's traditional public carnival culture turns into a private, electronic, living-room culture. Not only would it be patently ridiculous and psychically suicidal for Waters to go back to the old way, but it would also be – worst of all – bad business sense. Nonetheless he stays fully plugged into the latest filmic outrages from today's Underground and uses his high public profile as a bully pulpit to publicize young filmmakers like Nick Zedd, Todd Haynes and Todd Phillips who are fighting to get known. He still has credibility with a lot of the old time crowd, and is lionized by a new generation of punkos and troublemakers, folks like the Lunachicks, a kick-ass lesbian punk band who rate DESPERATE LIVING as their favourite movie of all time and would move to Mortville in a second if they could. And if you don't know where Mortville is – fuck you!

Of all the changes that Waters has observed, the new attitude of his old neighbours shocked him the most. SERIAL MOM was filmed in the upscale Baltimore suburb where Waters grew up, but this time residents gave him a welcome he'd never received for his earlier films. "I realized it was their parents who hated us," ruminated the old juvenile delinquent. "My age group lives in those houses now." His age group is also running Hollywood now. Producers no longer sit in shock when he shows them his old films – they saw them all in college.

It might be argued that Waters' films have lost their power to shock because modern-day America, glutted on "reality TV" horrors and the daytime talkshow freak parade, has turned into a John Waters' movie. What his actors used to deliver to outraged hoots and hollers at midnight, common folks today are thrilled to confess on the Oprah Winfrey show. In a bizarre twist, Waters' brightest new female discovery, Ricki Lake, now has her own successful daytime TV talk-show.

John Waters directs *Serial Mom*

At the time of this writing, Waters reports he has finalized a deal for a new film about a kid director who kidnaps a movie star. Entitled CECIL B. DEMENTED, the production will be financed by French money but as usual he'll shoot it in Baltimore. Casting is not yet set, but maybe John will hook some real A-list Hollywood talent like Richard Gere, Jodie Foster, Meryl Streep, Mel Gibson or Sharon Stone – actors he's

John Waters

indicated a desire to work with.

Amazing to think of John Waters working with these people. But not so amazing any more, actually. It would be more amazing to think that maybe, finally, he'll be able to come down off the cross of his past cinematic sins and transgressions and make a movie free of the stigmata of his old outrages... a movie judged by what it contains, not by what it once **might** have contained.

A lapsed but still ever-so-guilty Catholic, John Waters would appreciate the image.

Chapter Two

THE JOHN WATERS INTERVIEWS

Part I: A written interview with John Waters that he filled out on an airplane in November, 1981.

JACK STEVENSON: Do you believe with more money you can make a better movie, or can technical limitations themselves provide certain effects or feels, and to what extent can you control that?

JOHN WATERS: The more money you have the harder it is because you're dealing with more people, crews, and have more on your shoulders. Money does not equate quality, certainly, but it enables you to try more. Technical limitations can force you to be more original in your script.

JS: Some people would say your best movies were your cheapest and with the move to legitimate budget 35mm [POLYESTER] you've lost that certain magic. Any comment?

JW: Reverse snobbism. Even in the most peculiar moments my films were oddly commercial – even eating shit. The cheapest movies I tried to make look as professional as POLYESTER, I just didn't have the money.

JS: You admire some directors who shoot in black-and-white; David Lynch for example. Would you ever consider shooting in black-and-white?

JW: I made some movies [MONDO TRASHO and MULTIPLE MANIACS] in black-and-white, solely for budgetary reasons. I don't mind black-and-white, but wouldn't do a film in black-and-white and add another commercial problem to my films. Black-and-white in 1981 is almost pretentious if you can afford colour. I thought ERASERHEAD [by Lynch] the most original film of the '70s. I thought ELEPHANT MAN looked great but wasn't wild about the liberal script that turned me into a reactionary who almost thought "the ugly fucker got what he deserved".

JS: You said in your book *Shock Value* that you were once appalled by the earthiness of San Francisco. Has your opinion of the city changed? Could you see yourself living here today? New Orleans?

JW: San Francisco is aptly called the Kook Capital of the world, and I like it for that reason. However, the earthshoe/ashram/healthfood people I consider my enemies. It's a great movie town. If I lived in New Orleans I'm afraid all I'd do is ride the bus named Desire over and over. [Ed. note: and he'd be the only white face on it as it headed for the country's largest housing project.]

JS: Does pornography [films] have any redeeming value? You've said you would never consider shooting hardcore pornography, but don't you think it has some subversive value, or the potential for such? Some of the best B-film directors got their start in pornography, while Russ Meyer admits he's a pornographer, a first-class one.

John Waters directs *Polyester*

JW: Porno, as an aid to masturbation, is redeeming I suppose. Hardcore is not that subversive, once you've seen it for the first time. I don't think of Russ Meyer as a pornographer at all. He has way too much style to be just that. ROCKY was porno to me.

JS: While your films are largely attended by gay audiences, you don't seem to champion homosexuality, but treat all sexual orientations with the same twisted sensationalism and blistering disrespect. Any comment here?

JW: I don't think any sexual preference is better or worse than any other. Since sex is so important in everyone's lives, I naturally like to slam it. Surprisingly, I do believe in love. Kissing is more rewarding than cumming.

JS: Don't you think stereotypes are dangerous and evil?

JW: No. They didn't get to be stereotypes unless there was a lot of truth in it. I revel in clichés.

JS: What are your favourite man-made and natural disasters?

JW: Ones that strike unsuspecting communities... the world.

JS: Do you believe that car accidents appeal to children more than adults?

JW: Yes, I hate them now and always turn my head. What a low-brow way to go! I have ultimate car paranoia if someone else is driving, but I think a lot when driving by myself. Most of my film ideas come from this.

JS: You've been to some of the most sensational trials of our day; what are the main ingredients for a media circus?

JW: (1) Murder (2) Good looking killer (3) Unrepentance (4) Lying (5) Defiance (6) Guilt (7) Press (8) Gore.

JS: Who is your favourite President and why?

JW: Gerald Ford because he was never elected.

JS: What do you think of Reagan cutting the arts?

JW: If it takes away ugly outdoor murals I'm all for it. I'm against art welfare.

JS: What do you think of: Jackie Gleason?

JW: Fat.

JS: Walt Disney?

JW: Genius.

JS: Organic foods?

JW: Poison.

JS: Baseball on the radio?

JW: Bring back Capital Punishment.

JS: Baseball strikes?

JW: I hope they last forever.

JS: Sports writers?

JW: Waste of paper.

JS: Woody Allen?

JW: Very funny but I wish he wasn't in his own films.

JS: Barbra Streisand?

JW: Married her hair dresser.

JS: Mel Brooks?

JW: Like him for backing David Lynch.

JS: The economy?

JW: I pay my bills – all I can do about it.

JS: The Gross National Product?

JW: Export sports fans.

JS: The sluggish housing industry?

JW: Don't buy.

JS: High interest rates?

JW: Don't borrow.

Part II: A phone interview with John Waters taped on March 7th, 1985.

JS: How are you today?

JW: Pretty good, I'm fine.

JS: What was your opinion of the three big blockbusters that came out of Hollywood last year: GHOSTBUSTERS, BEVERLY HILLS COP, and PURPLE RAIN?

JW: Ah... GHOSTBUSTERS was okay, I mean I laughed in it, I mean I just thought it was okay, I didn't think it was awful, I didn't think it was great... you know... I don't even remember it to tell you the truth. PURPLE RAIN... I don't mind seeing Prince sing, but I – I'm not a big person against sexism in movies, but **that** offended me – I thought it was the most sexist movie of the year. And I thought the plot line, with his whole family and stuff... was just embarrassingly ludicrous.

JS: What do you think the lousiest movies of the year have been? You've mentioned RHINESTONE.

JW: Yes, the worst, more nauseating than any gore film... even though I like Dolly Parton a lot. The movie I hate more than any movie I've seen in a long time is WITNESS. Any movie that takes as its heroes a group of people whose religion forbids them to go to the movies I think is a bad movie. And also I hated the audience thing, it turned me against Amish people.

JS: If you were working for some studio do you think it would be easier for you to get financing, if you were in the system?

JW: Well, if I was in the studio system I would be "assigned" to make movies – so of course it would be easier to get money because you don't have to raise money when you're in the thing – they give – assign you to a movie, or "hire" you.

JS: But then, of course, they control...

JW: Oh yes, yes... so I mean, it would certainly be easier as far as money is concerned because, when you're in those situations you don't even really care if the movie makes money or not because you get such a huge salary up-front. That's why those movies **cost** so much, because **everybody** gets their money up-front.

JS: What do you think of all the "splatter technology" that's been coming out in these recent gore films like TERMINATOR and NIGHTMARE ON ELM STREET?

JW: I loved TERMINATOR – I thought it was one of the best exploitation films of the year... I think I preferred it in the old days when it was really badly done. A perfect example is the movie THE THING, the new version of it. I mean you probably couldn't get better splatter and more "state-of-the-art" splatter than that but once it's done with so much money it loses some of the punch it had in the beginning. I don't know if gore has that much "punch" any more.

JS: Right, like NIGHT OF THE LIVING DEAD is an example of very crude...

JW: Yeah, but that was certainly scarier than any of those [recent] movies... I think the

---

low-budget aspect almost makes it scarier because it's like a documentary or something, it looks like.

JS: Did you think DUNE was a good David Lynch film?

JW: I didn't see DUNE. I really wanted to and it vanished so quickly. I'm not a big science fiction fan, I **am** a big David Lynch fan... and from what I've read, it sounds like he did DUNE exactly the way it should be done but I don't know if I'd like that, you know. I've never read DUNE and I never – don't have any desire to read it. But obviously some people love that kind of stuff. And I know a lot of people who were really DUNE fanatics liked the movie.

JS: Did you see any of the other Christmas blockbusters?

JW: Like which ones?

JS: ... actually I don't remember any of them.

JW: I don't remember them either.

JS: Well, there were probably a bunch of break dancing movies, what do you think about—

JW: No, I **hate** break dancing, I never see break dancing movies.

JS: So there are movies you won't go to?

JW: Oh, there's a lot of movies I won't go to you know, I don't go to see completely everything, I don't go to see... [sneering, disdainful tone] MICKI AND MAUDE... there are some I just **don't** go to.

JS: Harkening back to William Castle – one of your favourites – given an unlimited budget and immunity from prosecution, what would be the ultimate theatre gimmick?

JW: Well, I think the ultimate theatre gimmick has already been done by that guy who did MOM AND DAD when he put nauseous gas in the vents of the theatre so that people would pass out so he could get photos in the papers the next day of ambulances taking away "shocked" movie patrons... I don't think you could do any better than that... and they "four-walled" the theatres in these places, so they didn't have to wait to get paid.

JS: You've said before you like Fassbinder's films. Did you know him personally?

JW: I met him, I wouldn't say I "knew" him – I met him very shortly before he died, in Berlin at the Berlin Film Festival. And I **miss** that he's not here. I miss his films you know... there's one called MARTHA that's supposed to be released, one that I haven't seen, and I wish they'd hurry up and put it out. I've read all about it and it sounds great. But I met him, I can't say that I knew him.

JS: Previously you've said that you weren't surprised, actually, that he did die, considering his lifestyle.

JW: Well, I know a lot of the people that worked with him and the stories they tell! There's that book out now called *Fassbinder* by Ronald Hayman, it's incredible, the monster they portray him as. You should read it, it's really the most shocking book of the year... it's a biography of him and it is **unbelievable** what he did to those people.

JS: What did you think about the prematurely aborted Kathy Boudin Weathermen trial last year? Was that a disappointment?

JW: I read the book on her... well what else was she going to do besides what she did? I think that all those '60s radicals – the Weathermen and all – I'm still interested in them but they are really "humour impaired" people... so, the trials are only just so interesting when they will only do political [unintelligible].

JS: So you'd rather go to another "MOVE" trial, if we're talking politics?

JW: Yeah, if we're talking politics, I'd rather not have it quite so stale... something new... even though the people I hate more than any people are the ones that bomb abortion clinics and stuff – they interest me more because as that one girl said, "It was a Christmas present to Jesus".

JS: Ha, I never heard that one.

JW: That interests me a little more because it's something new at least.

JS: Right, and one guy said he was on a line direct from God...

JW: Yeah, I mean that kind of stuff. That's the new radical.

JS: Right, and hopefully some of them will be brought to trial so that we'll have some of these trials.

JW: Well, yes but they'll be boring... well, no, I don't know what will happen... although I mean, those people I'm really against. I mean, I **hope** they get time.

JS: Add those people to the Survivalists and the anti-tax crazies and the neo-Nazis and that's where the new terrorism is today.

JW: That's where it's coming from today... not from old Weathermen.

JS: Leftist terrorism is fading... Did you ever get that interview with Leslie Van Houten?

JW: I'm still going to do it, I'm in touch with all those people and everything... she has a parole hearing in April and we want to wait and see what happens.

JS: So most of the main characters in the Manson deal are still in prison?

JW: The main ones from the original trial. I just read an article today about Sandra Good, she was arrested along with Squeaky; the second phase of Mansonism, when they were very big on threatening polluters of the environment, that was their whole thing and it still is and Sandy got five years in jail and I was just reading an article today that said she just served all her time and she doesn't want to leave jail because she "still has too much anger" in her... even though they're going to kick her out of

---

jail... I know Clem is getting out in three years, he's got a date.

JS: Have you heard anything from Tex or is he still involved in the religious deal?

JW: I'm really not in contact with him any more. He's very big on the prison evangelist circuit, he's married, has two children – I wish him well.

JS: Well, now, he's out then, right?

JW: Oh no! He has conjugal visits. He has this huge mailing list with computers and everything, it's a business almost, I mean he's one of the top prison evangelists now.

JS: I wonder, a lot of prisoners cop evangelism to try to get time off their sentence.

JW: He **believes** it. I'm convinced. His wife is also a Jesus freak... I met somebody that delivered her baby, actually, and she said the whole time she was screaming Hallelujah... she lives in the town that the prison's in... You know that Manson documentary is coming out on tape, you ever see it?

JS: No...

JW: ... but you know, Leslie [Van Houten] though, she **should** get out, I mean she is really one of the few of them that is not into Jesus... I mean she **is** rehabilitated; she's been in for 15 years, she was 19 when it happened, I mean. she's almost a **yuppie** now!

JS: While we're on the subject – I'm sure you've stated it somewhere before – what's your opinion of Capital Punishment?

JW: Well, of course I'm against Capital Punishment. Too many people I like are sentenced to it. You know it's the age old thing where you don't teach somebody not to kill by society's doing it to them... and also a lot of people, like Arthur Goode, the guy I interviewed who got the electric chair, they **want** it as a means of – like Dawn Davenport in FEMALE TROUBLE – to get publicity. They're people that would commit suicide but don't have the nerve and want society to do it so they can go out with a bang. You know, I'm against it, except maybe I hope the "subway vigilante" in New York City gets it! I'm **so** sick of him, and this Archie Bunker-type outpouring of sympathy for him although I mean, I say in my lectures now I know what he means; I feel like killing people five or six times every time I walk out of the house... but I mean for different things, like wearing summer whites before Memorial Day. Would the readers of *Gentlemen's Quarterly* rally to my defense if I blasted such a person away?

JS: Right, and if you had a gun, who knows?

JW: Yes.

JS: And a few martinis.... I know I read in the *Times* or *Post* or somewhere, somebody wrote in after the subway shooting and said they were glad because now they could finally be proud to be a white male.

JW: I'm just so sick of the whole story.

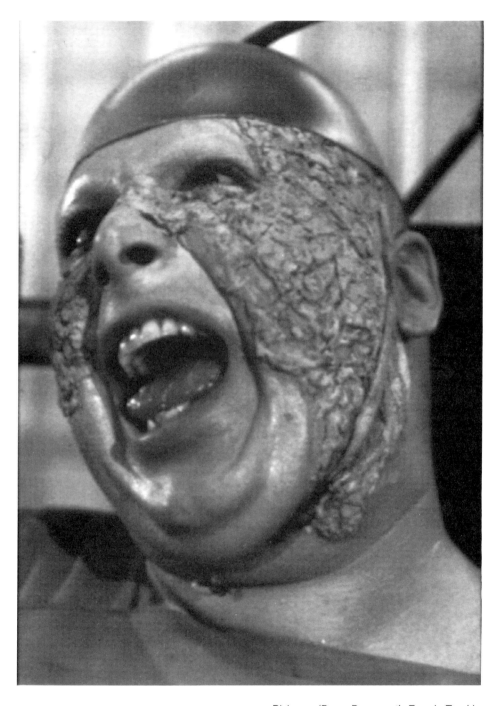

Divine as 'Dawn Davenport'; *Female Trouble*

JS: If there was a John Waters" calendar, what would the holy days be? You've mentioned—

JW: You know there's supposed to be one – someone [was] trying to sell the idea – I don't think he got too far with it, with the different stills... What would the **holy** days be?

JS: You've mentioned August 8th.

JW: August 8th and 9th [Tate-La Bianca slayings (Manson)]... God... I'd have to think about that one. You know the Mayor proclaimed it John Waters Day February 9th ['85] in Baltimore when I just had this retrospective at the Baltimore Museum of Art here... I got this whole proclamation, everything, sort of like the Wizard of Oz got, the scarecrow, you know... He said it was "John Waters Day". But I didn't find out until 9 o'clock at night, so I only got to reign for three hours, you know... if I had known that morning I would have put on the Imperial Margarine crown and Kleenex boxes on my feet, walk around shouting out orders all day.

JS: They didn't give you the keys to the city?

JW: Well, this was their version of it.

JS: This was the first time? They've had these events in Provincetown, right? – but this was the first time Baltimore's finally...

JW: Well, the Museum of Art, the last thing they had was a "Grandma Moses Retrospective"... I mean they're very establishment, right? So, here I was being honoured, so actually it was a great time, it was a "black tie" opening, my parents were absolutely thrilled [drolly]... and, you know, it was a very, kind of, "established" support for the same films that ten years ago I was worrying about getting arrested for you know, but the Censor Lady [Mary Avara], true to form – even though she's been kicked out of office – went crazy about it, said that her tax money was being used... and then said – I swear to God, she said this in the paper – that I was responsible for every rape and mugging in Baltimore – which was fair enough – **but then** she said I was also responsible for the dead rats in her cellar!!! And I thought... Wha... you mean you really think... ? And she said, yes...

JS: Oh man, you mean she's still around?

JW: Oh yeah, but she's not in any power, it's just this reporter – who was pretty smart about it – called her up **knowing**... you know what I mean?

JS: That he'd get some great quotes.

JW: Yeah, right, she's my best press agent.

JS: Yeah, that picture you have in your living room, I thought it was her at first, but—

JW: Similar type, she **looks** that mean...

JS: But then I found out it was that lady from *The Basement* [Kate Millet], which was a great book, of course...

JW: Why don't you write to **her**?

JS: I wonder if she's still alive?

JW: She is. I heard she's a Jesus Freak.

JS: Right... the Jesus Freaks I think they should keep in prison. Do you still go out trolling the bars any more, looking for strange characters?

JW: Well, if I'm making a movie, I do that, you know what I mean, like, eh, that's how we found Kenny, the foot-stomper in POLYESTER.

JS: Yeah, when I was in New York City last summer at the Breslin, me and Mink [Stole] and a bunch of other people went out that night and accidentally ended up in that bar in the East Village. They've cleaned it up a lot.

JW: Kenny's doing real well. He was in *Time* magazine recently, as a model for Stephen Sprause, he's doing a lot of modelling, goes to school, married, has a couple of kids – he's fine. Kenny King. He's from Boston, too.

JS: Do you ever get any strange mail, or people plaguing your house?

JW: [With enthusiasm] Oh Yes! When I went on this lecture tour... I mean **each** city: I got to Chicago and there were maps to John Gacy's house stuffed in my mail box, I went to Atlanta and the first place they took me was the corner where Martha Mitchell was run over... in Seattle they gave me all the press on the Coe trial. So each place I go they come out of the woodwork... yeah, I still get strange mail... nothing recently that's **that**, you know... I can't think, off hand... I mean nothing will top the dirt off Gacy's lawn.

JS: Right, and as you say, he might get the death penalty now after all.

JW: Well, the Supreme Court... they might fry **him**.

JS: Now, when he got the death penalty – I may be thinking of another mass-murderer – I thought he got the death penalty then it was abolished [in Illinois] and he got "life" instead?

JW: No, no, he's still got it; that was it, the Supreme Court just upheld his sentence.

JS: Right, that was in the papers, I should've read between the lines. What do you think of the Baltimore Colts leaving Baltimore?

JW: [Painfully] Oh, I don't care... good. I didn't follow that story, you know...

JS: ...as one of the most avid sports fans.

JW: I'm glad. I wish they'd all leave.

JS: Right, there's only the baseball team now.

JW: Yes. I wish that would leave too.

JS: Did you watch the Olympics on TV?

JW: No, I never even knew it was on to tell you the truth. I don't even know when it was on or what happened or anything...

JS: Right.

JW: I've been totally able to edit sports out of my life... I mean I never even take the sports section out of the paper. It's like... straight from my door to the trash without seeing one letter.

JS: That's great... do you agree with Reagan – I'm not going to ask you who you voted for – that a "new patriotism" is sweeping the nation?

JW: No... I think that sounds like a commercial. I think that the Reagan movie that they showed at the [Dallas] convention will be the new REEFER MADNESS in twenty years. It was so... berserk.

JS: The only bright spot in the Dallas convention – I don't know if you caught the article or not – but there were a bunch of, I don't know, they called them hippies, punks and anarchists. I don't know... a bunch of troublemakers; they stormed into the Neiman Marcus and ran through it spitting on things, knocking over displays and spray-painting swastikas and anarchy symbols and stuff.

JW: Well, I disagree with that because Neiman Marcus has some nice stuff, I'm not against Neiman Marcus. I think if they were going to run, they should have run through J.C. Penney's.

JS: And Barry Goldwater happened to be shopping in the store at the time and they asked him what he thought, and he goes, "Ah, they're just a bunch of god-damned nuts".

JW: He was probably right. I mean... he didn't care... you know he couldn't have cared less.

JS: The convention could've used more of that type of behaviour.

JW: It was quite dull. Both of them.

JS: Yeah, as a matter of fact I gave away my TV set that week... I regret it now but...

JW: I like Jesse Jackson's speech. When he talks about the despised, the depraved and the damned, I **identify**.

JS: So, politically, with all this election bullshit, basically you didn't get too involved with that I'd imagine.

JW: Well, I voted, I always vote. I hated both of them, I voted for Mondale, but with the **least** enthusiasm that I've ever voted for anybody. And I knew Reagan was going to win... but he was a better villain than Mondale was a good guy.

JS: What would you say was the dullest presidential election? Ford versus Carter?

JW: No, because I loved Ford. He was my favourite president because he was never elected. So, this was duller to me. There was, like, no suspense, there was no... Ferraro perked it up a little, and I **love** that she did a Pepsi commercial, which I think was "politically correct" – that's the "new patriotism" in my mind.

JS: Moving away from politics, you used to be – probably still are – a big Rock and Roll fan. What groups do you like now?

JW: I'm **not** a big Rock and Roll fan. Eh, I don't know much about music, either.

JS: Do you like, say, the Cramps or the Beatles?

JW: I **hate** the Beatles – I've **always** hated them, even when they were at – they were just honkies to me... I mean... 'cause I listened to the black groups and the girl groups and all that stuff and then they came along and ruined it.

JS: Yeah, they steam-rolled a lot of good groups, better groups that ended up playing for peanuts at "Beatle Rallies".

JW: Yes. The Cramps I like. Some of the New Wave stuff I like to see and I like hearing and reading about it, but when I'm relaxing in my apartment I don't put on Sid Vicious's greatest hits. [John would rather just follow him around lower New York City, as he did shortly after Sid was out on bail after murdering his girlfriend: "Young girls would constantly try to pick him up, and I was thrilled to see that so many people wanted to sleep with a killer."] Eh... what albums have I just bought? I bought that recent Velvet Underground album of previously unreleased stuff, I bought a Frank Sinatra album... I buy a lot of Glenn Gould. I don't buy too much pop music... I like Pia a lot, I buy all her albums. She was nominated for a Grammy.

JS: Right, right... who?

JW: Pia, Pia Zadora.

JS: Oh yeah, ha.

JW: Tina Turner... but I liked her better when she was married to Ike, had a moustache and travelled in a green school bus.

JS: Yes, and after she left him she gave him so much bad-mouthing in the press, you know, but she... had a lot more class back then.

JW: Well... he probably **was** a monster.

JS: Right. That's what she says anyway. Nobody's got Ike's version of it yet.

JW: Well, he got busted for heroin, that's the last thing I heard about Ike.

JS: What was just on TV, the Emmies or the Grammies or something?

JW: The Grammies. It was on, I wasn't really watching. I would look up every once in a while hoping to catch Pia in the audience – that's the only reason I had it on.

JS: You used to know members of the band "X". Have you heard anything from them?

JW: Oh yeah, I still know – well, John I know, I've met Exene and the rest but John I know, he's from Baltimore. I saw him the last time I was in L.A. He came to my William Castle lecture. That's another group I like, "X".

JS: What keeps you busy these days? You've mentioned a bunch of articles coming out.

JW: I'm travelling around the country with this "Evening With John Waters" thing. I've written four articles that are coming out, one's for the *National Lampoon*, *American Film*, *Rolling Stone* and *Baltimore Magazine*. I'm dealing with this agent, trying to get *Flamingos Forever* turned into a novel, we're trying to sell that. I think it will definitely happen... just trying to get the best deal on that.

JS: So this won't be like *Shock Value*?

JW: **No**, it's a novel. Because FLAMINGOS FOREVER was the movie we were going to make – the sequel to PINK FLAMINGOS, but when Edie died, I thought it couldn't be a movie. And also, we didn't have the money. [This must have been a real disappointment to Mink, who was insanely enthusiastic about the part John had written for her in that one]... it was **really** hard to get money for that movie because it was so much crazier than *Polyester*.

JS: Right, you were trying for quite a while...

JW: Yeah, for two years, you know – that was a big hassle. We had some of the money, then Edie died and I thought, I really couldn't make the movie without her because she had such a huge part in it. Well, I don't think you could do a sequel to it [PINK FLAMINGOS] without her. And I don't think audiences would go for a fake Edie.

JS: Exactly, there's no way you could...

JW: So that's going to be a novel, which I'm looking forward to since I've never had a novel out... And I'm writing another screenplay right now. Actually I have three of them and I'm trying to figure out – putting them all together and it's still at that stage. So I'm really just hustling together projects, which is, unfortunately with independent films, most of your time is spent doing that instead of making movies.

JS: And you've written a lot of articles, so actually you're almost as much a writer as a filmmaker.

JW: [Regretfully] Yeah, lately. And then I do these things around the country so that's like, travelling, and I have these updates, and I'm changing the lecture and everything.

JS: And at these lectures you show your films, right?

JW: Well, it's changed. It used to be at universities, now it's mostly at movie theatres. It's called "An Evening With John Waters" – which opens with my talk – then it's usually a weeklong festival of all my films, in various combinations.

JS: So this sort of thing pays the rent, eh?

JW: Yeah, I get residuals too.... There's new hassles every day.

John and Edie

JS: Are you still teaching in the prison?

JW: Well, I did it last semester and a year ago, that semester. I only do it one semester a year because I have to guarantee that I'll be able to **be there** every Thursday. I'm going back in next Thursday as, you know, the **substitute** teacher... I'm often, like, the "guest" teacher. But, you know, I've been to parties in prison, for different organizations, where you take a date and sit at a table and it's just like a banquet. So... I'm still **involved** in that prison.

JS: Now is this the same prison they let you film in for FEMALE TROUBLE?

JW: No, it's a different one. This one "60 Minutes" did a big thing on and it's really almost the only one of its kind in the country. It's for "emotionally disturbed" prisoners but ones that are not... [career criminal types], and when you're there you're under psychiatric care and if you're not responding you're flown back out to the regular prison system... well, it's like people who have had no criminal record and then kill six people. You know, that kind of case. Which is the kind of case that interests me the most anyway. I mean, believe me, I don't have any "possession of marijuana"s in my class.

JS: You probably run into a lot of interesting – are any of those people on death row?

JW: No, because if they're on death row... you can't go to college because they're gonna kill ya. I mean what's the point?

JS: Even if you are on death row for 12 years.

JW: Yeah, that's really ridiculous. But I think they can't use tax money to give you an education and then kill you. Talk about depressing... picking up your diploma.

JS: What do you think of the plans to demolish 42nd Street?

JW: Oh, I think it's just scandalous! I mean... that was the first place I ever went to in New York. I still go there. It's something [the new plans] I totally deplore. They're going to put in boring highrises and... bad plays, that cost $60 a ticket, that are for tourists.

JS: I'm not familiar with what they intend to put—

JW: That's what they intend, fancy hotels and stuff like [in a drawn out sneer] Broadway theatre, which – I hate plays anyway. It'll just move some place else, but it won't look as great. It won't be as classic as 42nd Street.

JS: Right. And as you say, you've been going there quite a while. Have you seen any changes over the years?

JW: I don't go that....I mean, I'm not a real **buff** on it......I mean, to be honest, I will only go to see a movie on 42nd Street if it's not playing anywhere else because: I don't feel like getting stabbed, I can't **hear** the movie – you know, that kind of thing. You know, the local colour is wearing a little thin sometimes. However, I **love** to walk down the street... I mean, it's part of New York. I don't understand – where are these people gonna stab each other on New Year's Eve when they watch the ball drop?

JS: That's true. Have you ever been there on New Year's Eve? I hear it's total anarchy.

JW: Oh God! I'd never go **near** it – are you kidding???... I can't imagine a more horrible place to be near, with every drunken lunatic... I mean I can't imagine a place I would **less** rather be.

JS: Right. I don't know if you've ever been to the Mardi Gras in New Orleans—

JW: No, I would never go to that either, for the same reason.

JS: It reminds me exactly of that [New Year's Eve in Times Square].

JW: I know I would **hate** the Mardi Gras.

JS: When I lived down there I was there for two of them and of course everybody who lives there gets the fuck away – the town is flooded with tourists – there's a lot of violence, like the police on horseback who can't control their horses, casing kids and bucking around in crowds on Canal Street... Flambeaus dripping kerosene, people getting pelted with beads and tokens. Now that I think back... at least it wasn't dull.

JW: Shooting Al Hirt.

JS: Right. Throwing a brick at Al Hirt.

JW: No, I've never wanted to go to those kind of... I don't know... "organized having fun" is not my idea of a great way to spend an evening.

JS: It's probably pretty tragic, actually, with all the people vomiting everywhere. In New Orleans the whole town is enveloped in a warm cloud of piss, sweat and vomit for a week.

JW: Yeah.

JS: Do you ever spend much time on 14th Street? I guess 14th and 3rd Avenue has a nice movie theatre called Variety Photo Plays.

JW: I know what it is, but no, I don't go there. Ah, New Line's office used to be near there, that's the only reason I went there. Believe me, when I go to New York I don't **seek out** those kinds of places. You know, that's the problem when I go on these trips, everybody always says, "Ah, we got a place to take you!" And they always want to take me to these horrible places and I really **don't** want to go to... 'cause I **know** what they're going to be like, you know what I mean? Unless it's something really kind of amazing. Generally it isn't.

JS: I just wondered about that theatre because—

JW: It's a great looking theatre.

JS: I stopped in there last summer, all sorts of prostitutes trolling the aisles, and—

JW: I've **seen** that and I've been in the other one, the Metropolitan and, I mean, I know what it is... and I'm certainly not going to... take advantage of it.

JS: Right.

JW: I mean... unless you want to actively participate.

JS: Like you said, the local colour wears a little thin. I walked in there and for the first five minutes the movie was showing upside-down on the screen and I thought, well, let's not be quick to judge, maybe this is the way it's supposed to be...

JW: ... no one cared.

JS: Did you ever see CAFE FLESH?

JW: Yes.

JS: Do you think that's the future of porno? It seemed to be a unique type of porno film.

JW: No, I don't think so. The people that liked CAFE FLESH... the porno business is for people that go once a week to those films, you know what I mean? It's not a hip audience – it's the opposite of a hip audience, real porno fans. Porno is made, not for someone who sees one porno film in their life, it's made for the people who go once a week, it's a habit, it's how they have sex. Those people, you know they probably don't have sex, except for that. So, I think it was too "hip" for the raincoat brigade – you know what I mean? I think the future of porno is certainly just video – that's the whole reason people buy VCRS, is so they can jerk off and not have to do it in public.

JS: Right. And not have to go to some theatre and listen to people snore. The mayor here [Raymond Flynn] is trying to get rid of the Combat Zone.

JW: That's where I finally saw Liz Renay, when I first met her, was in the Combat Zone.

JS: Have you heard from her lately?

JW: She has this amazing book out that I didn't even know about, that somebody sent me. It's been out for about two years, called *Staying Young*. You should see it. It's like a self-help, like, sex book for people over 50. And she says things in it about how fabulous her life is, like "sometimes if I feel like it, I fly from Las Vegas to Phoenix just for lunch". It has lines like that, and, rapturously describing how she had all the skin peeled off her head and put back on, for a facelift. And then at the very end she says, "If all else fails, be a stripper." And I can't imagine what the 60-year-old women who are reading the book think when they get that far. It's a hilarious, wonderful book.

JS: And how old would she be now?

JW: Fifty-five or so.

JS: But she'll remain eternally young in DESPERATE LIVING.

JW: Well, she says in the book that "Most people think I'm 26," which is... how I love her humility!

JS: Here's a hard one; if you were reincarnated, what would you come back as?

JW: Reincarnation would be my idea of what **Hell** would be... to have it never end, to have to just **keep** coming back, and then maybe one time to come back as, like, uh, some of these people who are so [unintelligible]... eh, if I could come back as like, anybody?

JS: Anybody or anything.

JW: From the future, you mean?

JS: Yeah... I was thinking of inanimate objects.

JW: I would come back as Pia Zadora's new baby. Because he will be financially secure forever. And how great to have Pia be your mother! Her name is Kady, by the way, named after her [Pia's] character in BUTTERFLY.

Liz Renay; *Desperate Living*

JS: Pia still appears in all the press.

JW: Oh sure! She was on "Good Morning America" about **two seconds** after she had her baby. They were right there in the hospital.

JS: Does she have any new movies coming out?

JW: She has one that's supposed to be coming out called VOYAGE OF THE ROCK ALIENS that was supposed to come out last summer, I don't know what happened. I guess now it's going to come out in the spring.

JS: What would you say her worst movie and her best movie would be?

JW: Well, so far she's only **had** two. BUTTERFLY was the best and LONELY LADY was the worst.

JS: She was in more obscure ones earlier on.

JW: When she was a child, yes. SANTA CLAUS VERSUS THE MARTIANS, they weren't really **Pia Zadora vehicles** like today.

JS: Would you say your living habits have definitely mellowed since the days when you had greasy long hair, shoplifted and lived in your car?

JW: "Mellowed" is not a word I would certainly use.

JS: Changed, then.

JW: Obviously I'm not running around, living in my car, taking drugs... yes.

JS: ... and your hair's a lot shorter.

JW: Yes, but I've always tried to keep in style. I didn't cut my hair because I got a surge of Republicanism... my life is... different now... but I think my sense of humour is the same. And I'm still interested in all the things you're not supposed to be interested in. It's a little easier now – to **get to** those things you're not supposed to be interested in. That's how it's changed. It's easier to research my obsessions. But my obsessions have certainly not changed. I mean, I'm going to go to the McMartin [child abuse] trial in Manhattan Beach, you know, which I would have done when I had long, greasy hair and lived in my car. The difference is this time I might get **paid** to go me it... which is quite nice... otherwise I would have gone anyway and people think you're crazy, now I go and they pay me.

JS: And you might be recognized yourself – by the judge, and the...

JW: That's the difference.

JS: Are there any other trials coming up that you're interested in?

JW: Some of these people sent me something about a murderer named John Waters – I sort of want to go to that one.

JS: Then you could clip all the articles the next day and let **him** go to jail.

JW: I think the McMartin one is the biggest one right now... I totally don't understand child molesters. How do you talk dirty to a child? "You wanna get tied up with a yo-yo string?" I mean it's... since everybody knows that the only reason you have sex is because cigarettes taste better afterwards. Don't child molesters feel stupid lying naked in bed with a pre-teen as they hack away on their first Lucky Strike? – That's a line from my lecture.

JS: Yes, you really hit stride with that one.

[Coughing]

JS: Sounds like you've been doing a little smoking yourself.

JW: [Gasping] I want a *Kool* coffin, like they have *Kool* sailboats.

JS: Did you ever hear of a guy called Michael Valdez, he was a criminal – this is a pretty obscure question – but he beheaded his girl-friend in 1978 and mailed her toes to Gerald Ford.

JW: No. Is it true?

JS: Yeah, I have the clipping in my scrapbook.

JW: Well, what happened to him?

JS: They wanted to let him out. I think he actually did get out on parole. But, ah, there were some pretty flamboyant articles about him. They pretty much treated him as "this guy's so crazy he's not gonna hurt anyone else."

JW: Well, didn't his girlfriend's family sort of dispute that?

JS: I don't know actually, it doesn't say in my information... So, have you been in communication with Divine much?

JW: Oh yeah. He's in Europe mostly **all** the time now. He's about to go on a tour in Japan, I saw him a couple of weeks ago when he was here, he came to visit. And I talk to him [on the phone], you know, he lives in Woodstock.

JS: Woodstock, New York?

JW: Yeah, he's always In Europe because he's a recording star there, so he's constantly appearing at discos, clubs and that sort of thing.

JS: So you've been keeping pretty much in touch with all those people?

JW: Yes.

JS: You probably don't watch too much TV, I'd guess.

JW: No, except I do watch "issue" movies, you know. Now it must be horrible to be a teenager because as soon as you pick up a problem to make your parents crazy, they make a TV movie to tell your parents how to deal with it.

JS: Like about the child abuse stuff.

JW: That, or being gay or being a transvestite, or **anything** – that's the new "exploitation" film.

JS: Right, only with a lot less style.

JW: "TV social issues"... I want to make one about "Grandslamming", which is beating up your grandmother, and have it with Gary Coleman and Katharine Hepburn.

JS: A TV movie, that'd be great... you might have a little trouble getting **that** one financed.

Part III: I spoke with John Waters over the phone on New Years Eve, December 31st, 1985. He is sitting at his desk in his apartment, chainsmoking from a carton of Kools he has just stolen. I am lounging in my one-room flat.

JS: Alright, let's start it off with what new films did you love or hate this year?

JW: Gee. GODZILLA 1985 was my favourite since I'm always trying to have a happy childhood as an adult. I love the colour and I think Gorgo, I mean Godzilla, see, Freudian slip there, Godzilla stomping on buildings is my idea of cute. I liked A MAN CALLED EVA which was a woman playing Fassbinder's life. I liked MAD MAX BEYOND THUNDERDOME, even though everybody else was disappointed, I thought it looked beautiful, I thought it was like a Fellini movie. I liked...

JS: How did you like the use of so many children in that film?

JW: I liked the kids in it. Didn't bother me at all. I liked... What did I like this year? I liked STREETWISE a whole lot. Did you see that?

JS: Yeah, that was a great one. That double-billed with MEAN STREETS.

JW: The scene where he puts the Coke can on the coffin was my favourite.

JS: Right, that almost looked, that funeral though was **weird**!

JW: Yeah, really! And I liked HAIL MARY of course, because I like to have holy water thrown on me when I go to the movies.

JS: Right, exactly. You hit all the protests in New York for that one.

JW: Right. So I think those were my favourites.

JS: How about for the bad ones now?

JW: Gee, the bad ones, you know, I hated WITNESS. I hated almost all the Steven Spielberg, I'm real tired of him, it's like it just comes out of a computer.

JS: Right, you said THE COLOUR PURPLE you were less than impressed with.

JW: Yeah, it was like watching a Hallmark greeting card for two and a half hours, you know, I expected E.T. to land and sit next door. People feel guilty about saying they hate that movie because of the subject matter.

JS: Right, it's the socially conscious type of bullshit.

JW: But as a friend of mine said, his heart turned to **stone** while watching it.

JS: Did you see THE BRIDE?

JW: No, I didn't see that. I'm really not tolerant... I sometimes just don't go to 'em any more.

JS: Right, I heard that one was just appallingly dull.

JW: Most of the worst ones I've seen on video for some reason. Because the only things I can find to rent are movies that I didn't see in the first place because they were so terrible. You know I just turn 'em on for a while, you can't **walk** out but you can **rewind, return**.

JS: From a technical standpoint, do you think that video technology, being so much cheaper, will eventually replace celluloid?

JW: No. Because people have to go out, people still have to go out. I think it will replace, certainly, porno movies. I think they look better on video, maybe. No, because people want to go out and they want to see a big screen and everything. I don't think it'll do that. The only thing it'll hurt or it does hurt is repertory theatres I guess. And it also hurts, a lot of people, if you're debating whether to go see a movie now people **won't** because they'll say I'll wait for it on video tape.

JS: Yes, you do hear that quite often... If a financier insisted that you create a role for Mariel Hemingway in a film of yours, what would it be and would you kill the character off quickly, maybe right after the credits?

JW: Well, I always thought the Kitty Genovese story should be Farrah Fawcett's since she gets such good reviews if she gets beat up. Mariel, I don't know, her in THE MEAN SEASON, I used to like her, I liked her in her first movie, in MANHATTAN I liked her. But then in THE MEAN SEASON you know, all she did was **whine** all through it. You know, I...

JS: If you could make a movie starring all the sons and daughters of American presidents, like Ron Reagan, Trish Nixon and Amy Carter...

JW: Oh, Amy Carter's my favourite, you know that.

JS: She's your favourite of all that crew?

JW: Oh yes. Because she hung around with the Ramones and she lived in a tree fort at the White House and I just think Amy's great. And I think she probably has turned out to be okay. I think I would like to use her in a film a lot. She's my dream date.

JS: Have you ever heard of Rosa von Praunheim, the underground filmmaker?

JW: Oh yeah. I met him before. I like some of his movies. Divine's in one of 'em. Well, Divine didn't know he was gonna be in one of 'em but he ended up in one of 'em. It was some sort of documentary thing. I didn't see it. I've seen a lot of his movies but I've usually seen them in Germany and they don't have subtitles so it's really hard for me to tell what they're like.

JS: The trend in Hollywood seems to be toward these lumbering brain-dead behemoths like Rocky and Rambo. Pretty soon it seems like that's all we're gonna have. Do you predict an eventual backlash against this sort of shit?

JW: Well, I don't know. I liked COMMANDO and I liked TERMINATOR, so, I **loved** them, I hated RAMBO. FIRST BLOOD I didn't mind too much when I saw it except for the end when he went into the speech, his moral speech.

JS: Anybody could've played his character, too.

JW: No! Nobody could be as much of a lug-head. No one. No one can play it like he can.

JS: Somebody couldn't help putting a little more style into it, even if they didn't want to.

JW: He is my most unfavourite movie star, most definitely, but **has** been for a long time. It's nothing new. RAMBO, I mean it was, no matter what you think of the Vietnamese they weren't **that** stupid, you know. I mean he'd be there and five hundred people would shoot guns and they'd all miss. I saw it though. I did not see any of the ROCKYs. I saw the first one and that still has me reeling ten years later. I'm not a masochist, I didn't go see the other ones.

JS: The stylized violence of movies like SCARFACE and RAMBO seems to run counter to the ugly violence...

JW: Well, I like SCARFACE a lot, I laughed a lot in that one.

JS: The violence was almost choreographed and almost like exaggerated on purpose it seemed. It's a lot different than the ugly type of violence that used to predominate and was really more shocking... someday someone's going to come along with a low-budget movie and everybody's gonna be grossed out, another John Waters 15 years later.

JW: But once you could do it, it lost its punch, you know, its violence. I mean now once Hollywood did it it just sort of, I don't know, once you've seen gore, you've seen it. It's like porno, when you couldn't do it, it had some sort of punch to it.

JS: So it's like a time thing in that maybe it's time has passed and we're heading in a...

JW: I just finished a chapter in my book about that. I really think the Golden Age of Trash may be over.

JS: Well that would be something to mourn for sure, and I'm sure you're the one to mourn it.

JW: Yes.

JS: Is it possible to go back and make a smaller film once you've hit the so-called big time, you know, could Lynch go back and make another ERASERHEAD after...

JW: Well he's going to go back and make something called BLUE VELVET, I think, which is a low-budget film. I think after DUNE he has no choice but to go a little backwards 'cause I mean how much did that movie cost, I mean to make one that costs more would be careericide, as they say. But, sure, I think he can go back and make, not an ERASERHEAD, not a film... I don't know, I mean I don't wanna go back and make a film that cost $25,000 a year, it's, in a way it's sort of stupid but you feel like you keep working and then, it's like going backwards to do that. Which may be stupid, maybe I should do that. I don't know. You get to the point where you don't wanna go through all the... making a movie is hard enough but doing it for nothing when you're forty doesn't have a lot of appeal.

JS: Did you ever have any problems with censorship as per your writing?

JW: No, not – yes, once... Well, I don't know if I should say this or not 'cause I haven't seen the final product but *Esquire* asked me to review this Tom Waits record, and so I did. But they cut part of it because they felt that it was too much for *Esquire*. They cut the opening line which was... I **think**, I don't know. I argued with them and then I never heard back and I got the check for the article so whatever happened, happened. Maybe they put it back in, I don't know. But the opening line was, "Tom Waits sings as if he doesn't change his underpants daily." That seemed to be a bit much for *Esquire*. **Why**, I don't know, I mean what did they expect if they hired me to review Tom Waits?! It seems like Tom Waits wouldn't mind. I don't know why they would.

JS: It seems like most of these magazines want the unvarnished Waters. Your Man of the Year nomination for the guy who removed Reagan's asshole. That's pretty hardcore.

JW: Well he saw it, he didn't remove it! No, I haven't had any, most of the magazines, no, they don't censor me at all about that, that's what they want. They don't expect, if they hire me, to write in praise of Whoopie Goldberg and her family. Although I liked Whoopie Goldberg, see I liked everybody in the movie, I just didn't like the direction.

JS: Which movie was that again?

JW: COLOUR ME PURPLE, as my mother calls it. A lot of people are saying that. I've heard, "Have you seen COLOUR ME PURPLE?" Not joking, I mean they think that's the title.

JS: You've interviewed people before yourself. Arthur Goode...

JW: Yeah, that's one article that **isn't** gonna be in the book because the editor said, well, you know, the whole book is a comic essay book and this one, I mean he said, I like the article but it just totally throws the whole book off. And he's probably right. And I said I wanna do these other stories. And he said well then one day we'll do a book *Waters On Crime*. I hope I get to do that one day.

JS: Have you interviewed anyone else?

JW: No, I mostly don't wanna do interviews per se, because you know...

JS: Except if it's somebody you really...

JW: Yeah, I mean I can't think of any, I really **what**? Not **hate**? Is that what you said? 'Cause I **love** Pia Zadora.

JS: Any people you just really want to, are **obsessed** with.

JW: Yeah, I mean I have no interest, say, in going to interview Madonna.

JS: If you were the mayor of Baltimore what would be the first official act, maybe to abolish all sports from the city limits or something of that order?

JW: No. I guess people should be allowed to do what they want.

JS: Right, consenting adults...

JW: Yeah, I guess I would maybe open the beauty parlours for a day and have free hairdos for the needy.

JS: Maybe have free cab rides to and from the beauty parlours.

JW: Well, there are no cabs in this city anyway hardly. It's one of the worst cities for cabs. You have to call them and they come a week later if you don't live in a bad neighbourhood.

JS: Or else go down and wait by the Greyhound Bus Station where I always catch 'em.

JW: Really. Are there cabs around there? I'm surprised.

JS: Oh, there was. I caught one. You're a collector of artifacts and mementos. I think any archaeologist would be interested in your collection which I understand includes soil samples from Gacy's lawn and the basement of the '65 Sylvia Likens torture slaying.

JW: Well that was a recent thing. I got them, you know I'm sort of a, I don't **go out** and **get** these things, people mail them to me. You know. It certainly beats *Readers Digest* sweepstakes entries in the mail.

JS: It spices up the mail.

JW: Yeah. I'm a reluctant collector of it.

JS: Sometimes an unwilling collector.

JW: The worst was when someone gave me an oil painting by John Wayne Gacy which even I had trouble hanging. I finally did it, in a very obscure part of my apartment.

JS: But that's hanging in your kitchen, do you ever choke on your food?

JW: It's not in the kitchen! It's in a little side room off the kitchen.

JS: You never choke on your food?

JW: No, but I don't look at it a lot because it is pretty creepy. He wasn't a real charismatic killer.

JS: Divine appeared at a club in Cambridge a few months ago, The Man Ray Club, and in a newspaper interview he said he wants to be a serious actor. Is he kidding, or what?

MAY 27-JUNE 2 1981

SIXTY.CEN

ꝹohoNews

WHAT FREUD DIDN'T TELL U.
ABOUT OEDIPUS

THE WIZARD OF SLEAZE

John Waters, leading lady Divine, Tab Hunter and a troupe of degenerates
have made a slick, big-budget movie about... suburbia!

Jim Farber/Bill Landis/Michael Musto

———————————— FILM ————————————

ZOE TAMERLIS: DISARMING MS. 45
Stephen Saban

TRACKING THE SUMMER RELEASES
Seth Cagin

MARY CORLISS FROM CANNES

JW: I don't know, you'll have to ask him. He's always been a serious actor, I think. I don't know what he means by that.

JS: We all know he's capable but somehow I just can't see him as the new Dustin

Hoffman.

JW: Well I can't see him in OUT OF AFRICA but **who knows**, I mean I think that he always has been a serious actor.

JS: What's more of a threat today; AIDS or organized religion?

JW: AIDS, certainly, because religion isn't going to kill you. It may try but you can kill that back. [Laughs] You can't kill AIDS, so I would definitely say AIDS.

JS: Do you think, skipping across continents and time, do you think they should free Rudolf Hess, was he your favourite Nazi?

JW: Yes, I don't know that I have a favourite Nazi; Ilsa, She-Wolf of the S.S., was my favourite Nazi.

JS: He was the craziest, though.

JW: It seems to me, yes, I have to be consistent in what I feel about all prisoners, no matter what the crime is. Yes. I think that he has served his sentence.

JS: Do you see any danger in the Meese Commission on Pornography?

JW: What is it? Oh, the one in Indiana?

JS: No, that's part of the feminist movement. Meese set up a commission, a lot of the First Amendment people are really going nuts about this, the head of the commission, it's to investigate to see if pornography is harmful, overturning the '73 ruling that it's not connected with violence; and the guy he put in charge of it is the prosecutor from Arlington County who is famous for getting rid of all pornography in that county and declaring it a porn-free county.

JW: He probably has a huge collection of it in his apartment. The way to get rid of pornography is to make everybody watch it for a week and then you get so bored with it you don't care about it any more. The way to make it popular is to not let people have it and then that will make the Mafia happy. It'll cost more and so people will think it'll be better. The more pornography costs, the more people think it's sexy. If it was a nickel nobody'd care. I don't know, censors, I mean the whole thing is such a **tired** thing, it's like if you want something to vanish, don't talk about it. That's what censors should do. They should go around, and have censor boards that try to influence the media **not** to review something, or to ignore something. That is how to end something.

JS: Right, and this is just bubbling up again.

JW: I mean look at HAIL MARY. An obscure French art film turned into an event.

JS: Turned into, probably, a great financial success, too.

JW: Yeah! I mean it had a $30,000 opening week gross in Boston **because** of the Catholic pickets. No other Godard film opened up strong. And this is not even an "easy" Godard film, you know what I mean, it's even **artier** than usual.

JS: Are athletes good role models for young people?

JW: **Hardly**, I mean... I don't really know because I don't know any young people or athletes.

JS: You don't have any time for the Yuppie phenomenon?

JW: Oh god knows I like to eat in good restaurants too, you know, I don't hate them, they're part of my audience in a way. No, I don't hate them, it's so fashionable to hate them. Better than Hippies, I'd rather live around Yuppies than um, what do you call them, those things in WITNESS?

JS: Oh, Amish people.

JW: Yes!

JS: You're gonna stay far away from those people after seeing that movie, you might get **bored** to death.

JW: Give me a Yuppie over Amish people any day.

JS: If you had a choice, would you go to jail or to the suburbs... if you only had two choices?

JW: For how long? I don't want to go to jail, certainly, and I also don't want to go to the suburbs.

JS: You'd rather just stay where you are.

JW: There's more mental death in suburbia. I don't want either really. I think jail probably sounds a little better than it really is. I teach there so I know. I like going there once a week but if you had to go every day it would be rather depressing. Living in suburbia would be rather depressing but I guess suburbia would be better 'cause you can always leave suburbia, you can't leave jail. I left suburbia once already in my life, I'll do it again. Or it would be very easy to get suburbia to kick you out but you can't be so bad in jail that they let you out.

JS: I think jail is almost a better creative writing type of thing than colleges are but I don't think anybody would choose to go to jail to learn how to be a creative writer.

JW: Well no, but also they say write what you know. You can only go so far with jail stories, you know.

JS: Right, it is definitely a very narrow experience type of thing, just about anything that comes out of jail would be pretty brutal I think.

John Waters

JW: Oh, not really. You should see some of the, I have some of the stuff that they write in my class. They're so sick of jail that they don't want to write about it because they're just so tired of it.

JS: That's true. Have you been to any of these recent second-wave "MOVE" trials? I know you followed them in '78.

JW: Ramona Africa's is January 6. That's really the only one. She's the only one left. I mean Alberni is now somebody else, he's been adopted by his real father. And Tree-Tree is dead.

JS: And those were the pillars of the movement.

JW: Yeah, so I think Ramona's trial ought to be interesting. I tried to get a magazine to send me to it but they all felt "MOVE" was **old** news, whereas I think it can **never** be old.

JS: No, certainly not. I can understand the police a little bit. A lot of people don't like their neighbours and would like their houses burned down.

JW: Well, "MOVE" **was**, I mean they did have bull horns on top of the house, twenty-four hours a day, screaming obscenities [laughs].

JS: And garbage and they used to hassle people I guess.

JW: They were the filthiest people alive for real. They would win if we made a sequel to PINK FLAMINGOS and came back and challenge... **they** would win.

JS: It's been said that the family unit is destroying the fabric of this great country. What do you think about that?

JW: Oh no. Because the family unit is always responsible for so many neuroses that it keeps the country going. I think that when people use the term family as a defense against anything that they are dangerous, certainly. I like **my** family. I don't have anything against families. I just think when it's used defensively as a word for morals and people...

JS: The whole value structure that comes from it...

JW: **That** I don't believe in, certainly.

JS: But the family itself you are a believer in, you probably see your parents at Christmas.

JW: I think the most fascinating thing is to meet somebody you know's parents because it tells so much about the person that you think you know when you meet their parents.

JS: Do you have any advice for the disillusioned youth of America, in closing?

JW: Are they so disillusioned? I guess they are. I guess the people that buy this magazine will be. [Laughs] You ought to become a caricature of yourself and give in to all your obsessions and whatever you wanna do if you can manage to not give up and do it for ten years, eventually you'll be successful 'cause then people can't get rid of you and they accept you for what you are.

JS: You haven't been to Boston for a couple of years.

JW: No, I haven't been for a while. Who knows? I like to come up there, I always have fun there. [Laughs]

JS: You know there's a massive following up here.

JW: It's been a very good city for me always.

JS: Right, the films have done well here. You've been protested here and everything.

JW: That was years ago. I don't think I'd get too many these days because I'm not about Jesus. That's the only thing that can really get people hopping now. [Laughs]

JS: Is to hit the Catholics. [Laughter]

JS: Okay, I guess the first question – don't think I could start with anything else – but what was your reaction when you heard Liberace died?

JW: Oh well, it was really weird because before he died two newspapers, the *Philadelphia Enquirer* and the *Baltimore City* paper called and asked me to write an obituary for them, which really made me feel weird because I didn't know that they had "free-lance" obituary writers – you know, what am I going to do, write some funny little "witty" article in the **obituary** page? – I felt very SAD that he died and I think, ah, he was a role model for me [chuckles] since I was a kid, I mean I **always** liked him. I'm glad he died quickly rather than – **if** he had AIDS – you're never gonna know that, they'll never admit it if he **did** or not. It doesn't **matter** If he did. [Ed. note: two days later county coroners verified the cause of death to be AIDS-related.]

JS: That's the thing, they said he lived a private life, let his death be private.

JW: Yeah... So I think, unfortunately, I imagine five chauffeurs are writing tell-all books right this minute.

JS: But you turned down the chance to write those obituaries?

JW: Oh yeah 'cause I had written about him in *Vogue* so I did that whole thing in *Vogue* and there was nothing left to say. I thought about it, and so you know... I **met** him before and because of that *Vogue* article his press agent called and told me that he **really liked** it!

JS: Oh yeah!??

JW: Surprised me 'cause I sort of poked fun at him a little bit. And so he invited me to his party at the Radio City Music Hall; I went.

JS: This was all quite recently?

JW: This was very recently, yeah.

JS: Did he seem to be in ill-health?

JW: Well... he looked skinnier... you know, he sort of had a tiny bit of that Hubert Humphrey look. Which is, If you have cancer or any of those things like that, so he didn't look sickly but he did look different.

JS: And of course he was elderly.

JW: Yeah.

JS: So, what were your most loved and hated films of the year? I think you mentioned BLUE VELVET as being on your list of favourites.

JW: Well, I liked BLUE VELVET very much, I liked SALVADOR very much – wait a minute, let me get my list – I can't remember them all, hold on. Okay, let's see, my favourite movie of the year is THERESE. It's a **wonderful**, arty French movie about Saint

---

Theresa, but it's very bizarre – it's one of the most bizarre movies I've ever seen in my life – it's a big hit in New York, aahh, I think that's my favourite movie by far. I liked SALVADOR a lot, I liked TEXAS CHAINSAW MASSACRE 2 – which nobody else did, I don't know, I thought it was **funny**, I thought the art direction was great – did you dislike it?

JS: Actually, I missed that one. It played quite briefly up here [a lie].

JW: Well, it's coming out, TEXAS 2 is coming out in video any second... BLUE VELVET I liked, MARLENE I liked very, very much.

JS: That documentary, MARLENE?

JW: Yeah. Surprisingly – well, I didn't expect to like it but I like LITTLE SHOP OF HORRORS a lot. I liked PLATOON, I liked MENAGE.

JS: How about some of the more top-grossers, like TOP GUN or...

JW: I never saw TOP GUN. [Laughs] I heard, people without their shirts flyin' airplanes. I don't know. I didn't see it. I almost went a couple of times – I actually should've seen it, it was such a hit. The worst movie by far was UNDER THE CHERRY MOON, the Prince movie, which was directed by himself and his direction consists of **a close up of me**.

JS: Even more indulgent than PURPLE RAIN if it's possible.

JW: Yeah. LEGAL EAGLES I couldn't stand, TWICE IN A LIFETIME made me literally retch.

JS: How about CRIMES OF THE HEART?

JW: Oh. Well, Diane Keaton to me is the Sandy Dennis of the 1980s... and she played a retarded Annie Hall in it – I had trouble with that film. [Laughs] I thought Jessica Lange was great, as always, I mean I love to watch her on the screen, but I wasn't too crazy about the whole thing. And there are many bad ones, I mean those are just the ones that came off the top of my mind – I try to forget the bad ones. It's just part of the gamble of going to the movies.

JS: You saw PLATOON, didn't you?

JW: Yeah, but I liked SALVADOR better. And I really can't comment on TOP GUN. I didn't see it. A lot of people I know saw it and didn't like it so I guess I was a victim of "bad word of mouth", and also a film that's become **that** big a hit, if I don't see it in the beginning I never see it. I usually have to go to a movie right away, or... they have to change ad campaigns, or something to get me to go see it, or some review I'll read much later that... generally if I haven't seen it in the first couple of weeks, I don't.

JS: What do you think of this recent film "colourization" scandal? I mean, what would you do if Ted Turner tried to colourize MONDO TRASHO or—

JW: I'd be happy! I don't know – I'm against it, but I'm almost becoming a reactionary about it. The bottom line is: turn your television to black-and-white. Adjust the colour dial if you don't like it. I'm against it but there's more important problems in the world than that, I mean it's treated like it's, ah, the most – The Three Stooges in colour? So who cares, you know? I wouldn't like it if they did it to PSYCHO, but yeah, I'd rather see it in colour than not see it.

JS: I just saw THE HONEYMOON KILLERS last night and was amazed by it.

JW: **They** did it in colour?!

JS: No, no – that was in black-and-white but that's an example of one that should be left black-and-white.

JW: Yes, but they'll **never** put colour on that. That not the kind of thing that – you know what I mean? [Laughs]

JS: Right, the whole thing exists to make movies more commercial, but the subject matter of **that** one [THE HONEYMOON KILLERS] is hardly commercial.

JW: Yeah, I mean I'm very much against it but I'm so sick of reading about it that pretty soon I might be for it.

JS: If a backer insisted that you use Barbra Streisand in a film, how would you cast her and when would her character die, right after the credits?

JW: Oh no! If I could use Barbra Streisand... oh no, I mean if I had to use her I would have her in the whole thing, I would have my make-up man give her certainly a different look, and, oh I could have fun with her, I mean any big star you can make fun of their image. So I don't know what I'd do, but **that** wouldn't be the worst thing in the world, God knows.

JS: Is there **any** actress you hate bad enough to kill off right after the credits, or, 'cause last year I asked you the same question about Mariel Hemingway and you didn't hate her that much, so I'm fishing for somebody you hate.

JW: I mean you say the word **hate**, I mean I don't want to **slaughter** some actress... there's nobody that gives a performance so much that I **literally want her to die!**

JS: Exactly, I guess the word is...

JW: Diane Keaton is the one I have the very most trouble with. And, of course, Sandy Dennis. All that kind of mumbling acting where you know they got home and practised by sitting around and pretending they're a **tree** and that kind of "acting exercise" which I find kind of maddening.

JS: Did any strange things happen to you on your recent book-signing tour? I noticed at your Boston signing that gifts were piling up on your table.

JW: Yeah, people gave me lots of nice presents, it was great. The woman at the bookstore said, "I've never seen an author leave with a bag of presents."

JS: There's a lot of Art Linkletter paraphernalia here in Boston.

JW: Actually, somebody sent me a TV commercial of Art and Diane for mixed nuts, which I had **never** seen.

JS: Oh my God.

JW: You know, she comes up to him [mimicking], "Yeah Dad, they're pretty fresh!" In Los Angeles somebody was waiting in line and they had a little box, like a ring box, and they said, "I collect celebrity spit, will you spit in it?" and they had all the ones labelled, you know, "Bette Midler", so I mean who knows if they were real, but I made sure he bought a book and then I spit in it. Also, somebody was there – you know in the book there's one of the letters about, "I collect sex with celebrities and I want so and so, and so and so, and so what if they're dead" and stuff – well, I walked in and this person handed me a note that said, "I'm the person that wrote that and what can I do to please you?" and I just... thanked him. [Laughs] Well he looked like he was about 12 years old. [Laughs] So that's just what I need. It was surprising to finally **meet** him. He was happy that the letter was in the book.

JS: And you heard from him a good while ago! Years ago wasn't it?

JW: Yeah, I mean I'm sure he wasn't 12, he just looked...

JS: That chapter has become part of the Waters folklore.

JW: No, this was a different one, this was the one that just wrote and said he collected sex with celebrities... which is different than the one that was in *Shock Value*... my different Pen Pals.

JS: If you had a film budget of 200 million dollars, what would the setting be, the stage props?

JW: God... 200 million... maybe I should name it "John Waters' House", you know, and spend it all and build myself a mansion. [Laughs] Two hundred million – I don't know, that's so impossible to imagine because I mean, my new movie, the budget's going to be about 2.4 million. But a lot of it's for music and a lot of it's, ah... I don't know, it's something that I doubt will ever happen because no movie costs 200 million. I guess what I would do is hire every star I could think of and make it like WON-TON-TON and just have like every star in the world that sort of has some kind of weird image. Like AROUND THE WORLD... – all those movies that have like a million star cameos in them. They never seem to **work**, but I like the idea of that, of just having every extra that walks by, you know, like **Perry Como** – **every** kind of star. In the entire movie, every face would be a star. That's what I'd do. The screen actors guild would love me then.

JS: It's astonishing that you did POLYESTER for, what was that? Three hundred thousand?

JW: Yeah.

JS: That's utterly amazing.

JW: Yeah, but I could never do it again. I mean, that's the same with all of 'em, you can't go back, you're in a certain stage of your life, the people you work with and everything, you **can't** go backwards unless you use all new people and all – people with no experience.

JS: Would you ever be interested in doing a movie cast entirely with transvestites or transsexuals?

JW: No, you know I'm kind of **bored** with that, mean I don't even think of Divine as a transsexual. He's not – I mean he's somebody who puts on that outfit to make a living.

JS: Exactly. Before I talked to him on the phone [August 1986] I had trouble, I'd always say "her", not "him", but after I talked to him on the phone I now say "him." Once you know him a little personally there's no confusion.

JW: I only call Divine "her" when he's in costume as somebody, like on a movie set or something I do call him "her." But in real life I – if I had to have drag-queens I would get people you wouldn't expect in drag, you know like Sylvester Stallone's brother... who's dating Liz Renay now, by the way.

JS: [Shocked] Yeah?

JW: Yeah, and I saw this book called *Whatever Became Of...* and there's a picture of her and him in there – they're dating – and also that Liz Renay's daughter committed suicide on her birthday in 1981: I never knew that!

JS: So this is the last word you've got on her?

JW: Yeah, I didn't know that, I felt bad because I met her daughter.

JS: Oh right, they had a mother-daughter act.

JW: They had a mother-daughter strip act, yeah, Liz just said she was "perplexed" at what caused it in the article [chuckles], I thought that was kind of a light word. It might not have been "perplexed" but it was something, you know, like... I don't know, she had a bad birthday. Some people react like that on their birthday.

JS: Speaking of people who have done themselves in, in one of your articles you wrote about the sleazy underbelly of L.A. – did you ever think of doing a "crime tour" like Greyline Bus does package tours for old people, except you go out to crime sites?

JW: Yeah, we always joke about that in Baltimore. I've always said I want to do the John Waters Tour in a bus, 'cause we always take anyone that comes here **on** it. You know what I mean? I mean just in my **car** to show 'em.

JS: Yeah, you could well do that, you could even franchise them in different cities.

JW: I had an offer today! – from a Los Angeles guy that wanted me to, you know, be like, do a mondo kind of I'm the on-screen narrator about L.A., you know, all the hideous places. When that article came out I had offers from **lots** of city magazines to come to their city and do it, but I thought, "Oh God! Then I'll be like the trashy Michelin guide to **each city,** and it would become forced.

JS: Exactly, and L.A. is your favourite city, it was a labour of love.

JW: Yeah, so it was fun, I mean I went in with enthusiasm, the other way it would just be a **job** to find, you know – "Akron, Ohio: The Trashiest Places!" [Laughs]

JS: Right, it would get sort of seedy, a deadening conveyor belt of sex-murders and suicides. You once threw a theme party around Kate Millet's book, *The Basement*. Are there any recent books worth doing theme parties on?

JW: [Thoughtful silence] Let's see...

JS: Or was that a one-shot thing?

JW: Books... I haven't planned any **parties** around them, there've been a lot of books that I always liked. But I guess that one really obsessed me at the time. Also, it was summer and I was in Provincetown and a lot of people were reading it at the time and talking about it.

JS: You made everybody read the book before they came to the party.

JW: Yeah, before they came to the party...

JS: What did you serve for food? *Kool* cigarettes and dry toast?

JW: No, we had a cake that said, "I'm a prostitute and proud of it," which was kind of **horrible** because I had to ask the woman in the bakery to put it on there and she said, "Oh, you'd be surprised in this town what people ask for on cakes." I have all the Gertie [Gertrude Baniszewski] tapes. She's **out**, you know.

JS: She's active in some degree?

JW:·Well... I felt **bad** for – I think she should have been released. And she's religious, naturally, and she left with a preacher who looks exactly like Bo Diddley. I was in Washington at the Pia Zadora concert and afterwards her husband had this reception, all congressmen and those kinds of people, **fatcats**, right? So I'm standing in line with my friend Ken, and he says, "God, that guy is my congressman from Indiana," so I said, "Oh, hi, are you from Indiana?" – he was really Mister White Bread kind of guy – and he said, "Oh yes, yes!" and I said, "I just want to congratulate you on your courage for releasing Gertrude Baniszewski from prison," and his **face turned** to just, he said, [deep blustering, mumbling tone] "Well, well, that was a very tough case," and he moved away from me so quickly, he thought I was gonna say, you know, something about what a good job he was doing [laughs] or something – it was the **last** thing he expected to hear in Washington D.C., 'cause it did cause quite a stink in the town, naturally.

JS: Right, in the town... nationwide, although it was probably not too big.

JW: No, nationwide, I don't think, well, *U.S.A. Today* is the best paper to read for **those** kinds of stories. They won't always have an in-depth article but at least you'll know it happened... they cover crime, I mean, they were the only paper I know of that covered the Larry Layton trial – People's Temple guy in San Francisco. I don't know any other paper that did, I mean the **San Francisco** papers did but I can't get them every day... although somebody sent me all the articles [chuckles]. All my **great** pen pals that clip things for me!

JS: So there weren't any books...

JW: I would have a **theme** party but I don't know maybe I'm too **old** for that. I don't know. [Laughs] I did it once, you know... the last theme party I had was my 40th birthday which I had in an old age home. That was the last "theme" party I've been involved with.

JS: Right, and the next one'll be when you're 80.

JW: Who knows. I hope the next one will be a film party. The next party I'm looking for is a "wrap" party when it's over.

JS: What historical era would you rather have been born in? Or do you cringe at the thought of being born into a world before movies? Would depraved Roman orgies or bloody Indian massacres substitute satisfactorily for movies?

JW: I wouldn't have minded being around when Absinthe was popular. That is the only drug I never tried that sounds fun. I think somebody could make a fortune today by dealing Absinthe to **very rich** night clubs, for people that are tired of cocaine because Absinthe is like – you can't get it anywhere in the world. It's so romantically decadent when somebody famous – literary people died from it.

JS: What exactly is that, anyway?

JW: It's addictive and it's a kind of liqueur. And, Oscar Wilde – so many people were big on it. [Thoughtfully] God, I'd have to look it up, but **lots** of literary figures had a problem with it. And I think dealers should concentrate on that these days: bring a comeback to Absinthe.

JS: Yeah, get off crack, get into something classier.

JW: I've never met anyone in the **world** that took crack. I feel really **mature** since it's the first drug that's ever come along that I've never even **met** anybody that's taken it!

JS: Back in the present day, do you think anything can be gained from film schools or should a filmmaker go it on his own? Where would you be today if you had gone through four years of N.Y.U.?

JW: I'm not against film schools. It's a good way to get the equipment. I think it's good to go to film school to get your hands on free equipment, I think that's the whole point. And you know, good people have come out of film schools, I'm not against them. At the time, in 1966, there weren't that many film schools, and the ones there were would **never** have allowed the kind of movies I made. **Now** you can make the kind of movies I make, **then** you couldn't even say in a film class that you liked... ah, SHE SHOULD HAVE SAID NO [laughs] or any of those movies. You were just **wrong**, you couldn't say that in film school. Now you can write a treatise on... Ann-Margaret's high heels in KITTEN WITH A WHIP and it would be okay.

JS: Right, exactly, things have changed with the cult films coming to prominence.

JW: Well, I mean when I go to film school now, when I go and do lectures at them I'm not against them, I just have a problem with school period, **personally**... that I never cared for it too much. But I think it's great for some people, I think it's a waste for others. It just depends. I didn't **want** to go to school so obviously I wasn't going to get anything out of it. Some of the schools I went to it was their fault 'cause it was so bad. At N.Y.U. it was my fault – I never – I only went to two classes! And then I just went to Times Square all the time. You know, I went and I **knew** from the films I saw, I'd **seen** every one of them, and they were all the most obvious kind of – but it's completely different now.

JS: It's opened up a lot now. Now they're having things like Karen Finley at the Institute of Contemporary Arts here. She's one of the Richard Kern people who does all sorts of depraved things on stage, and now it's **art**, you know.

JW: I haven't seen Richard Kern's films, what are they like?

JS: They're quite vulgar, they're, ah... Lydia Lunch is—

JW: Well, she **opened** for me [laughs] in Toronto! I'd like to see them [the films], I haven't.

JS: I guess his latest video was rated triple-X and the SST record label was going to distribute it but they backed off because there was a scene in there where this, sort of the main, the head guy, the hero – if you can call him that – bends Lydia Lunch over the hood of a car and rapes her with a pistol. It's definitely triple-X rated. We put it on at a show at a bar where, fortunately, the owner was out buying beer most of the night and wasn't there.

JW: Well, isn't Lydia's thing called FINGERED?

JS: That's it.

JW: It's a great title. I like the title. And another title I've always liked very much is THEY EAT SCUM [Ed: by Nick Zedd].

JS: You've heard about some of this stuff then?

JW: Yeah.

JS: It's hard – you aren't going to see it really unless he's putting on a show. I think – my opinion is – that his stuff is influenced by a lot of your stuff.

JW: I haven't seen it, I don't know, but I sort of like the idea of it.

JW: Right. And that was the first time you met Lydia Lunch, in Toronto?

JW: Yeah.

JS: You did a cameo in SOMETHING WILD. Do you plan to do anything else along those lines?

JW: Well, you know what happened was, I did it 'cause I'd met Jonathan [Demme] and I thought it'd be fun to do and it **was** fun to do. I mean, I just went there for a day. I could be on a movie set and I didn't have to **worry** about anything!

JS: You did wear make-up, right?

JW: I can't remember if they did make-up or not, there was so much – when I was on the Joan Rivers show they put make-up on my **hands** even. That's the first time I've seen that; if you put your hands to your face, it matches. I don't remember if I had make-up on or not, probably... yeah, I did! I did. Which is fine with me 'cause you look awful without it. Ah, it was fun. The only difference from my set was that a **panic** wasn't there, which on a low-budget film it is. They had **great** food, which with mine you were lucky if you got a glass of water. What happened from it actually is, an agent from ICM called me and sent me to Bonnie Timmerman who was casting for BEVERLY HILLS COP II and I went back three times! I didn't get it but I had three call-backs [laughs]. Which I thought was funny – I went in and she asked me to do the whole scene onto video tape and you know, I don't really wanna be... I mean I'd **do** it if it's something funny. But it was just such an off the wall thing I just did it like a lunatic, she was laughing and stuff, so it seemed to work, who knows? [Laughs] I could have a third career on the side. I would more than anything love to play in a Disney film.

JS: Do you think that Hollywood might be imitating you possibly a bit now with films like RUTHLESS PEOPLE – I don't mean to an extreme degree but just sort of **leaning** in a direction that you pioneered?

JW: Well, certainly not on purpose. I think Bette Midler **screamed** as much as people did in my old films, [laughs] it was a very "screamy" movie.

JS: Exactly. In fact, when I talked to Divine, he said that he could have done a much better job and played both her role and Danny DeVito's role.

JW: [Laughs] I didn't see the new one yet. I like, well, everybody tells me that Disney is a very hands-on studio, which is the **scariest** term to any film director, which means they want to be **closely involved** and all that [laughs].

JS: Your whole thing basically has been that you didn't want to be "hired" to do a film, but rather, similar to what David Lynch did with BLUE VELVET, they gave him total artistic freedom.

JW: Yeah, and I mean that's a perfect example that I use all the time, I mean when you're trying to write a movie they send it to these professional script readers that do a report on it, and I always say, "Well, what do you think the script report was on BLUE VELVET? You know what I mean? 'Cause **all** my films are – they say make the characters **sympathetic** – all of that kind of stuff. That new one... I actually got good script reports which made me very nervous [laughs].

JS: If there was a Waterstown, a.k.a. Jonestown, where would it be and what sort of activities would you subject your disciples to?

JW: [Awed] Gee... well I wouldn't want to do that to people, but I guess that, ah... if it was beautiful women I'd go back to one of my oldest ideas, of modelling themselves to death.

JS: Would the food be like Krishna food, or...

JW: Oh no, if it was – well Jonestown was like a town built of people to idolize you, right? You're the leader. So you're – now I'm not saying I want to do this, you're asking me a question if [laughs].

JS: Yeah.

JW: I guess if I wanted to do that stylishly, I would have all the women be over six feet tall. They would model themselves to death, while the men... [thoughtfully] Geez, let me think... wore good-looking shoes. [Laughs] Gee, that's a good question. Maybe something to do with planes, like hijacking a plane and crashing it, each one, like a load, taking off and then purposefully crashing it over and over, you know, as many plane loads as you could get.

JS: Right, fairly spectacular, while the women all lay dead on the ground.

JW: Well they'd be **modelling** the whole time, so you could look up in the air, or could look down, either one. But they'd be **tall** so they'd be nearer the planes.

JS: Bhagwan Rajneesh bought one hundred Rolls Royces...

JW: [Impatient, demanding tone] I want that book! And I can't find it anywhere, about the guy that quit and wrote a book about it – it's out now. I love these books where they, you know, a "defector" tells all. I forget the title of it...

JS: If you were gonna buy cars I don't imagine you'd buy Rolls Royces, you'd probably buy used Cadillacs.

JW: Yeah, well you know I just bought another car and it looks like a **nun's** car, that's my favourite kind for myself, I have a **plain blue sedan**, and before I had a **plain white sedan**. I don't like to attract any attention when I'm in my car, and it goes back to maybe when I did illegal things [laughs] – you know, who would ever want a "vanity" license plate?

JS: Right – of course you always did those illegal things in **other peoples' cars**!

JW: Yeah, but who would want a vanity plate – people can remember your license when you're trying to get away! I always want the hardest license plate... although you know I hardly do anything illegal these days.

JS: People always think you drive around in a—

JW: People always think that I have a Cadillac or something, always expect a '59 Cadillac. I mean, you know, I'd like to have one but I'd put it out front here and it'd be stolen the first night.

JS: On that Australian TV interview with Susan Atkins I sent you, where she recants her role in the killings, do you believe she didn't actually stab anybody?

JW: It could be possibly true, because, no, I mean she went in the houses, she **held** people, she was enthusiastic. Whether she literally plunged the knife, I don't know. Tex Watson, in his book, says he did it all. I don't think she drank [Sharon Tate's] blood and all that, I think it was her trying to be the filthiest person alive, just bragging, you know, **acid lunacy bragging**.

JS: Exactly, and she said things like when she stabbed Sharon Tate it felt so good she had an orgasm, that kind of thing came back to haunt her.

JW: Well, she said that kind of stuff in jail when she was just trying to be a **big shot** and get attention. Same way on that whole thing, of all that stuff where they were going to gouge out Frank Sinatra's eyeballs – that was all bullshit, that was just her being a lunatic, just scaring her cell-mates.

JS: Yes, and Bugliosi put it all in his book. If I talked to Bugliosi I'd say to him—

JW: **Bull-yo-see!!**

JS: What's his name?

JW: He gets very mad when you mispronounce it – it's a silent G – Bull-yo-see. He always said that in the trial and they'd always call him, purposely, [snottily] Bug-li-yo-see to get on his nerves. Well, you know he did that Lee Harvey Oswald trial.

JS: Right, he did that. And the thing is, it seems his whole career – he hitched his wagon to Charlie Manson's star – and if Manson had never come along you never would have heard of this guy.

JW: Well, he made lots of money on that book and the TV show and the documentary and then wrote another true crime book that was terrible and then a novel that I didn't read.

JS: Right, so you're not a great fan of his?

JW: Well, I mean *Helter Skelter* did have some bullshit in it, but...

JS: It seemed to sort of idolize him, especially—

JW: Well, I certainly didn't **idolize** him [laughs].

JS: I think he was idolizing himself in his book.

JW: Yeah. He made lots of money.

JS: Do you want to go to heaven or hell?

JW: Heaven.

JS: ...Heaven?

JW: Of course... [laughs]

JS: Okay!

JW: Not the answer you were expecting?

JS: [Laughs] Oh yeah, yeah...

JW: If there's one of the two [laughs].

JS: Are there limits to depraved stunts on film, is it possible to be too excessive, to go too far?

JW: Oh sure.

JS: When does a shocking act or display degenerate into unredeemable stupidity or moronism?

JW: When it's not funny. When it's just made to make you sick, without being original, witty, funny or most importantly, ironic in some way. You know, I don't too much think about "outrage" on film any more, even **trying** to do that, because I did it a long time ago, and if I just kept trying to do it... you have to... keep going, in a different way. I'm still trying to make people laugh for all the same reasons I did when Divine ate a dog turd. But I certainly don't think that would even work now. I mean that was in that time period and that's the way I was thinking at the time [laughs]. But I don't really every day for, ah, what is the newest outrage, because basically I don't... the only way you can do that is sacrilege. I means there's **gore** and all that other stuff – it's kind of over with because Hollywood does it. As soon as Hollywood does it there's no punch.

JS: As a film director, do you have a casting couch?

JW: No – you know I almost think I've never slept with anybody in any of my films. I may be wrong. Yeah, I am wrong. But the person I slept with I didn't sleep with 'til **after** the film was done. I've never done that. I would be nervous doing that, because... I'm just not that type, I don't know – I just couldn't.

JS: And you've also said you – I think it was a great quote – could never shoot hardcore pornography because it reminded you too much of open-heart surgery.

JW: Well I, I **enjoy** hardcore pornography once in a while. I wouldn't want to do it, it would be too embarrassing.

JS: I think **shooting** it is different than watching the finished product.

JW: Yeah! But I'm certainly enough of a voyeur where I like it – ah, I really wish that I could invest money in it these days because I'm sure with all the horrible diseases and everything that it's **very, very** lucrative money-wise, now. I think today would be the perfect time for it. Many people are dating their VCRS.

JS: In the first issue of *Pandemonium* you were in with William Burroughs, Al Goldstein, Charles Manson and Charles Bukowski. How did you like appearing cheek-to-jowl with those four on the cover?

JW: Well, I think we need some **women** in there.

JS: Right, exactly. I know we need to represent women and blacks, I'm really sensitive to those issues.

Cookie Mueller

JW: [Laughs] Well, I really am intrigued by eccentric women, certainly and I think there are some great ones.

JS: For a long time I had the line that there just weren't any women **bad** enough to be in the magazine, but that's certainly not true.

JW: Oh sure there are. Ah... I mean off-hand I can't give you a suggestion but – I'm not going to name names but some of the people in the first issue I like very much, and some, I didn't **hate** any of 'em, but, ah...

JS: You were less than enthused about them.

JW: Yeah.

JS: You met Cookie Mueller back when you were shooting your early films. She lived in the Haight-Ashbury before you met her, right?

JW: Yeah, I met her when she had come back, she'd been out there for a couple of years.

JS: She hardly seems like she was a peace-freak kind of hippie...

JW: She hardly was [laughs].

JS: I think in *Shock Value* you describe her as a "mean hippie".

JW: Yeah, she was a **mean hippie waitress**. But that was the great thing I loved about her. I mean she was really **young**. I mean where else – that's what all young women do at that age – waitress. It wasn't like that was her lifetime work. Cookie certainly has a toughness with which I'm very, very much in love. Did you see the other day in the *New York Post*, they had an article I couldn't believe: *"Ingrid Superstar Is Missing"*.

JS: No.

JW: Well, if you even remember her, she was sort of a very obscure Warhol star. And they had this huge article about it, and I thought does any-body know who she is but me? [Laughs] And I called up my friend and I said, I whispered, "Ingrid Superstar is missing," and he went berserk 'cause he knows about her too... but she just walked out the door to buy cigarettes and never came back. That was December 7th [1986] and today is **February 6th** [1987]... no-one **reported** it 'til now?!

JS: I have to confess, at the risk of embarrassment, that I don't know who she is either.

JW: Well, she was an obscure one, but this was a **huge** article in the *New York Post*, which I thought was amazing 'cause Pat said to me, "Did you hear that Ingrid Superstar is missing?" and I said, [laughs hilariously] "Who printed that?!! How do you know that?" That's been my favourite story of the week. Did you see all the pictures of Cookie in the book called *The Ballad Of Sexual Dependency*?

JS: No, is that—

JW: It's a photograph book, I think it's *Aperture*. I think Nan Goldman did the book. It's got pretty good pictures in it.

JS: I'm going to have to check it out. Now, Oral Roberts is having a fund-raising drive on TV in which he needs to collect another few million bucks or God is going to call him home, he'll die—

JW: Let's hope he does.

JS: You ought to try that strategy to finance your next film.

JW: [Laughs] No, I think – all these people tell me they watch these preachers and they're annoyed but I can't even watch them, I don't **care** about them. I'm **not** Intrigued by 'em, I think they're a bunch of assholes and whatever happens to 'em – I don't even find them so awful that they're good. One time when I was on the book tour, I was in a station and I **had** to watch one of the, oh! And that woman, that wears like, all her eye-lashes are, **so** heavy make-up – you know who I mean?

JS: No.

JW: She's one of these evangelists. She cries all the time and her eye-lashes are too heavy. So much eye make-up on her, I couldn't believe my eyes! That's the only one I've really seen. [Disgusted tone] I mean I've never seen all of them.

JS: People like Frank Zappa monitor them, they record 'em on video and stuff, there's a lot of people who monitor all those... but you're not too crazy about them.

JW: No, I don't even care. I mean I think they should take 'em all off the air. [Laughs] I'm **for** censorship. Because I'm violently – it's that whole thing with state and religion – I violently want them separated. The last really lunatic person that I followed and cared about was Father Divine.

JS: Right... Father Divine??

JW: Yeah.

JS: How about Pat Robertson, I—

JW: I don't even know who he is. I mean, I've heard of him. Is he that... "Club" or something?

JS: He's the clown that's – might be running for President.

JW: Oh God!

JS: You're thinking of Jim Bakker and his slutty wife, Tammy.

JW: **That's** the blonde woman with too much eye make-up on.

JS: Oh, her! She's nice in a way, she's probably the cheesiest of the Evangelists. She's really slutty looking.

JW: Yeah, I just don't care about 'em.

JS: What's your idea of a grand exit? How would you want to die if you could direct your death like a movie?

JW: How would I like to die for **real** or for, image reasons – it's a very different thing. I would like to die peacefully in my sleep is how I'd really like to die!

JS: And go to heaven.

JW: And go to heaven, yes. If you want me to say how I would like to die... **splashily,** it would certainly be in an airplane that hit the Empire State Building... and **live** for a day to give interviews about it – and be the only person [laughs] to go on Letterman on my death bed to describe what it felt like, and then drop dead on television.

JS: Also, you mentioned in *Shock Value* riding in a rollercoaster that goes off the tracks and hits a cotton-candy stand.

JW: Well, that almost happened. When I was a teenager I got on the Wild Mouse and went up the hill and the chain broke and the car slid back down – the guy just hooked the chain back up and we tried again [laughs]. So, it really was a frightening ride. But

I was too uptight to say, "Let me out!" 'cause he was just saying, "Alright, alright," and I thought, "Oh my God, I don't believe this!"

JS: Rumour has it that you once tried to talk Mink [Stole] into setting her hair on fire.

JW: Well, that's true, that was in *Shock Value* even. Yeah, at the time I wanted her hair to be just so red that it spontaneously combusted. And she said yeah until the day came. Then she said, "Well, how you gonna do this?" and I said, "Well, we're just gonna set it on fire and we'll have a bucket of water right off camera." And she put her foot down and said no and looking back on it she was right. She might have had scalp burns or something. I mean I didn't wanna do that – I would've had a TWILIGHT ZONE trial [laughs]. And then Cookie, one time I wanted her to smash a TV while it was on, and she called all these places and the TV people said it would blow up. Those are the only two things. And I'm glad we didn't do it... although it still would have been a good scene, with her hair just suddenly catching fire.

JS: Exactly – on film for posterity.

JW: I think she wasn't worried about that as much as the humiliation of somebody throwing a bucket of water on her. That was what she was worried about [laughs].

JS: Do you think all artists should be judged on the merits of whether or not they're good role models for young people?

JW: Good or **bad**, yeah, I mean, no, I don't think artists should be... judged as role models. Well, they're only gonna be a role model if they strike a chord somewhere. You know, it depends what kind of role model to what kind of kid. I mean you can have – Sylvester Stallone is a good role model to jerky kids. So, I can judge that and think that they deserve each other. Same way, they can say, ah, The Beastie Boys are bad influences on 13-year-old kids. Well, I'm more for **that**, you know, if I was 13 I would probably like The Beastie Boys too, you know, sort of to liberate me from my suburban life maybe. I mean I certainly don't go out and play their records, but I'm **for** that! Because it's still pissing off certain people.

JS: Are there any records or groups that are young that you listen to?

JW: I don't even know if I've ever heard their records, I just like what—

JS: You hear about them.

JW: Yeah. No, I don't ever even listen to any of those groups, I don't even know who any of 'em are. The only – I get so many magazines that I know what they look like and say but I never hear their music and that's the way I like to keep up with music [laughs]. Knowing what they say in interviews and how they wear their hair but not having to hear them.

JS: [Laughs] Okay, I guess the last question is – do you have anything to say to the future generations?

JW: [Long pause] ... to future generations...

JS: To the future generations of uncorrupted young kids who aren't even born yet.

JW: [Silence] Well, if they're not even born yet, I mean, you know, they're not gonna hear me, so no [laughs].

JS: Very good. We're gonna take this interview and put it in one of those time-capsules and have it dug up in 100 years, maybe you could—

JW: Well, what I would like to do in any time-capsule is put **wrong** information in it to confuse history. To say "this is what happened here, this is what happened there" – and have it all be wrong. That's what I would love to do 'cause I think most history books are wrong anyway so it'd be much more fun to **purposefully mislead** a different generation.

JS: Right, yeah, I think you'd probably have to have private funding to do something like that. I don't know if you could talk City Hall into—

JW: Maybe I could get my first grant! "How To Mislead History"!

JS: Yeah, it's a great idea and I think a lot of people might be wise to pick up on it. So, I guess on that note we'll close, and thanks a lot for your time.

JW: Sure.

JS: This interview's going to be a little bit different. You're going to be in with a whole new cast of characters and I'd like to get your point of view some of these folks for the sake of some insight or friction. Some of the people are Johnny Eck, Jean Hill, Mary Vivian Pearce, among others, so it'll be something like a Baltimore homecoming issue.

JW: [Laughs] You should get Spiro Agnew.

JS: Johnny Eck, now he lives in Baltimore. Have you ever had any communication with him?

JW: I've never ever met him. I saw him recently in this movie called PAINTED SCREENS which is a documentary about this phenomenon in Baltimore, and he is actually one of the most famous painted screen artists.

JS: I guess he lives with his brother, Rob. Do you know what part of Baltimore he lives in?

JW: I think they live in East Baltimore – I'm sure they do. He is famous here for the painted screens. I'm sure that most of the people that know him don't even know that he was in FREAKS.

JS: And painted screens is strictly a Baltimore thing?

JW: Yeah, it's like Folk Art. I mean, it's in a lot of the houses in East Baltimore where I've certainly filmed a lot of my films, including HAIRSPRAY. What they are is they're all these like, I think kind of corny scenes of **ducks**, and that kind of thing. But they're all on the screen so that you can have your windows open and look out but people can't look in. For those hot summers here.

JS: This movie that he was in, was this a local documentary?

JW: Yeah. I was in it but they cut me out [chuckles].

JS: Did it receive play anywhere else?

JW: Yeah, I think it's gonna be on PBS – I think it **was** already on PBS.

JS: Was it a mondo Baltimore type of thing?

JW: No, it was a serious PBS type documentary... and that's how he's known in Baltimore, painted screens. I mean, film people know [of FREAKS], but I think for many, many years he has refused to discuss FREAKS. And this new breed – they don't know what FREAKS is.

JS: Do you remember the first time you ever saw the movie FREAKS?

JW: I probably saw it... I saw it in New York, at a theatre on Times Square... and I saw it in about '64. But then you know when underground movies first came out they played it a lot. I think maybe that was the first real revival of it, and I think that was when it was **the** most popular ever, then. And then I showed it to my prison class... they liked it [chuckles].

JS: Do you think a remake of FREAKS [proposed several years ago by a major studio] would be a feasible thing?

JW: Well, it's feasible. I'm against the idea personally, but financially it could work.

JS: It seems like freaks have totally gone out of style, though.

JW: You know I used to always go to the freak show, I was obsessed by it. Last time I went it was with Pat Moran, her husband and her kids. And I remember the guy came up and stuck a nail up his nose with a hammer and said, "You think it's fake but it's not!" And then Pat caught her daughter trying to shove a nail up her nose. [Laughs] I think that's a reason they don't have it any more. But, there were no **real** freaks – most of it was all kind of fake. There was one guy, that was like flippers he had. Seal Boy. But mostly it was just bad tricks with the most **pitiful** costumes that needed to go to the cleaners so badly!

JS: I think, also, a sort of social consciousness-type atmosphere has taken over that says "these people should not be exploited".

JW: This one, there was the barker out front, and you went in, and it was **so hot** – that's all I remember. See, I could never go to state fairs because all I can think of 'em is **bees** and **trashcans**... it was like 110 degrees in there, and believe me, this was **not** a highbrow audience. The midway always had a freak show. That's where I saw my first fat lady, too. I used to go and look at her every day. She sat in a polka-dot dress eatin' a peach and she'd just **glare** at you. And I'd just stand there by myself.

JS: Speaking of underground films, we also have some material from George Kuchar. In speaking of your teenage years when you were coming up to New York City to see some of the underground films, you often mention George's film HOLD ME WHILE I'M NAKED.

JW: Yes, and SINS OF THE FLESHAPOIDS, which I think is Mike's. **Both** of 'em – they made me want to make films, **they** are the reason. Because they were like – and I hadn't even seen Douglas Sirk yet – they were the first people that ever idolized Douglas Sirk, they were so ahead of their time. And their films were that **lurid** colour, and they were the biggest influence on me, of the underground filmmakers.

JS: More so than Warhol, and...

JW: Yes, because... I saw them first, and the Warhol movies then were just like SLEEP and EAT and stuff, know what I mean? That was before the Superstar thing. Then, of course, the early Warhol – I saw the Warhol première of CHELSEA GIRLS. But I had seen some before that, like COUCH and HARLOT and – you always had to go see them in churches and stuff, and weird – well, The Bridge Theatre, that's where they had a lot of that stuff.

JS: As for the lurid colours, you certainly used that yourself in FEMALE TROUBLE and DESPERATE LIVING.

JW: Oh yeah. And just all their... I don't know, I still love their stuff – I still visit them when I'm in San Francisco. You should see their apartment. They have the **best** portrait of themselves, it's an oil painting that I've always wanted to break into their apartment and steal! But George, I've seen his new stuff – you know he still makes movies all the time. He still teaches at the Art Institute and all the students that sign up for his class **have** to be in his movies, [chuckles] which I love! And George is also obsessed by tornados, you know. And so we talk about that and he's told me all these great books to get on tornados. *Those Terrible Twisters* – that's my favourite one, where you had to send to some post office box in Oklahoma, and make the check out to "Those Terrible Twisters" – I love doin' that! And he made this video about – every year he goes and sits in this motel and waits for a tornado, and I think when one finally came he ran and hid. [Laughs] I'm not sure, he might have

It isn't very pretty.....

Starring LIZ RENAY · MINK STOLE · SUSAN LOWE · EDITH MASSEY · MARY VIVIAN PEARCE · Introducing JEAN HILL From NEW LINE CINEMA

been joking. But that's his vacation every year – he goes by himself to a sleazy motel in Oklahoma and sits and waits for a tornado.

JS: He's done a lot of video recently, too. You've never been inclined toward video yourself?

JW: No... **porno** looks better on it. But, ah – no.

JS: Speaking of porno—

JW: I knew **that** would get you going! [Laughs]

JS: Yeah, [drily] my favourite... subject. What did you think of his collaboration with Curt McDowell on THUNDERCRACK!?

JW: I liked the movie very much. I thought uncut it was a little long. But I think it's **sexy**. I think the sex scenes really are sexy for real. And I think it's funny and I love how it looks – I liked it very much.

JS: If you ever shot a porno film... but you've never been inclined to take that up...

JW: No. No... it's too limiting [chuckles]. If I ever shot one I'd keep it for my personal use.

JS: Yeah. I think they might've been trying to expand the boundaries of what's a very narrow form.

JW: But they **did**, but it's very hard, though, to make a good porno movie and be **funny** because they're sort of the opposite. Good porno isn't funny. It's **dirty**, you know... to **me** at least. You know, I'm not interested in, ha – finding a "meaningful relationship" [chuckles] – I don't think it's what most people are lookin' for in pornography.

JS: Well, speaking of "dirty" pornography and pornography that has a dirty look to it, did you know Curt McDowell at all?

JW: Yes, and I saw LOADS, which I was **shocked** by. That was a little more [laughs] "self"... what's the word I wanta use for that one? Well, I kinda was **amazed**, especially in interviews when he talked about "these are the tricks that I got," and filmed them!... You know, I thought "**God!**" Maybe I didn't want to know that, I think maybe that's how I felt.

JS: Yeah, George said his [Curt's] calling in life was pornography, and that's why God put him on earth.

JW: [Chuckles] Well he knew him better than I!

JS: George has referred to FEMALE TROUBLE as "a quite magnificent and sweeping saga, worthy of Edna Ferber".

JW: Oh! That's nice, so **big**! [Laughs] I think I have a biography of her called, ah... George wrote me the sweetest of all the notes I got when Divine died. And I really got a lot of 'em. And his was maybe the **most** touching. What was his star's name? He had a **great** star.

JS: Donna Kerness?

JW: **That's** the one! She's my favourite – I had a picture of her from *Film Culture* magazine in my apartment for many years – wonder where that is – in a prom dress. She was great. You know there was really great stuff in *Film Culture*, they really covered them [the Kuchar brothers] really well. That was the **best** underground film magazine. It was really good in the Warhol years and underground film years. It was really the only magazine that ever wrote about them. And it had **great** stills and really, really good stuff – I have a lot of them.

JS: And I think maybe the reason *Film Culture* went out of business was because that whole scene ended in a way.

JW: Well yeah, it did. People saw too many movies with colours jumpin' around, you know. That wasn't what they had in mind for underground movies.

JS: Speaking of that period of the underground, did you ever see any Kenneth Anger films?

JW: Oh yeah! The première of ROMAN CANDLES which we had during the Flower Mart in the afternoon in a church, and the Flower Mart then was a thing that all the lunatics came to. It was really a flower show for old ladies but it was a big **beatnik** scene at the time, too. We showed ROMAN CANDLES and Kenneth Anger's EAUX D'ARTIFICE because we wanted to use his name but we didn't want to show anything

too rude in a church, then, because ours was rude – we didn't want to be out-ruded. And, we used his name to lure people in.

JS: In the best tradition of exploitation...

JW: Yeah.

JS: And SCORPIO RISING, did you see that one?

JW: Oh yeah! I mean, I loved it. Kenneth Anger was the very first person – and I don't think anybody ever did this before – that used pop music the way now every movie does. I copied him – everybody copied him.

JS: Yeah, like BLUE VELVET...

JW: **Everybody** copied him, he did it first.

JS: Do you know him at all, personally?

JW: I met him once, I don't know him, no.

JS: You've read his books [*Hollywood Babylon I and II*] though, of course. Bonnie was reading a copy of *Hollywood Babylon* on the bus [The opening scene in MONDO TRASHO].

JW: But she was reading the **real** one, the one that was banned. That wasn't the – the two *Hollywood Babylon*'s that came out in this country – that is different. That was the French one, that was published underground.

JS: Can you ever envision a *Hollywood Babylon III*?? Because he has said that maybe in ten years he'll need more money, so he has to...

JW: The **problem** with it is – you know I sort of feel bad because I gave *Hollywood II* a bad review [chuckles]. Well I think that if you're gonna tell gossip you have to act like you're upset about it and not glad. And I just read the Clara Bow biography, which is really, really good, and it disproves every single thing that he ever said about her. So, I'm not sure how much you can believe a lot of it. Which, I'm sort of against the idea that when you die you lose all rights. I even know that when I've written books, when the lawyers go over it and they go berserk... With *Shock Value* when the lawyers first read it they almost had a heart attack. But, if someone's dead they don't care what you write. You could make up every lie and there's not one thing anybody could do, so, I'm against that.

JS: Didn't you have a line in your review of *Hollywood Babylon II* that the book was so bad nobody should pay for it with cash?

JW: No, I didn't say it was so **bad** – I said it was the kind of book that no one should pay cash for, everyone should charge it on their MasterCard. I'm not saying it was **bad**. I thought the **tone** of it was different that the first one, I thought it was **too** mean. And I think you can be mean, more mean, if you're not as happy that these horrible things happened to these people.

JS: I'd like to talk about Hubert Selby. You've read some of his books – in fact you turned me on to *Requiem For A Dream* in 1980 – what do you think of him?

JW: Well, **most** of 'em are **great**, there's a few I don't like. *Demon* I didn't like. Certainly *Last Exit To Brooklyn*, *Requiem For A Dream* are good... I liked his stories [*Songs From The Silent Snow*]. I think he's really great, and I'm happy they're doing this movie [*Last Exit To Brooklyn*].

JS: Yeah, I wanted to ask you what you thought about the idea of this movie.

JW: Well, I'm dyin' to see it.

JS: Do you think there will be any problems bringing unvarnished Hubert Selby to the screen? I mean is it possible?

JW: Well, certainly less problems than there would've been when the **book** came out! I can't wait to see who plays Tralala!

JS: Did you read *Last Exit* when you were young?

JW: I read *Last Exit To Brooklyn* when I was in highschool – it was a **major, major** influence. And I like his books very much. I like the **idea** of Hubert Selby, Jr. because everything I've read about him... I still have never been able to figure out what he's like.

JS: Just theoretically, how would you shoot *Last Exit To Brooklyn* if you were going to do the movie?

JW: Well you know, I'd have to re-read it – I haven't read it in twenty years. And somebody **did** make it, I mean Ricki Lake's in it – I mean there's a 7-page ad for it in this week's *Variety*. It's a German-American film.

JS: It seems to me like it would almost have to be shot in a grainy documentary style.

JW: Well I don't know, you know Cronenberg's gonna make *Naked Lunch*. In *Variety* this week it says that. So... maybe these kinds of things, everything comes back [chuckles].

JS: Also, I think Charles Bukowski is another example; there are three movies out about him but they're all like, art movies, they're all shot by Europeans.

JW: But I **like** the movies, I liked all three of them a lot. I really loved LOVE IS A DOG FROM HELL – it's my favourite movie of the year practically. And I like TALES OF ORDINARY MADNESS and I liked BARFLY.

JS: You always run into these Bukowski fanatics who just bitterly **hate** those movies, because – I think they take him as some sort of... saint.

JW: Well anybody who loves a book that much, they're **never** satisfied with the movie. A movie is a different thing than a book, and it can never be what they expect. That's why I don't have much desire any more – I used to want to make *A Confederacy Of Dunces*, but I think that would've been a mistake because that book has **such** a following that it's never gonna be what they want.

JS: I think NAKED LUNCH will be... it'll be very interesting to see how that's filmed.

JW: Well Cronenberg could do it.

JS: Jean Hill is another star of this issue. She was in community theatre before your films. Didn't you go to one of her plays at one point?

JW: Yes, it was called *Little Ham*, and that's how I met her. The guy that works the desk in my building – 'cause it's a highrise – I kept saying, "I'm lookin' for a fat black woman that weighs 200 pounds," and he said, "I know one that weighs 400 and she's in this play." And so, she came over and then I went to see the play. And she was **totally** – I mean no one had a **chance** when she walked on stage. And sometimes she forgot her lines and it didn't even matter 'cause she'd make up new stuff that was better than the play anyway. But the actors [laughs] looked like they were scared of her.

JS: Yeah, she says she never really "acts" – if you ask her to do something, choke somebody, she will **do** it, she **will** choke them.

JW: Well, she did knock somebody unconscious in DESPERATE LIVING.

JS: And so she lived in your building for a while or was staying with somebody there?

JW: Yeah, that was the guy at the desk. But no, I don't think she ever **completely** lived here [chuckles]. Her presence was felt heavily.

JS: But that's rather astonishing that she was living in the **same** building...

JW: Yeah, I was lookin' all over everywhere for her when we were casting DESPERATE LIVING and she was **literally** right in front of my own nose [chuckles]. But I had never seen her before.

JS: Jean lives right in your neighbourhood today, doesn't she?

JW: Yeah, she lives the closest to me of anyone I know in the world. And she **always** has.

JS: Have you been to her house that she's in now?

JW: Yeah – it's very tastefully done, very pretty, it's a very nice apartment. She always has people **lurking** around in the background but I'm not sure who they are [laughs]... usually her house boys.

JS: Not to pry into personal matters, [mutters] which of course is absolutely what I'm about to do... but, ah, she mentioned some notorious 18-page letter of some years ago that she wrote to you. Do you remember it?

JW: Yeah, I remember, but she actually didn't give it to me until way afterwards, so, you know... it was like a moot point kind of. And I don't remember everything in it. It was right after DESPERATE LIVING, I think. And I think that Jean maybe at the time

Jean Hill and John Waters

thought everybody that was in a movie made millions of dollars, or something. I'm not quite sure if she quite understood the independent film world I was in at the time.

JS: What was your first encounter with Jean's mother like? To quote Jean, she said that her mom can be hell on white people. Jean told us to ask you about her, ha ha.

JW: Jean's mother in my mind is a racist. She said, "How dare you exploit my daughter," and I said, "Jean made more money on that movie than I did." That shut her up. But her mother **constantly** was against me. And a lot of people's parents have been against me in the beginning with the movies... so I'm used to that. But her mother was so rude to me – her mother basically doesn't like white people. Usually parents don't like me because they find the scripts, or they see one of my movies, but usually not because I'm white. I guess also in a way it's good for white people to feel that prejudice. But it was the first time anyone was really so blatant about it. You know, she might have changed, because a friend of mine is in the hospital, who is very white, he has long blond hair, and she was on the same floor and he said that she was absolutely lovely and they really got along. And I did see her once at Jean's birthday party. But now I kid her when I see her: [yelling] "Oh, Mrs. Hill! It's so **good** to see you!!!" – and she even laughs, so I think over the years she probably calmed down about it. In the beginning she was... not exactly a stage mother [laughs].

JS: But I guess Jean has always had white friends.

JW: She **always** has! And I think her mother's probably always hated that. But in any case, I haven't seen her in a long time. Her brothers and her father are really very lovely.

Susan Lowe, Liz Renay, Jean Hill, Mink Stole; *Desperate Living*

JS: Did her mom ever see DESPERATE LIVING?

JW: I doubt it [chuckles]. Who knows, you know? I don't know. She wasn't at the première. And Jean has a very **close** relationship with her mother. She goes through all sorts of changes with her, but she's certainly very close to her mother... Well you know, in the beginning, everybody's parents were against it. The only person's parents in the very beginning that weren't against it all were David Lochary's. Well, it was his mother – you could **always** go over there. I mean, she loved Divine from the very beginning – we always used to go over there. And David would hook school and she worked, so we'd go over there in the day. But she always was nice. She died a couple of years ago, but I stayed in touch with her way after David died. You know, she went back to art school and everything, she was always very, very lovely.

JS: Jean was featured in the porno mag *Jumbo* a few months ago. What was your gut reaction when you saw this magazine?

JW: Well, she told me about it first. She called up and said she didn't know – suddenly her mailbox had like **hundreds** of letters in it. And she just gave an interview to one of those magazines like *Penthouse* or *Gallery* – I don't know, one of those kind. But yet, no dirty pictures or anything – it wasn't dirty. And then they sold it to that magazine, and when I **saw** the magazine! I mean, the title I think is very, very funny. But I read the letters she got and I felt like washing my hands afterwards. I mean, there are really a lot of chubby chasers, and **she** is the Marilyn Monroe if you're a chubby chaser. But the letters were like, "I'd like your thighs to crack my neck"... and stuff. And people sayin', [anguished cry] "**please** let me see your ass, **please**." Begging, you know. It was like, there are so few magazines I guess if **that's** what you're into, that, when you finally see it you're just crazed about it. They just were **rampant**

chubby chasers.

JS: And the other girls in that magazine—

JW: Oh God! But they like **them**, too. A stretch mark is sexy to them.

JS: And those other girls, I mean some of them didn't look too **happy** to say the least!

JW: Oh, I couldn't even look at it [voice trails off in disgust], I mean, you know...

JS: And I guess readers of that magazine wanted copies of her "nude film" which boils down to DESPERATE LIVING!

JW: Well, they probably **assumed**, not knowing anything about Jean, that she was like the rest of the women in the magazine, that she had a porno career. And you know, there was some black woman called "TV Mama", and there was some other one, a big black woman that has done porno. People get mixed up sometimes.

JS: And I think somebody who reads *Jumbo* probably has never seen any of your movies.

JW: Well, I don't think any marketing team has done a survey of *Jumbo* readers. You know? How much they earn, what kind of liquor they drink, what **airlines** they fly... I really don't think that there's been a marketing survey of *Jumbo* magazine.

JS: Correct me if I'm wrong, but sometimes DESPERATE LIVING seems to be your least favourite of all your films.

JW: Yeah, probably is. I **like** it, though... but, ah, I think it's the least joyous. And I wrote in the screenplay book that really maybe it's a film to watch if you're crashing from a glue high [chuckles]. Well, that makes it sound more negative than I feel about it – no, MONDO TRASHO is by far my least favourite. Every year I'm tempted to snatch that one off the market!

JS: Did you actively try to get away from a "midnight movie" style after DESPERATE LIVING? Or was that just something that happened?

JW: Well, midnight movies were over, you know? I'd be a **fool** to make a midnight movie now – there's like one theatre in the country that shows 'em. Video is midnight movies now. See, you go into a movie with your friends and say, "look at this hideous movie," and **that's** what a midnight movie is now. So certainly... I know the business well enough now to know that that would be like saying I want to make an underground movie. You know, the **times** are different.

JS: Some people have said that DESPERATE LIVING lacked a little because it didn't have Divine in it, but I always thought that any movie with Jean Hill and Edith Massey didn't need Divine.

JW: Well you know, Divine was supposed to play the Susan Lowe role [Mole McHenry – lady wrestler and botched sex change] and everybody assumes it was supposed to be Liz Renay's part. Well, it's easy for me to think that was some of the problem of it, because there is something not very **joyous** about it. Maybe I was in a bad mood when

Divine; *Mondo Trasho*

I wrote it [chuckles]. You know, in Europe they like it a lot, and some of the really hardcore fans like it best. So, I don't know that – I can't really tell. I probably like it least because it did the worst at the box office. That always colours how I feel about one of my films [laughs]... in hindsight.

JS: Jean said that she knew Divine a long time ago, the early '60s or something, at a place called Eddie's Bar in Baltimore. Now, is it possible that two future Waters stars could have collided before you came into the picture?

JW: **Yes**. I know what Eddie's Bar is – I was in there once in my life, too. And I'm sure that Divine had been in there in his life, yes.

JS: And very possibly Jean, too?

JW: Oh yeah, well Jean I'm sure was.

JS: Did you ever go to the Royal Theatre back then?

JW: **All** the time, you know, it was my favourite. And I would go, and I'd always be the only white person and I'd get beat up and it'd be worth it. Because I saw, like, Little Stevie Wonder when he was 12, I saw the Jewel Box Review... The Marvelettes... I saw Tina Turner when she still had a moustache. I mean, it was quite good. And it's really a shame, because after the riots they tore that whole neighbourhood down, which was really stupid. 'Cause that really was the Apollo Theatre of Baltimore. **Everybody** played there. Ruth Brown said she played there a lot – it was really a **famous** black theatre.

JS: How's your relationship with Jean been over the years? She's pretty feisty

---

Hairspray

sometimes, isn't she?

JW: Jean can be difficult, but I think my relationship's been good with her. Oh... yeah, we've had some ups and downs but never anything I'd think of as serious. You know, I love Jean, I mean she's great fun to go out with because no one ever looks at you [chuckles]. She's better than wearin' a camouflage outfit. And Jean, you know, underneath it all, is... can even be conservative. It's hard to see what she's really like because she can be so aggressive... but underneath it she's a good Catholic girl [wry chuckle].

JS: It's ironic that HAIRSPRAY was a "black movie" for you but was made without your only black star. Surely there would have been a part for Jean in that movie?

JW: She broke her leg, though. You know? Really, a month before we started shooting it. So, and – the insurance people – there was no way. I mean I even talked to her doctor and he said "she will not be able to walk." So right up to the last minute I tried every possible way to get her in it.

JS: We also have your old friend Mary Vivian Pearce in this issue. Now, your parents and her parents are back on speaking terms again?

JW: Oh, they're best friends again. [In a tone of bemused chagrin] Her mother asked me for my autograph at her father's funeral, to give to some friends of hers... so times **do** change. Her mother's very lovely to me now. I've known... well, **Bonnie** is what everybody calls her. Mary Vivian Pearce is her name in movies, and you know, she just had her first published article that came out in the paper, about being a clocker and it's by "Mary Pearce". So she's "Mary Vivian Pearce" in the movies, "Mary Pearce" in the press, and "Bonnie" to everybody that knows her. And this piece in the city paper is very good. I've really known Bonnie since I was born. Our fathers were friends in college.

JS: You know her sister?

JW: I know all of 'em – she has a million sisters. But there are lots of things in all my movies that come from growing up with Bonnie. We weren't allowed to see each other for a long time, by the **police** I think, for a while. Well, at least they threatened that, I don't know. We ran wild together as teenagers.

JS: In those early movies, did you pattern Bonnie's character after any particular Hollywood star?

JW: No, she came up really with that look of that white hair and bright red lipstick before anyone I'd ever seen in my life wear bright red lipstick. That's what she really looked like. I remember when we lived together on 25th Street where we made the movie – that house she walks out of – I think she walks out of a basement apartment, but we lived upstairs – but in that house was also, on the first floor, a plumbing school. And you had to walk right through it. Plumbers would sit there working on pipes and we would walk through with, like, Divine in **drag**, you know, and I remember the head plumber came to the movie. We were making EAT YOUR MAKE-UP there and the whole beginning is this girl just going [in a breathless panting grunting moan] "make-up, make-up – Oh God – make-up!" moaning about make-up for about three minutes, right? We had to try to synchronize it on a tape to the lips, which was impossible... but I didn't know that then, so we did it for like four or five **days**, she was up there going "make-up! make-up!" and the man in the plumbing store finally said to me, "Well, I heard that up there but I just thought it was one of

Eat Your Make-Up

Mary Vivian Pearce; *Hag In A Black Leather Jacket*

your friends havin' a baby so I didn't say anything." [Laughs] I couldn't believe that. But Bonnie lived there then and she looked like that, and I remember her just walkin' out of the house and people would go **crazy**!

JS: Do you remember back when she used to hang out at Windy Valley?

JW: Yeah! She used to hook school and I used to meet her there. And I remember mostly meeting her when I lived at my parents' and she lived at her parents' and the quickest way for us to meet was walking up the railroad tracks. So we'd both walk up these railroad tracks and see each other in the distance [chuckles]. It was very... Tennessee Williams [laughs]. Bonnie is the **only** one – Bonnie is in HAG IN A BLACK LEATHER JACKET. She's the only one of all the people that was in **all** of them. None of the other people were. At the end of HAG IN A BLACK LEATHER JACKET she was doing the "Bodie Green", which was the dance that was later used in HAIRSPRAY.

JS: Oh, the Bodie Green was in HAIRSPRAY?

JW: Yeah, they do it in the record shop. The "Dirty Boogie" – it's the same thing.

JS: Now, did you guys invent that or was that an existing dance?

JW: No, it was the one dance you weren't allowed to do. And Bonnie and I used to go to a Catholic Youth Organization – it was the only time we could see each other – and steal pocketbooks and do the Dirty Boogie and be asked to leave. No, it was a real dance. We carried it to unheard of lengths [chuckles]. She was **really** good at it!!!

JS: Yeah, I remember when you were in Boston, here at your show, and somebody asked you to do it up on stage and you said you weren't **about** to do it by yourself—

JW: [Tone of dry conviction] Well, I **certainly** wouldn't. I did do it some with Divine when we were teaching Ricki Lake to do it, in rehearsals. Divine could really do it, too. Matter of fact, one of the first memories I have of Divine is him doin' it. At a swim club. But yeah, Bonnie was even in THE DIANE LINKLETTER STORY with a very limited cast [Lochary, Pearce and Divine], so she's been in every one of 'em. And I think she was really impersonating her mother in THE DIANE LINKLETTER STORY. It was the same stuff her mother was saying to **her** at the time.

THE GIRL. . .THE TRAGEDY. . .THE GAP

JOHN WATERS'

THE DIANE LINKLETTER STORY

STARRING DAVID LOCHARY, MARY VIVIAN PEARCE AND DIVINE AS "DIANE"
a dreamland short subject - 10 minutes

JS: Now, "Miss Cotton" in PINK FLAMINGOS – she was the "travelling companion" and I think psychologists have debated and studied this role for many, many years... what exactly was her relationship to them, was she **related** to—

JW: No, she was Cracker's... ah... girlfriend, but they never touched. So she was Divine's friend and Divine's son's girlfriend. So I guess Divine in that movie was a common-law mother-in-law [chuckles]. And in the sequel you see Divine has married his son and had a baby. And Cotton is **more** of a voyeur in this one 'cause it's fifteen years **later**. So it's all the same character – Cotton, Crackers.

JS: In some of those early movies, I think even PINK FLAMINGOS, a lot of people used

Mary Vivian Pearce, Divine; *Pink Flamingos*

Cookie Mueller

Divine; *Pink Flamingos*

their own names, like **Cookie** [Mueller].

JW: Well, Cookie may have been the only one, and that was because she was new and I wanted people to **remember** her [chuckles]. That's how we did it in the beginning, to **break 'em in**. But the main characters... well, Bonnie's name wasn't **Cotton**! God knows where that name came from – maybe her hair looked like cotton.

JS: Yeah, Cotton and Crackers – Crackers was a brilliant stroke. And **Noodles**, I mean this is like, ah...

JW: Well, that name came because Cookie **was** going to name her baby Noodles, because her last name is Mueller, it was gonna be like "Mueller's Noodles", and the hospital people told her she couldn't. They wouldn't do it. And that **is** her baby in the movie. He's now seventeen. And the baby that Divine has in FEMALE TROUBLE is Susan Lowe's son, who is now sixteen. I even saw "Taffy" the other night at the movies, and she's in her twenties now. You know, the one that played "Little Taffy" in FEMALE TROUBLE? She looks great. I said, "Does anybody ever recognize you? And she said, "No, but my boyfriend and I rented it [FEMALE TROUBLE] the other night and he was **so appalled**, [laughs] he said, 'That's you??!!! **Oh my God!!'**" – he just couldn't believe, like, what was her life like? and her parents? at the time that she was in this movie. [Laughs]... She's very pretty.

JS: Those first three films: EAT YOUR MAKE-UP, ROMAN CANDLES and HAG IN A BLACK LEATHER JACKET, do you **ever** show those any more?

JW: I showed EAT YOUR MAKE-UP to some friends a couple of years ago... the problem is that HAG... is 8mm with the sound on tape and you need a reel-to-reel tape

---

recorder. My 8mm projector is broken and I don't have a reel-to-reel tape recorder. ROMAN CANDLES is three of 'em shown at once – like an obvious rip-off of CHELSEA GIRLS – and same thing – I need a reel-to-reel tape recorder. And both of those, there are no prints, they're the originals. EAT YOUR MAKE-UP is 16mm, black-and-white, filmed at 16 frames a second, because I didn't know the difference, so you could never put it on video... and it also has a very, very closely synchronized soundtrack on a reel-to-reel tape recorder but I would be the only person who could ever **attempt** to show it, to make it sync right. And I did show it to one of the stars [in it], Marina Melin, a couple of years ago when she came down to visit – and I hadn't seen it in a long time, and... it's fun to show – it's like showin' home movies to your old friends. In my apartment, to people I've known for twenty years, it's fun to watch. To put it in a theatre, or in front of an audience, I'm sure that... there'd be a few people that would enjoy it. But basically it's much better to imagine it [chuckles].

JS: What's the condition of these movies?

JW: HAG IN A BLACK LEATHER JACKET is really bad... ROMAN CANDLES is, literally **is**, home movies. I mean, it's random shots of people, there's no story or anything. And it's got Mink in it, praying at some grave, **sobbing**, it's got... I really haven't seen this one in ten years. It's got Alexis eating an apple. Alexis was this other huge girl we knew at the time, who was really good friends with Divine. It's just random shots [chuckles]. EAT YOUR MAKE-UP is the only one that **sort of** has a story. [Laughs] **Some** would call it a story.

JS: And MONDO TRASHO is one that you—

JW: Every once in a while I'm tempted to take it out of distribution. But... what the hell – it's already out there. And there are parts of it I like. It should be twenty minutes long but it's ninety, you know? I think if you've seen all my films it's okay to see that one. It played here recently, in a theatre, and the audience **roared** all through it, so, I don't know.

JS: It always struck me as having the most **complicated** plot in the history of cinema or no plot at all – I can't figure out which.

JW: [Laughs] All my plots are complicated, but I remember one reviewer in the very beginning said that all my plots are mere clotheslines to hang my dirty wash on. And I even think of that today when I'm writing a script, I never forgot that one [chuckles]. It's maybe true.

JS: So John, I guess the last question is more just directed at you. I just figured I had to ask it... in our last interview I asked you if as a movie director you ever employed a casting couch, and you said you never slept with anyone in your movies except one person, and—

JW: No, I... it was one person and it was years **after** the movie. I've never slept with anybody before a movie and I still haven't.

JS: Who was it?

JW: Ah, I won't tell you that one.

JS: [Laughs] That's what I figured.

JW: Did someone else tell ya – I'm tryin' to think of...

JS: No, people just always ask me, they say, "why didn't you ask him **who** it was?" – that's the **logical** question. I guess then I have to...

JW: Good try! [Laughs]

Chapter Three

AN INTERVIEW WITH DIVINE
August 13th, 1986, 7PM

JACK STEVENSON: In a recent interview Joey Ramone asked Pia Zadora what she thought of John Waters and she said she loves him because she wants to be the next Divine. I suppose **you** want to be the next Pia Zadora.

DIVINE: I don't think so [laughs]... I'm quite content actually... I'm quite shocked that she would ever say that, isn't she happy enough being Pia Zadora? I mean, I'll trade places with her, but... in some ways... but I don't think she could **be** Divine and I don't think I could be Pia Zadora.

JS: Right... I think she was probably kidding a bit, too...

D: Oh yeah! But I would gladly sit there with her husband and help him spend some of that cash.

JS: Exactly. I guess he's quite rich.

D: Yeah... I would think she would be busy just havin' fun doin' that.

JS: You tour a lot outside the U.S.; you've taken Europe by storm and you toured Japan recently, I think; how did the Japanese like your show?

D: No, I was in **China**.

JS: You were in China?

D: Yeah.

JS: My God... behind the Iron Curtain.

D: I haven't gone to Japan yet... it went over quite well there [China]. Yes, I've been very lucky to play all around the world; Israel, Australia...

JS: And of course, America regularly, too.

D: Yeah.

JS: But I guess you're perhaps a bigger star in Europe.

D: Well, I think for records because the movies are just starting to play there... but I think for my records – I have platinum and gold records in a lot of those countries and, of course, I don't really have a recording career in this country but for the movies I think I'm more known here, you know, not so much for the music.

JS: Okay, here's a theoretical question: Suppose John Hinckley had shot President Reagan for **you** instead of Jodie Foster, do you think it would have given your career a boost or...

D: [Laughs] Oh God...

JS: I mean, to ask a loaded question.

D: That would've been a loaded one. I guess I could have gotten some good... a lot of press out of it. I don't know how "good" it would have been – I was gonna say "good press" – but I guess I could've got a lot of press out of it. I don't know what it would have done career-wise actually. It could have gone either direction, especially with me I think... I met her when I was just out in L.A. the last time and she's very nice.

JS: Oh yeah, Jodie?

D: Yeah.

Sun

Vol. 3 — No. 5 January 29, 1985   55¢

Behind the cameras:
How top celebs film sex scenes

Desperate citizens flee in terror as ...

GIANT FLYING CAT TERRIFIES STATE

Cure backache just by rubbing on your head

BIZARRE SCANDAL OF AMERICA'S GAY WRESTLERS

Thousands of truckers to get tax refunds

DOES YOUR WIFE SPEND FOOD MONEY TO BUY ROMANCE?

Magic power of dollar sign can make you rich

NEW BLOOD TEST PREDICTS IF YOUR MARRIAGE WILL LAST

Garlic restores faded sex life

SICKO TORTURES HOOKERS WITH TRAINED ROACHES

If you thought Boy George was strange, LOOK AT THIS!

JS: I don't think she talks **at all** about that any more.

D: No, I didn't bring it up either, no I have learned discretion over the years. I thought maybe it was best not to bring that up.

JS: Exactly, although I bet a lot of people **want** to bring it up.

D: Oh sure – they're dying to, yes.

JS: You've been on the cover of – speaking of publicity – infamous scandal sheets such as *Weekly World News* and *The Sun* – when will the *New York Times* finally recognize your genius?

D: As far as being on the **cover**?

JS: Yeah.

D: I think because they've written about me many times on the **inside**...

JS: Yes, you've been on the cover of both of them, the *Weekly World News* and *The Sun*, above which they headlined it "GIANT FLYING CAT TERRIFIES STATE" [issue of *The Sun*, January 29, 1985].

D: [Laughs]

JS: That's publicity you can't buy.

D: Well exactly – that's publicity the *Times* could never match! It's all different, but I think more of my audience probably reads that paper than reads the *Times* [laughs].

JS: Right... and the highest pinnacle would be to get on the cover of *TV Guide*.

D: Well, once again, I've been on the **inside** of *TV Guide* but... with time all things can happen.

JS: Okay, to get on record straight from the highest source: who was the sexiest, Mansfield or Monroe?

D: [Thoughtfully] Mansfield or Monroe...

JS: Or is there a possible third candidate?

D: Well, there's always me [laughs]. Well, they were so completely different: one was... more like a little girl and one was more like a real **star**, you know, being Mansfield.

JS: Was there one that you were more...

D: My preference was always Mansfield.

JS: Right, people say you're more patterned after the Mansfield [prototype].

D: But I always thought her more a, what do you call it, "of the times", what's that word?

JS: Phenomenon of the times?

D: Yeah... ends up being a **victim** of the times, too, which they both did... but I think... Mansfield was more animated and... which I've always thought of the character of Divine being, you know.

JS: Monroe, they always said she had legitimate acting abilities... could play subtle...

D: Oh yeah, and all that, whereas Mansfield was actually really smart but just had the dumb act all the time [Ed. note: which she brilliantly parodies in THE GIRL CAN'T HELP IT.] ...I'm not saying I'm Einstein, but I mean it's more or less like the whole Divine thing too because I think a lot of people think I actually **am** like that character that I've played... and I think that's the same thing they thought about Mansfield, whereas actually she was quite different.

JS: Right, and she could take that all the way to the bank.

D: And **did**... her whole, she was a character actress too actually, you know, she was doing a whole act... whereas, with Monroe, there was a lot of sympathy involved, she was in and out of the hospital and divorces and all of that, which I mean, sold a lot of tickets to the movies, but I was always interested more in the – "good time", the animation – the...

JS: Exaggeration.

D: The exaggeration. I think that was Mansfield.

JS: If Ronald Reagan had asked you to perform at his inauguration, would you have gone?

D: Well, I'm willing to sell out if the right deal comes along, you know, but I don't think that would've been the right deal, no – I don't think number one, he wouldn't ask and if he did, [dreamily] I don't know.

JS: I think Frank Sinatra was in charge of getting those acts lined up... so I don't know.

D: I don't think I would have had ...

JS: You don't think you appeal to the over-sixty crowd, maybe?

D: Well, some, but I don't know if it would be the Reagans and the Sinatras.

JS: What do you think of Nancy's wardrobe – it seems to be in the news quite a bit.

D: Well, It's **safe** but, I guess anyone can put on a $4,000 whatever... and look, have that look which I'm not gonna say is right or wrong – it's a very "safe" look, but I guess with her job that's how she has to look – but I think from what I've read, she's always had that look.

JS: Right.

D: I don't know, I would think something with a little more imagination would be more my...

JS: Something more along the Divine scale, or perhaps not as—

D: [Chuckles] I don't know how good she'd look in toreadors or a big fish tail, you know. But it's just a very safe look. I admire people who have a bit more imagination.

JS: For a President's wife I guess she's maybe a little daring, I don't know... but that isn't much daring.

D: Well, Jackie was, too. Mrs. Kennedy.

JS: She was probably, maybe your favourite of the President's wives troop?

D: Well yeah – not that I've ever been really into **politics**... but I think... I like Lady Bird Johnson a lot; **dyed black hair**... two hideous daughters.

JS: On the serious side, you knew Harvey Milk, you were a personal acquaintance of his. Did you feel any extreme emotion when Dan White committed suicide?

D: Well... just that – when did he do that?

JS: About two years ago. He [White] lived in seclusion in the San Fernando Valley after he got out of jail.

D: He deserved that [jail]... well in a way he got in the end what he should've gotten. I mean, I do believe if you're going to take someone's life then you must pay with yours. Because that's the most precious thing you can take from someone, isn't it?... and for this bullshit story that Twinkies drove him to it... it's exactly what I said: it's bullshit. And for anyone to get away with the murder of **two** people... I mean I really think the man should have been punished severely. But because of the circumstances he wasn't. And by "circumstances" I mean people being gay. I think it's left a very bitter taste in a lot of people's mouths... that might not be the right words to use either [laughs]. But you know what I mean.

JS: Right, poetic justice, or something along those lines, eventually caught up with him.

D: Yes! You get back what you give out. I'm a firm believer in karma. I think what's meant to be is meant to be, and he had to pay.

JS: He put out a tremendous amount of bad karma and he got it back one day.

D: And it's very funny because I think he had it beat, but you know – by getting off more or less – because he certainly did. I mean a lot of people that go out and murder two people would get the electric chair. And I think, like you say, he lived in seclusion. I think it was probably on his mind constantly and he just couldn't live with it any more, and so he was executed by himself. I know Harvey didn't deserve that, nor did the other man.

JS: I guess when the news broke that he had committed suicide there was utter jubilation in the gay district and some people said, let's not gloat, it's a wholly unfortunate thing, but other people were just... glad he was gone.

D: Oh yes, like I said before, I don't wish any bad on anyone, you know, because I don't want anyone to wish it on me. And... like I said, karma – it's strange – sometimes it works immediately and sometimes it takes a while. Just when a lot of people think they've gotten away with whatever it was they were getting away with they find you've got to pay – there's no way to beat it.

JS: Speaking of karma, more or less, when you were growing up in Towson, Maryland, did you really live in the same house that F. Scott Fitzgerald used to live in when Zelda—

D: I did, yes. We had a lovely place that I grew up in, it was a small estate, it had a very big house on it, we had twenty-eight rooms. At one time F. Scott Fitzgerald and his wife Zelda had lived there for a couple of years while she was in and out of a mental hospital right near there called Shephard-Pratt. So I guess she had a few problems. But, yeah, they did live there.

JS: There was a fire there at one point?

D: Yeah, and she had set the top floor on fire so that part of the house did have a newer roof than the other part... and we did meet their daughter, Scottie, at one point. My mother wrote her a letter and she came to the house.

JS: It would probably be a little far-fetched to ask if there was any feeling of any "presence" in the house... I mean were you aware of the history of the house at a young age?

D: Well, yeah... I mean, there certainly was strange... "vibes" there, whatever you want to call it, especially on the top floor. But I was sort of a weird kid – I used to love to go up there. My cousins and things wouldn't when they would come to visit.

JS: It was a very large house, as you say.

D: Yeah... and the third floor originally had been like a servants' quarters, or maybe children's rooms or whatever.

JS: To this day, have your parents come to grips with your fame?

D: I think so, yeah, it took a while. But I think they're quite happy now, and finally with TROUBLE IN MIND – my father's watched that seventeen times, he just got it last week, so I said, well good – I'm so glad he finally got one that he didn't mind watching. I think he sort of cringed every time he'd see me come around the corner in a mini cocktail dress [laughs]. But they both have come a long way in their thinking, believe me.

JS: I noticed in the *People* magazine review of TROUBLE IN MIND that they referred to it as your "first male role" – I guess they never saw FEMALE TROUBLE, eh?

D: I think they meant the first one where it was a male role all the way through, not just a cameo thing.

JS: I guess you were hassled a bit in junior high and high school for being different, do you ever feel vindictive toward the people that hassled you, thinking like, "Well, I'm wealthy, successful and famous and they're still pumping gas and working in sub shops"?

D: Yeah... well I – no, I don't feel vindictive, I mean at the time I did, when it was happening. But I was young, just a kid, and you don't know what's happening – I mean, you know what's happening but you don't understand **why** It's happening. And, when you get older and have time to think about it and realize, you know, that... but it's still hard to understand **why** people have to go to those extremes. Why they have to beat people up just because they're different and things, I never understood that and never **will**, but it's very funny you should mention that because when I went back to Baltimore a few months ago I did see a lot of them and some of them were doing, ah, menial labour and things, and I thought, "Well, you see, once again!", "Here we go", you know, you all have to pay, it's what you get, in a way, you know... and in a way I felt very bad for them. And these also were people – not only the ones that used to wait to beat me up – but also I saw some other people that used to laugh at me and tell me I was, excuse me, but an "asshole" and a fool and I would never get anywhere in this business and they were still doing **exactly** the same thing they were doing at the time... and I thought, you know, and I felt very bad for them, too. So, some people are just very narrow-minded and... stupid. But it all boils down to, I mean I'm a firm believer also if you want something bad enough and you're willing to go out and work for it... nobody is gonna **give** it to you. 'Cause if they give it to you you're gonna have to pay for it again and again anyway somehow. So you might as well work for it and do it on your own.

JS: Right, do it on your own, no matter—

D: And then it's yours.

JS: Perhaps the more original you are the more you have to fight for what you... see.

D: So, you know, if you want it bad enough and want to work for it, it'll come your way. It takes time! There'd been many times I'd felt like throwing in the towel, and saying "forget it". But I mean, I don't know what else I would do – I mean I love to make people laugh.

JS: Right. So it's not like if the offers ever dried up you'd get a job in construction or something.

D: Well, I've been very lucky now that I wouldn't **have** to. If I wanted to live very frugally I could quit tomorrow. But it's not just the money any more... after... when you're very poor and don't have any, I certainly did go through **that** for many years because I didn't make any money until five years ago. But then after a while, when you realize you can make the money, of course you need the money for different things, you know for **living** for instance, and... just the expense of being in this business. Costuming and travelling and blah, blah, blah. But then it's just, when you get **so** far, you think, "I got **that** far and people told me I couldn't, maybe I could go all the way." And so – I'm very ambitious, I'm gonna go for it, you know. People told me I'd never get on television. I just wrapped my first television show last week. *Tales From The Dark Side*. So I thought, "there's nothing gonna stop me now", you know.

JS: And you've been on the Letterman show a few times and other talk shows.

D: Well, I've been on all of them except Carson.

JS: Oh, you've been on every talk show?

D: Yeah, all the major ones.

JS: And this is a series that you finished?

D: It's called *Tales From The Dark Side*, it's a series that's on every week but every week it's a different episode with different actors and different stories.

JS: Right, when might this episode be aired, did they give you any idea?

D: I'm not quite sure... probably not until January because the new season doesn't start until September, you know.

JS: Are you working on any film projects at the moment?

D: Well, I have two films lined up and I have one for later on in November and one for the spring.

JS: What will Divine be like in old age? Will there be MOMMIE DEAREST scenes, just to ask a gonzo question.

D: No, I don't think so, I mean, there aren't any kids. So...

JS: And you wouldn't adopt any kids just to slap 'em around?

D: Huh?... No... I wouldn't want to. Maybe once in a while, yeah [humorously]. When the baby cries it's like going out and opening the door and throwing it out or something... just because you don't get time to sleep all the time, and I think they're living a normal life, they don't know what this is like, you know.

JS: But you can't see any... I mean it's not the sort of thing where age is going to be a factor for a long, long time, that you can see, I mean.

D: Oh well, I don't know that I want to—

JS: Like you just said, the sky's the limit.

Divine

D: Yeah. I mean I want to go for it – as long as it takes – I'm hoping it doesn't take much longer, I mean it's already been twenty-four years. So I'm hoping maybe within the next **ten**, we can peak and get that over with and... just ride a little wave right through there, you know.

JS: Right through to glory.

D: And be able to pick and choose what we want to do, maybe do one real good movie a year and just lay around or – and I would like to produce other people. I know many talented people that really deserve a good break. I really would like to be in a position to help them out. I could also make a lot of money off of that! [Laughs] Because that's what people would say the whole reason was, but it isn't. It's just different **challenges** and things that you want to sink your teeth into after a while.

JS: Is that twenty-four years – that's twenty-four years you've been in show business? Since the first of John's films?

D: Yeah, yeah.

JS: Yeah, that's a while. So actually these people you went to high school with and stuff, they must, that was a good while ago – **not** trying to make you feel old or anything.

D: No, I'm forty.

JS: So you're just about exactly the same age as John is.

D: Exactly the same age, yeah.

JS: Which of your films do you consider your GONE WITH THE WIND?

D: [Chuckles] My GONE... would be POLYESTER I guess, wouldn't it?

JS: Yeah, I would vote for POLYESTER. With your amazing character transformations from Earl Peterson to Divine to Hilly Blue, De Niro's RAGING BULL performance pales. Do you think he's even in the same league with you?... just to ask another loaded question. [Ed. note: although I completely and utterly believe it.]

D: [Laughs] You're trying to make enemies for me!

JS: [Laughs] I'm just seein' how ya handle yourself.

D: No, no! None of them are more fabulous than, I am! That's why it aggravates me every time I go to the movies, it's that I think I should have had this part... [defiantly] I would have been better. RUTHLESS PEOPLE with me could have been **unbelievable**! I could have played Danny DeVito **and** Bette Midler's parts! Even though two or three reviewers did say that she was playing me **anyway**. So that when you read that – I'm sure it pissed her off – and at the same time made me think [practically shouting] why didn't they just give **me** the part!!??

JS: When CHAINED HEAT came out the Boston reviewer wrote that the lady convict gang leader should have been played by Divine and it would have come off a lot

Divine, Edith Massey; *Polyester*

better, so I think your name pops up in a lot of reviews.

D: Well, yes, I'm telling – I go to movies all the time and say, "Oh, this is for me, this is **written** for me!" It's so funny... And then you go to movies like this last Gene Wilder film. With Gilda Radner and Dom Delouise.

JS: Right, it's like a take-off on a '40s mystery movie or something.

D: I thought it was the worst thing I've ever seen in my life. I fell asleep. And I'm such a fan of Dom Delouise, I was so disappointed. But I thought with **all that money** they could have given it to John Waters – we could have made **ten** good films.

JS: Exactly. You're not a great fan, probably, of Gene Wilder and Gilda Radner, maybe, or don't have much opinion...

D: More Dom Delouise I like a lot. No, that kind of humour I guess just doesn't... isn't for me... I don't know. No, I'm not a big fan of either one of them [laughs].

JS: You say you're a fan of Dom Delouise. Are there any other early comics that you would say have been an inspiration to you? Rodney Dangerfield or any of those?

D: Oh, I think he's hysterical. And I **loved** BACK TO SCHOOL. It had some slow moments in it but basically it was very funny, I think. And he's good. There was a time I couldn't stand him because I think maybe the material he did was mostly about his wife and things, you know, that sort of humour. Don Rickles I can't really bear.

JS: How about Jackie Gleason?

D: Jackie Gleason I've **always** really liked. And Lucille Ball. I mean, I think they are two of the funniest people that ever walked the face of the earth. And also George Jefferson, on *The Jeffersons*? I think he is **so** funny. I don't know if you ever watch that programme...

JS: Right, yes I do.

D: But he is hysterical. I mean, and Dom Delouise – not to keep repeating myself – but just to see him do that ad for ziplock bags, or something, is funnier than the whole Gene Wilder movie.

JS: Right, you say that's one of the worst because of the way they played it. Are there any others that stick out, recent movies, that stick out in your mind as being incredible or incredibly bad?

D: Oh, the **very worst**: Stephen King's movie, that **truck** movie!

JS: I've read reviews of it, I haven't seen that one yet.

D: Oh don't. I mean I'm gonna write letters and ask for my money back! I mean this was six dollars I had to go on stage and work for and I want it back. I **couldn't** believe, what a waste of film! I mean the man should be locked up – well not **really** you know, but it's just like [in a crazed wail] "Why did they give him this money?!" This money just makes me crazy. And then I saw ROOM WITH A VIEW which I think is one of the most charming – is a beautiful movie – with Maggie Smith.

JS: I think a lot of the money that they give to these people they give to them because it's a "safe" movie to make, they have name stars or something, whereas John Waters seems to be having a little, you know, he could make much better movies but there seems to be a risky element, Hollywood seems to think, with him.

D: Yeah, but I think after seeing RUTHLESS PEOPLE especially, not that it was John's style at all, but getting, leaning more toward that. I definitely thought so. **Did** you at all?

JS: I haven't seen that one yet.

D: Oh well, when you see it or if you see it – you've seen John's movies?

JS: Oh yes.

D: Well then you don't need to see those movies, forget it.

JS: Knowing the outrageous collaborations you and John Waters have been involved in, do you think that you two are blackballed in Hollywood to any extent?

D: No, not at all. I don't have any problem getting work. In fact I just got a Hollywood agent... No, the two of us are very professional and easy to work with, quite the opposite of our screen images but I definitely wanted to play some other types of parts, you know? I mean, I've always wanted to. Everyone else has always said, "Well,

Female Trouble

he's a transvestite, a drag queen, a sex-change, a pervert, a blah, blah, blah" but I've always said I'm a character actor. It just happens the parts I was offered were women's parts. And...

JS: So you were victimized by stereo – role models?

D: Well, I think yeah, it's the cliché Hollywood story of being typecast. And I certainly am the victim of **that**. But I would always work with John. He's one of my favourite writers, and I think he's a brilliant writer and director and friend and all of that, but "friend" doesn't even come into it when we're working. I love to work with him and I love his style and he knows me so he writes for **me**, which I'm very, very lucky, any actor to have that is a lucky, lucky person. A luxury, it's a luxury.

JS: He seems to have had a little trouble getting money up for some projects in the last few years...

D: Well, like you say, I mean, he doesn't want to write E.T. We're all willing to sell out to a certain extent, it's just like I told you before, but not all the way. I mean you have barriers, it's like "this is as far as I go."

JS: I think it's, maybe he's not **capable** of selling out like that, he just couldn't bear to put the words down for something like that.

D: Well exactly, it's not in his mind. He's too brilliant to do that, you know, so I think **time**, because he's in there all the time, he doesn't give up, so eventually it'll come around.

JS: Can you recall off-hand what was the strangest thing that ever happened to you on a film location – didn't you have to swim across an icy river in FEMALE TROUBLE?

D: Oh yes, [half in fondness, half in horror] across the river and then in LUST IN THE DUST I had to go into this river that was **completely black**. And who knew what was in there, you know.

JS: Right on location.

D: Uh huh, with all the cameras going and things. "Okay, get in! Get in!" And you had to be **nude**, too, "Okay, take your clothes off and get in there!". And there are forty-five people standing around, you know, on the set. I'm thinkin' "What am I doin' here," you know, with five pounds of make-up on, three pairs of eye lashes and my dong hangin' out, you know, at seven o'clock in the morning with a pair of falsies is just like – it's a bit disillusioning at times.

JS: [Laughs] Not all glory, eh?

D: Not at all.

JS: Where was that shot on location?

D: Santa Fe.

JS: And that was the second film you starred in with Tab.

D: Yeah.

JS: You've starred with him and Kris Kristofferson, of course, in TROUBLE IN MIND, and others: Who would you most like to co-star with now, perhaps Meryl Streep? Or...

D: Yeah! Jack Nicholson, Warren Beatty, Elizabeth Taylor... I mean let's go the whole route, you know.

JS: Are there actors or actresses you would refuse to star with?

D: No, because you never know what they're really like until you've worked with them and been around them! I mean, I've read things about me that were so completely untrue. A couple of times it made me mad and a couple of times I just sat there and laughed, you know. I thought, well they're writing that about **me**, what are they writing about Elizabeth Taylor or... Mick Jagger or who knows, I mean... so I think the best way, that's why I'll **go** anywhere and love to meet anybody because I think these are things you have to make up for your own mind.

JS: You probably do know a lot of the Hollywood stars, I imagine.

D: Well I've been very fortunate to meet quite a few of them, yes. And that's been a lot of fun 'cause I've always been quite a movie buff.

JS: Did you ever meet your favourite, Elizabeth Taylor?

D: Yeah, I did. Yes, that was quite a thrill.

JS: Was that a recent meeting, or...

D: Oh, it was about five years ago.

JS: I know because you mention it in John's first book [*Shock Value*] in that interview John did with you.

D: Yeah... so it might have been longer than that. When did that come out?

JS: Oh, that was about 1980 or 1981, 1 think 1981 that it came out.

D: So I guess I met Liz seven years ago or something, time goes by... Yeah, it was six or seven years ago I guess. I think I told John it was like looking in the mirror.

JS: I think in his book you actually said you hadn't met her yet, you said you saw Polaroids of her on an airplane... Elton John was on the airplane.

D: Oh right, yeah, because I'm friends with Elton and Elton had invited me to go on the plane to Philadelphia and the producers wouldn't let me off work that night from the show because, I guess, people just don't do that [laughs] but I wanted to go to a party and concert in Philadelphia on a private jet and I really couldn't understand. I thought they were being very unfair [laughs]. But actually I was the one who was being unfair. You don't think of it that way at the time. The next day I went over to have lunch with Elton in his suite and there were all these people there. They started showing me all these Polaroid pictures of Elizabeth Taylor [laughs] and Elton said,

"Yeah, you should have been on the plane!" And then I could have **killed** my producers, you know, had they been in the same room at the time. I thought there I would have been, up in the air with her. How long does it take to get to Philly, an hour?

JS: Yeah, something like that.

D: Forty-five minutes? Where she couldn't get away from me? So I mean, we would have **had** to have some sort of conversation. I thought that would have been my break, I could've been her best friend. But it didn't happen, I was quite angry.

JS: Right. Did you meet her after that?

D: Yeah, I did.

JS: These early stunts, on film locations, I guess John has put some people through some pretty amazing stunts, but like they say, he's never held a gun to anybody's head. I mean everybody has always agreed to do what he... suggested, in the spirit of the script. Would you say this is pretty much true?

D: Oh definitely! I mean he wanted Mink to set her hair on fire, and of course he was quite disappointed when she wouldn't. And if you know Mink, we were quite disappointed she wouldn't either 'cause we thought maybe she'd go up [laughs]. But she was too smart for us and wanted to stick around, so she refused. But, no, he doesn't make anyone, he can be quite persuasive though, I think a bit more persuasive than he would, might **say** he could be. He knows the right words to use, he knows what to say and how to get to your heartstrings.

JS: And he had the right bunch of people around him, who would do daring stuff like that.

D: **Yeah**, and we were all, like I said, little dare devils, sixteen and seventeen years old – what do you care about anything when you're that young?

JS: Right – speaking of those early movies you made with him.

D: Yeah. I mean you think, well sure, why not? Who cares? I mean nothing's ever gonna happen to these movies anyway. We live in Baltimore, Maryland, we're not going to become **movie stars**.

JS: Right, why not go all out.

D: Yeah, you know. It was just all done in fun and for friends and for our own laughs, you know. I mean if anybody ever told me I'd be giving interviews and making movies with Kris Kristofferson and making records and touring around the world I would have told them they were crazy! But that's what I mean: **anything** is possible. Go for it!

JS: If you were putting on the ultimate dream show with millions at your disposal, what would the stage props be?

D: The stage would be empty – I'd be in Rio with the cash in my pocket!

JS: You're a nightclub sensation, known to millions. If you had to do it over again, would you do anything different? We've already touched on this a bit.

D: Oh that's so hard to say because it happened the way it happened and... I wished it'd happened in different ways; I wish my records had become successful in America, I wish I could have toured the way Elton did and some of those people do, instead of playing discos and small clubs. I've had a taste of playing stadiums and things.

JS: You played Madison Square Garden.

D: Yeah. And I've also done them [headlined] on my own in Mexico and in Europe. And of course when you get a taste of playing that size and to that many people you don't want to ever give that up... and I had my own band and things. Then you come home and it's very depressing because here they don't even know the records.

JS: So you play mostly small clubs and discos here?

D: I play a lot of small gay clubs here in the States and also mixed clubs and straight clubs, depending on where you are and whether they'll mix with each other or not, whereas in Europe I find that most of them have a, a... combination plate – **everything's** in there, you know, and nobody cares.

JS: But in America it's more all gay or all straight?

D: It's more groups, you know, it's gotta be gay, straight and sometimes a very mixed crowd; mostly in bigger cities.

JS: Certainly, I imagine, your lifestyle has changed since your wild teenage years of drug taking, shoplifting and dragging at the Chicken Hut in DC.

D: Oh yeah, well now I can go out and **pay** for things, so it's [laughs] no fun any more.

JS: To get caught shoplifting an angora sweater with $200 in your pocket...

D: Well, we all do foolish things when we're young. And as far as drug taking, I mean it was **pot** you know, so it was no big deal. I'm glad I never got addicted to the coke and crack and all the things that are popular now... angel dust and...

JS: Of course there was the tragedy with David Lochary and angel dust.

D: Yes there was, and we all tried to help him through that period but it seems that... angel dust won out in the end. That was one of the main deterrents for me and angel dust, to see what was happening to one of my dearest friends. And like I said, it finally did him in. But you never forget those things. Now when someone says do you want some coke – and **yeah** I've had some coke, I'm not going to sit here and tell you that I've never done it because it would be a **huge** lie.

JS: Well, I think every athlete has done it, too and they all deny they—

D: [Shouts] Yeah, they **all** do it, the athletes!

JS: It's the most lied about drug on...

Pink Flamingos

D: I don't do it on a regular basis and I haven't done it in quite a while. It's not my drug. I mean, you do think about David and things like that when people offer it to you.

JS: They're having this big crackdown in the government about giving people drug tests and the only two people that've agreed to testing are Ronald Reagan and George Bush.

D: [Laughs]

JS: I mean we know **they** don't take drugs.

D: They should give them alcohol tests! I mean this is just as dangerous. You know, the booze, the booze, what about the booze? It's socially acceptable – especially in Washington. But some of those people are the kinkiest...

JS: Are you often recognized on the streets today?

D: Yeah, so I stay in a lot [laughs]. No, I figure if you go out and if you are in show business and, let's face it, show business is, part of it is, to **exploit** yourself. People always complain that someone exploited them, well, get with it, you know, get real. That's what it's all about, isn't it? And you do belong to the public – not to sound crazy – but you are a, you know, just something else that they can have.

JS: But even out of drag they recognize you?

D: Yeah. So unless I'm really up and want to go out and sign autographs, because people will ask, unless I want to talk to strangers, because people will come over and say hi and talk to you...

JS: Do you find that aggravating?

Desperate Visions 1: Camp America

D: No, that's what I'm saying, if I don't want to do it I stay in the house, 'cause you can order anything you need, and, if I want to go out, late at night, sometimes I go out with friends for a walk around wherever I am and have a look in the shop windows or something because my shows are very late – about three o'clock in the morning – when I get home there's no way to sleep. Thank god I'm not on coke because I'd be up for three or four days instead of three or four hours. I do my walking and things then, you know, if I'm really up for it I'll go out during the day because people will approach you. But I love that! Because, as I say, when they stop approaching you that's when you start to worry.

JS: These club dates you play in the States, do you ever do any female impersonation, or have you **ever** done that... you've never really done that...

D: No, I just do Divine, my own character, and songs that I've done, that's it.

JS: Do you have any outside hobbies, stamp collecting or...

D: No... I **do** collect pottery from all over the world, and toys, and I like gardening, I like cooking...

JS: Your home base is in New York City and you pretty much commute...

D: Well, New York, yeah and I'm getting a place in Los Angeles, so I'll be back and forth. And I have two dogs, Beatrice and Klaus, English bulldogs. I quite like to be with them, they're good friends.

JS: So this pretty much conjures up a private life that's... **considerably** different than the Divine persona.

D: Oh yeah, I mean I don't go to clubs and things. I'm in those every night when I'm working and listening to that music and things – the last thing I really want to do is to throw myself into that atmosphere when I don't have to, you know. So I'm very much a private person and keep to myself. I have groups of friends here and in L.A. and in London that I hang out with, that I visit with, and we usually just have dinner at each other's houses or flats or whatever, and visit.

JS: I was talking to John a while ago and he fears the Golden Age of Trash might be finished. Do you agree with that or...

D: [Thoughtfully, slowly] The Golden Age of Trash...

JS: I think he meant in the context of, for instance, his early movies or the early movies in the 1960s that he admired and that Hollywood is doing that now and they're doing it with an immense budget like this Stephen King movie you talked about...

D: Yeah, well I guess in that respect—

JS: And that they're really butchering the gore movie.

D: Yes, for sure. I would say in that respect it is over.

JS: Maybe in another twenty years, after Hollywood gives up the genre again, maybe another John Waters will come along.

D: Oh, I'm sure.

JS: With another group [of lunatic friends].

D: Well, hopefully, if the world's **lucky** enough to have two. Only time will tell.

Chapter Four

AN INTERVIEW WITH MINK STOLE
April 15, 1986, 8:00PM

JACK STEVENSON: I'm gonna ask you some questions, if you don't like any of 'em just give me your rudest possible answer.

MINK STOLE: [Laughs] I'm not in a very rude mood – but go ahead.

JS: I think there is a natural tendency to think of an actress in the context of her roles. Do you think your fans would be disappointed that you don't live your "real life" like one of your film characters, like, say "Taffy" out of FEMALE TROUBLE?

MS: Well, I don't know about Taffy particularly because **nobody** lives like Taffy, but... I think a lot of people would be disappointed if they realized that I don't live like Connie [Marble]...

JS: Right, and maybe – do you think that's your most lasting film role as far as people recognizing you?

MS: I think of all the people that have seen these movies, more people have seen PINK FLAMINGOS than any of the others, so... in that respect... yes. It's funny 'cause I met a person the other day, a guy who works in the store downstairs from me, and he was introduced to me and I said, "Yes and I'm Mink Stole" and he went, "Oh God" and flipped out, and he goes, "I know that your taste runs to the outlandish so I'm gonna keep my eye out for outlandish things for you!" [Laughs] And I didn't have the heart to tell him that my taste actually runs to the rather normal. So there is, yes, most definitely a very distinct... people do tend to think of me as someone who if not like any one particular of my characters... then someone quite extravagant and flamboyant, which I am not.

JS: You said at your old job there was a transvestite you worked with who when she found out that you were Mink Stole, deemed that it was safe for her to tell you she was a transvestite.

MS: Well, she's a **transsexual**, and it's not just because I was Mink Stole – we had also worked in the same theatrical company, only years separated... but, uh, the theatrical company that I worked with dealt a lot with transvestism, you know, the main character, a man, very often played women, so she knew that I was at least, ah... not—

JS: Right, not a Reaganite.

MS: Not upset by the idea. Yeah, I think people who identify me as... you know, would be surprised to learn that my panty hose get runs in them... you know, things like that, that I wear flats and not spike heel shoes all the time.

JS: Are you pretty much recognized quite a bit, or...

MS: No, not so much because in all the characters that I played I changed my appearance so drastically, from, not only from the average normal person on the street but even from my **own** normal... so in PINK FLAMINGOS I had flaming red hair and in FEMALE TROUBLE I had distorted make-up and wore children's clothes, in DESPERATE LIVING I had black hair, in POLYESTER I wore corn-rows, so my appearance was drastically altered for each one of my roles. I never, except for the beginning of DESPERATE LIVING when I was still the housewife before going to Mortville, I never really looked like myself.

JS: As far as being recognized on the street...

MS: My recognizability, I **am** recognized occasionally.

JS: And certainly the **name** is recognizable.

MS: The name is recognizable. Anyone who has seen the movies will recognize the name.

JS: And that probably draws, like, "Oh my god!"

MS: [Sweetly] Yes, it does. [Emphatically] "No shit?!! That was you?!!" I get that a lot – I even got that today.

JS: You still get crank phone calls, and if I might be so bold as to ask, what's the average crank call like?

MS: [Laughs]

JS: You're probably less than thrilled with them.

MS: Well, nobody's **obscene**, I mean generally people – actually a few weeks ago somebody called up, I answered the phone and they said, "Is this Mink Stole?" I said yes. He said [startled tone] "Oh... um... it really is?" I said yes. He said, "Oh, okay – thanks," and he hung up. And the next day I got another call from a person he sounded like a **young** man, like maybe a teenaged man, and the guy said, "Is this Mink?" I said yeah, and he goes, "oh," and hung up. I got a feeling that the second call was confirming the first call.

JS: That's one of the stranger...

MS: That's basically... I mean, people will call me up and they want me to entertain them over the telephone and I, I don't really know what to say, you know... they want to know what I'm doing and what I'm doing is clipping my toenails [laughs] or something really prosaic... it's not...

JS: Right, and these aren't like the really crude type of...

MS: No I don't get the really creep type of calls, I don't get people calling me up and making obscene... statements.

JS: Right, they just want to see if you're for real, maybe...

MS: I guess. I don't know **what** they want. I mean, they don't **want** anything, you know, they don't seem to really want anything, but, to know that's who I am, so...

JS: You appeared at a John Waters show here in Boston in November, 1983. Have you done anything Waters-related since then?

MS: No. Actually I haven't. No... as a matter of fact actually I've done nothing at all... theatrical.

JS: Since POLYESTER, eh?

MS: Well no, I worked – I did some theatre after POLYESTER. But I haven't done any theatre ever since... ah... probably 1983. I am now a private citizen.

JS: Right, a "private citizen" but still recognized.

MS: Seldom enough to enjoy it when it happens.

JS: Right, but maybe not walking out onto the street and being besieged by people...

MS: [Laughs] Oh heavens no! No, I think you have be somebody **a lot** more famous than I ever was to be **besieged** on the street. You know **Meryl Streep** is besieged on the street.

JS: Which role in a Waters film was your favourite?

MS: Oh, Taffy without any question.

JS: Taffy... that's funny because that's my favourite role, too.

MS: Yes, Taffy was wonderful because she was bad, you know, she was just so **rotten**.

JS: She was so **extreme**.

MS: So **extremely rotten**... that she was just... she was **fun**, I really enjoyed playing Taffy. You know, all my malevolence, my own **personal** malevolence...

JS: It was an amazing experience, just to sit there and watch you scream at Divine for about ten seconds, and you started to get a physical reaction in the crowd, I mean I thought it was one of the most... mind-blowing...

MS: I enjoyed it. I mean it really was extremely therapeutic.

JS: Were you inclined toward a career in drama – or should I say psycho-drama – before you met John, or was this...

MS: Actually no. When I met John I had no theatrical aspirations whatsoever, and he had only made at that time one film, which he'd filmed in 8mm, so when I met him he was a budding filmmaker... and we were friends, we became friends, and then when he started making films he used his friends, so he used me along with a lot of other people... and so I enjoyed it very much.

JS: And went on to theatrical work.

MS: Stage work, yeah... and I worked with Charles Ludlum and the Ridiculous Theatre Company here in New York for a couple of years.

JS: Anything in the future that you'd like to...

MS: I, ah... don't know... to tell you the truth. Like I said, I'm a private citizen now – I don't know if I want to **stay** one, but probably for the next period – and by a

On the set of *Desperate Living*   In a stage production

"period" I don't know how long that is. That could be the next two months, or the next six months or the next year or so. But for the next period – until I decide otherwise.

JS: Is there any sort of branch you'd like to get into, maybe commercials or anything...

MS: Well, I would like to do voice-over work very much... yeah, I like voice-over 'cause I do **love** commercials... and, ah, I don't want to appear in them.

JS: So it's just your voice that's in 'em?

MS: Yes, I would just like my voice in them.

JS: Right... maybe screaming as loud as you screamed in—

MS: [Laughs] There aren't too many—

JS: Maybe selling soap powder...

MS: There aren't too many commercials where people scream. One has to be gentler, in commercials.

JS: As far as John's projects, I guess he did have a script for FLAMINGOS FOREVER which he was trying for a long time to get money for, and you did read that script...

MS: [Dreamily] Oh and **loved** it... yeah, I really did.

JS: About your part in it.

MS: Well, it was a reprise of Connie Marble and it was a wonderful, wonderful script. It's heartbreaking that it will never be produced.

JS: He talked about getting it out in book form, but I haven't seen anything.

MS: I don't know. I know he has finished a book but that wasn't it.

JS: Yes, he has a book coming out this fall which is more of a compendium. [Ed. note: His book is called *Crackpot*.]

MS: He may put it out in book form. I don't know. It would be interesting if he did. I mean it's certainly... the story that he wrote was very clever, and I thought it had a lot of very funny stuff in it that would have been wonderful on film.

JS: Right, to see it come out in some form would be nice.

MS: Yes, it would.

JS: Have you had any communication with your veteran co-stars lately, like Cookie or Susan or anybody?

MS: I spoke to Cookie recently. Oh, we just chatted about our personal lives. She's still writing and may or may not be planning to get married, I'm not sure. [Ed. note: She did.]

JS: Since he [Waters] – when he was making all those films in the late '70s – he used a lot of people, had a large circle of friends, so there's probably been some of those people who've more or less disappeared I'd imagine – gone on to other things, or...

MS: Well, Divine is the success story of our group.

JS: Right, with the movie TROUBLE IN MIND.

MS: And Susan Lowe, who plays "Mole" in DESPERATE LIVING is an artist in Baltimore... and she has her artwork, which is wonderful [stuff].

JS: Yes, I imagine she'll be at his birthday party [Waters' 40th, April 26 1986].

MS: I would imagine so. I would imagine that Susan would be there and Pat would be there.

JS: So what are your, like, pastimes? Do you still do a lot of motorcycle riding?

MS: No, I do not. Motorcycle riding was a phase I went through.

JS: An enjoyable phase...

MS: Partly [laughs].

JS: Except when your ass gets numb.

MS: Well, I spent six months in Europe on a motorcycle. And during that period I was rained on quite a bit. One sort of loses one's sense of enjoyment when one is freezing cold. You know, it becomes **less** attractive. So basically I stopped. I haven't been on a motorcycle since I came back from Europe.

JS: But more or less you enjoyed that trip, huh?

MS: I did...

JS: Even though you got your stuff ripped off in, what town was that?

MS: Barcelona, and also in Seville, Spain.

JS: And wasn't there one time when somebody on a moped snatched your purse...

MS: That was in Seville.

JS: And you chased him down the street and he was so shocked that he dropped everything.

MS: Well, actually the time he dropped everything was not on a moped, that was in Barcelona. We chased him, and...

JS: Did you yell at him when...

MS: Oh **absolutely!** "Stop thief, come back!"

JS: Maybe if he'd seen you in one of your movie roles he wouldn't have done that.

MS: [Laughs] Well, as a matter of fact, PINK FLAMINGOS was playing in Barcelona that very weekend... when I was there, and it was also the week when I learned that Edie had died [sombrely]. And so I went to see PINK FLAMINGOS in Barcelona with Spanish sub-titles. Sort of, as a way, personally, to say goodbye to Edie. And, you know, visit with her one more time. It was very sad. [Pause] And it was all very strange to see PINK FLAMINGOS in sub-titles. But PINK FLAMINGOS is extremely wordy, and they couldn't fill the screen with as many sub-titles, to keep up.

JS: Yes, It was like machine-gun delivery.

MS: So, at one point, one scene with Divine screaming about the mobile home being burned, going: "Oh my mobile home! My fabulous trailer!" and Bonnie's going, "My theatrical wardrobe!", and just ranting on and on and on, and all that's on the bottom of the screen is **"Casta."** [laughs]. Twenty minutes' worth of dialogue and it says **"Casta.".**

JS: It must have had the effect to blow-away the uninitiated...

MS: Most of the audience was English-speaking.

JS: The spirit, I'm sure, had to shine – or should I say blow torch – through despite any

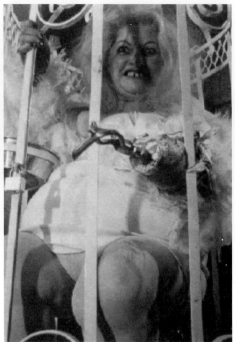

Edie in *Female Trouble*

language barrier.

MS: Well, **visually** it's...

JS: I'm sure everybody who knew Edie was much taken aback at the news of her death.

MS: It was very sad.

JS: Did you know her when she used to work at the hotel, where she bar-tended?

MS: Oh yes. That was when we all met her... she was tending bar, and ah...

JS: What was the name of that hotel?

MS: Pete's Hotel.

JS: Is that still around in Fells Point?

MS: Well no, it's not. The last time I was there – I don't know what it is now – but the last time I was there it was sort of a Greek bar/restaurant. In fact, maybe it was pizza. I forget. But it was run by Greeks.

JS: And it doesn't say Pete's any more.

MS: No, it's something else entirely.

JS: I understand she moved her thrift shop out to California recently.

MS: That I couldn't tell you. I don't know if she took the thrift shop with her. She had a thrift shop across the street [in Fells Point] from where Pete's Hotel had been... and she was there for many years and, but when Edie went to California I doubt she took any of it with her.

JS: You've lived in New York City for quite a while now. Do you plan to stay there or do you have any intentions of – would you like to live anywhere else?

MS: Yes, I'd like to live almost anywhere else.

JS: But, ah – you don't have any real yearning to move back to Baltimore?

MS: I do not. I love Baltimore, and I love the people I know who live there, but—

JS: And you go back frequently.

MS: And I go back whenever I can to visit... but no, I don't want to live there.

JS: Okay, I guess the last question – with your increasing involvement in feminism lately, and the work in Kate Millet's camp, do you see any incongruity with that and your past involvement with John's films?

MS: No. I don't. Oh, it's funny because I took the film FEMALE TROUBLE up there [Kate Millet's farm] and showed it, and... several of the women thought it was very funny, and a couple of them just sat there tight-lipped while they were watching it. But honestly I really don't. His parodies are of **everybody**, you know. His men aren't such great shakes either [laughs]. I mean, he doesn't **single out** anybody.

JS: The reaction is interesting that you got there because I think each person's sense of humour is different no matter what group you're with. Like, take five people who are politically – believe in exactly the same things, but that doesn't mean their sense of humour is going to be the same.

MS: No. I mean there are certain things that I think are absolutely not – that I consider **not funny**. But I don't think, with John, as far as... It's **real** hard for me to be objective. I mean I was there, I was involved in it, and... I'd be... [laughs]. So, no, I don't. I really don't see where there's any [clash].

JS: Was that your most enjoyable film to make?

MS: FEMALE TROUBLE?

JS: Yeah.

MS: Absolutely. Absolutely. We had a ball. We just laughed all the time.

JS: That's probably something that's not really possible with one of the bigger budgets, like a POLYESTER or something because there's so much – I imagine there'd be more pressure.

MS: Well, I don't know. I had a good time with POLYESTER as well. But I didn't work as much. In FEMALE TROUBLE I had a lot of screen time which means I had a lot of time involved in the script. And we were also at this point, John did not write the whole movie beforehand... he wrote it in sections and then we would film it as he wrote it. So that every time we would rehearse it before filming we were rehearsing material we'd never seen before, so it was very **fresh**.

JS: So you [the cast] probably had some input in it?

MS: I wouldn't say that. I mean I wouldn't say we had input insofar as we could say, "John, I think this or that should happen." No way.

JS: People might sometimes get the idea that the films are just wild... parties.

MS: Ad-lib parties.

JS: Right, ad-lib parties.

MS: Absolutely not!

Chapter Five

AN INTERVIEW WITH MARY VIVIAN PEARCE
March 13th, 1988

Mary Vivian Pearce, known to friends as Bonnie, is a long-time "travelling companion" of John Waters and a star actress in his early films. As maladjusted teenagers, they scandalized local C.Y.O. dances, hooked school, crashed parties and just generally indulged in juvenile delinquent behaviour that would go on to provide inspiration and subject matter for some of the most hilarious scenes in John's films.

While only appearing in brief cameo roles in John's last two big-budget mainstream films, POLYESTER (1980) and HAIRSPRAY (1988), Bonnie was one of John's first stars and an important weird character in his earliest (and greatest in my opinion) films where she always appeared as a platinum blonde.

HAG IN A BLACK LEATHER JACKET (1964), a 15-minute, 8mm, black-and-white film, was Bonnie's stunning world debut – even if no one's ever seen it and John keeps it locked in his closet today. John uses terms like "terrible" and "mercifully short" to describe it, yet credits Bonnie with salvaging it from complete shitheapism as in one scene she launches into a wild rendition of an obscene dance known as the "Bodie Green" garbed in a cocktail dress young John purloined from his mother's closet.

Bonnie went on to co-star in John's next film, ROMAN CANDLES (1966), a twisted take-off of Andy Warhol's CHELSEA GIRLS, complete with three-screen projection and tape sound of obnoxious radio ads, rock and roll, and press conferences with Lee Harvey Oswald's mother.

Bonnie played a kidnapped fashion model who is forced to "model herself to death" in front of a pack of screaming maniacs in John's next film, EAT YOUR MAKE-UP (1968). This endeavour, his first in 16mm, was shot mostly on his parents' front lawn and in John's newly rented slum apartment in the Baltimore ghetto.

These first three films are today unobtainable in any form and comprise the "holy trinity" that hardcore Waters fanatics would kill to see.

John made his first feature film in 1969: MONDO TRASHO. Bonnie, dolled up in hot pants and stockings as a jailbait Hollywood slut, co-stars with Divine and is the subject of much aimless camera time and ends up being carried around "unconscious" for much of the film. [She claims she boycotted the Oscars that year – and all years.] Waters proudly calls this a "gutter film" and promoted it as a "combination of cheap theatrics, obsessional fantasies, and a true love of all that is trashy in film today." The soundtrack is a run-on mash of every conceivable type of music, spliced in with radio snatches. The plot is either the most complicated since War And Peace or there is no plot at all, I can't figure out which.

Bonnie's career didn't go down the tubes like Clara Bow's when John started shooting "talkies" in 1970 with THE DIANE LINKLETTER STORY. Shot as a 10-minute sound check the day after Diane "tripped" out her window in the throes of a bad LSD trip, this quickie stars an overweight, five o'clock shadowed Divine dressed in ridiculous hippie glad-rags as the little lady. Bonnie and David Lochary play the concerned parents, mouthing ridiculous "parent talk".

Later that same year, John made his first talkie feature, MULTIPLE MANIACS, heavily influenced by the Manson killings hysteria then sweeping the nation. Bonnie plays David Lochary's "brainless chatterbox" girlfriend who steals him away from a vengeful Divine. This movie is as rampant, gritty and manically paced as MONDO TRASHO, yet, now able to employ dialogue, John's obsessions are more belligerently manifest. And after this, dialogue would never be the same. The film had showings in 16 cities, including London, but its longest run as a midnight film was at the Palace Theatre in North Beach, San Francisco in 1971.

Finally, in 1972 Bonnie and her co-stars exploded on an unsuspecting world with vomitous force in the now legendary PINK FLAMINGOS. Bonnie plays Divine's "travelling companion", Miss Cotton, the voyeuristic sexual deviant accomplice of Divine's hippie white-trash son, Crackers (Danny Mills). With her blonde looks, expressive eyes, and soft voice, Bonnie was able to evoke a twisted weirdness that the movie-going public had never seen the likes of before.

Playing the elegant and arrogant Donna Dasher in John's next movie, FEMALE TROUBLE (1974), Bonnie was again cast as the wife of David Lochary. Bonnie had a god-given talent for portraying frail, effete, psychotic society wrecks... wealthy, genetically exhausted, haemophiliac blue-bloods, and Lochary was an excellent complement to such a role. True chemistry. Donna Dasher, just like Miss Cotton, is a frigid, sex-hating, sex-fearing gal who compensates with an out-of-control and perverted-to-the-core imagination. And she was born to wear a fur coat. Wrapped in furs and silks and shawls and big hats, sneering at a world full of morons and inferiors, she was the essence of arrogant corrupted perversion. Her costumes took on this "society bitch" look from the end of PINK FLAMINGOS through FEMALE TROUBLE (until the money ran out).

Bonnie's last and perhaps most incredible starring role was in John's insane fairy tale, DESPERATE LIVING (1977), a genetic celluloid mutation of the French Revolution, Disneyland, Jean Genet and the Baltimore skid row. Here Bonnie is cast as Princess Coo-coo, the rebellious daughter of evil Queen Carlotta (Edith Massey) who rules over Mortville, a shabby make-believe trash town crawling with winos, criminals, psychotics and lesbians. This is my personal favourite of Bonnie's roles. She is perfect as the unhappy, cloistered, medieval princess, resplendent in doily-laced gowns and looking like something that fell off an over-embalmed wedding cake, buried under tons of eye make-up. There are threads of the Miss Cotton and Donna Dasher characters in Princess Coo-coo taken to the extreme. This was John's best looking movie yet, quality-wise, and the colour photography is lush to the point of gushing.

While never targeted for the attention and fame of other John Waters stars such as Divine, Edith Massey, Jean Hill and Mink Stole, Bonnie was perfect for certain types of roles and often came off as the strangest character of the bunch.

She was a perfect counterpoint to the massive jabbering grotesques who hogged all the notoriety in John's films, yet her characters were equally striking in the perverted and sickening scheme of things. Bonnie projected a more introverted personality, and John was always keenly aware of exactly the type of character she should play and he wrote these custom-tailored roles into his movies. Bonnie's characters remain a basic part of John's early film successes and she commands the fanatical devotion of a hardcore underground sub-cult of Waters junkies who would gladly bring her the severed head of anyone she named.

DESPERATE LIVING was John's swan song in a sense. It was his most excessive movie and the only money loser, and was followed by a conscious attempt to assault the mainstream, to expand his audience. Since Bonnie is not a trained actress and never especially wanted to be one, her starring days appear to be over as John adopts more conventional approaches on all fronts. I personally liked POLYESTER and HAIRSPRAY very much, but the five bastard children he raised from MONDO TRASHO to DESPERATE LIVING are some real sonofabitches.

I have come to know Bonnie at some of John's parties over the years. She's a

---

friendly, soft-spoken person, yet extremely quick on the up-take, with a slightly (?) twisted sense of humour. I talked to her by phone at her apartment in Baltimore near Pimlico racetrack – ironically, only a week after Divine's death.

JACK STEVENSON: Well, I guess it's hard to start with anything else considering this tragedy that happened a week ago – Divine's death. I just wondered where you were when you heard about it and what your gut reaction was.

MARY VIVIAN PEARCE: It was really **awful** the way I heard about it. It was Tuesday morning and I didn't get a newspaper, it didn't arrive as usual, so I went over to the track and got one out of the machine. I put a quarter in I had all my stuff with me – and the door slammed shut! So I had to go back to my car, get another quarter [laughs] and I – just read the race results. And I got really busy at work, and I never looked at the front page. And then this trainer comes up and starts saying – tells me that he had died and saying all these **terrible** things about him! About him being gay, being overweight and stuff, and I turned over the paper and I thought **oh my god** and I just started screamin' at him. I thought that was just **so** rude! [Laugh of disbelief] You just don't **do**... I mean you know somebody that had a friend that **died**, it was – was really horrible.

JS: Yeah, I **guess**...

MVP: So I went stormin' in the track kitchen after work, I was hoping he would be there so I could **yell** at him some more 'cause I was really upset... and I really thought I had things under control, and he wasn't there, but these two *Washington Post* writers were... "What's the matter with **you**!!!" so I told them that Divine had died and... one of them knew who Divine was and stuff, and that we had grown up together – and they were really sympathetic so that was nice to run into... I was sort of glad that I didn't run into the other guy... but I was really upset all day on Tuesday... and Wednesday was pretty rough.

JS: Did you talk to John?

MVP: I talked to John on Wednesday.

JS: I'm sure he must have been taking it bad, of course.

MVP: He took it pretty bad. But he's... in pretty good spirits. First... few days were pretty rough for him. But he's, ah... he had a **beautiful** speech written yesterday, at the funeral.

JS: Yesterday [March 13 1988] was the funeral, so... probably you saw a lot of people you don't normally see.

MVP: Oh yeah. Yeah, there were about 300 people there.

JS: Oh yeah?

MVP: Yeah. A lot of people I didn't know. And a lot of people I hadn't seen for a long time... and he was buried up in the, ah – Towson Cemetery, near where we all grew up, where we used to play hooky and... get into the graveyard and drink beer, and [laughs] Divine used to steal flowers from the graveyard there, because he used to decorate his apartment for parties – always Easter Sunday was the best day [to get flowers].

JS: Rather appropriate... and John had a speech that he wrote?

MVP: Yeah, it was **really** nice.

JS: It was so ironic that it happened just now, and I'm sure that struck everybody...

MVP: Yeah.

JS: So you knew Divine way back when, I guess... you knew John, like...

MVP: Yeah. I've known Divine for about 25 years. And I've known John all my life. Our fathers went to school together.

JS: Right, that's what he says [in *Shock Value*].

MVP: Yeah, but he didn't, uh – you know we just saw each other at family gatherings until I was about 13 or 14, and then we started hanging around together... gettin' in trouble.

JS: Right and then your parents started not speaking to each other.

MVP: Right [laughs]. We were juvenile delinquents. And, ah – we were forbidden to see each other, so naturally we... kept seeing each other. We didn't have "dates", we went out like, as kind of a group? So to sneak out we'd arrange a fake date. We'd get somebody real straight lookin' to come to the door and pose as my date? And the guy would be really embarrassed... and a little bit nervous, which my parents thought that – was **nice**, you know? They thought that nice boys were nervous when they met the date's parents. So it really fooled them, and the next day they'd say, "Oh, that was a really nice boy you went out with!" [Laughs] And so one night I couldn't set up a fake, and I wanted to go to this big dance called "Night Train" after the James Brown song, it was popular at the time, so this guy that I didn't like at all, but he had been **naggin'** me to go out with him for a long time, and so I said, okay... when I got to the end of the driveway I bailed out! [Laughs]... just to get out of the house. [Very brief attempt at seriousness] That was really mean. [Laughs]

JS: Yeah, that was the inspiration for that scene in POLYESTER.

MVP: Yeah.

JS: So did you know David Lochary, or did you meet Divine—

MVP: Oh yeah, I met David Lochary about the same time I met Divine... twenty, twenty-five years ago.

JS: When you were in your early teenage years?

MVP: Uh-huh. Yeah, I was 14... when I went to David Lochary's.

JS: And then those – John started to shoot those early films, right? Like HAG IN A

BLACK LEATHER JACKET?

MVP: HAG... yeah, about three years later.

JS: Right, in his book he describes – says he has that one [HAG...] locked in his closet and he doesn't want to show it, he refuses to show it, but he says it's pretty dull actually except the best part is when you do a dance in it.

MVP: [Laughs] Yeah, I do the "Bodie Green" in it... always getting in trouble for doing the Bodie Green.

JS: Oh yeah?

MVP: Well, the Immaculate Conception, of course that was a C.Y.O. dance, you know you weren't... we'd always do it and Father Morrison would [laughs] we'd get caught, and... at Beaver Springs, when we had dances there in the summer time – it was a swimming club, out in Cockeysville – and Josh Cockey would catch us doing the Bodie Green and he really would get furious. [Shouts in imitation] **"You can go from side to side young lady but no bumps and grinds!!!"**

JS: So there was no chance the dance would go unnoticed by... people of decent morals?

MVP: No.

JS: Do you have any memories of those early films, like ROMAN CANDLES?

MVP: ROMAN CANDLES, yeah, I remember that. That was the triple projection. It happened on Flower Mart day.

JS: Right, that's—

MVP: Well, it was a "one day only" [laughs]. Lou Cedrone reviewed it – he gave it a nice review. Said it went off with, not a whimper but with a bang, or something. It was pretty nice... it was the only nice review he gave any of John's movies – except for HAIRSPRAY. And he really wasn't nice about that.

JS: He gave a mixed review to HAIRSPRAY?

MVP: Well, he said he liked the first forty minutes but that was all.

JS: Huh... yeah that's weird. Yeah, it's been getting unbelievable reviews – it's really been, ah... did he say how – when you saw him [at the funeral] – how it's been doing or give any news on that, on HAIRSPRAY, or...

MVP: No. [Dead silence]

JS: I guess the earliest film that is being rented out now is THE DIANE LINKLETTER STORY – do you remember shooting that one?

MVP: [Fondly] Oh yes. Yeah, that was our first "talkie."

Mary Vivian Pearce

123

'Princess Coo-coo'; *Desperate Living*

JS: All the others were silents?

MVP: Uh-huh. The sound wasn't on the thing, there was a **tape** that went with it. So that was just a rehearsal to practice... **talking** and we'd just read a thing in the newspaper and it was improvised.

JS: So that happened the day after she jumped out the window, right?

MVP: Uh-huh.

JS: So it was **all** improvised?

MVP: Well, we just read the story we... had a basic idea of what we were gonna do, you know... yeah, it was a lot of fun! [Laughs]

JS: There are some great lines in that one. You [as the mother] trying to talk Divine into going to "the club"... [in a shabby Divine imitation]: "I don't **wanna** go to the club!"

MVP: Yeah, I thought David Lochary was really good.

JS: Yeah, he was great in all those... I think... which was your favourite of those films? You mentioned MONDO TRASHO as...

MVP: [Thoughtfully] MONDO TRASHO...

JS: A lot of people who've worked with John say they liked FEMALE TROUBLE. Is the—

MVP: FEMALE TROUBLE, yeah, I like that one a lot too. I like 'em all [laughs].

JS: Me too! I think your greatest roles were as "Cotton", [PINK FLAMINGOS] and "Princess Coo-coo" [DESPERATE LIVING].

MVP: Princess Coo-coo?!!

JS: Yeah – that was unbelievable, that was – you're not like that in real life, are you?

MVP: What?!!

JS: Like Princess Coo-coo?

MVP: [Helpless laughter]... No.

JS: I just had to ask that. Do you remember what that green bile was made out of that you dribbled out of your mouth at the end of that movie?

MVP: Yeah – it's Alka Seltzer and green food dye, and you just mix 'em together and put it on your tongue and it – you foam, because when Alka Seltzer mixes with saliva it just... foams out, like when you drop it in water.

JS: Well that's a great recipe, and I hope maybe some people will take a hint from that...

MVP: [Laughs]

JS: ... because it looked almost phosphorescent, that was really a wonderful last scene.

MVP: Yeah, it does look... [laughs]

JS: Of course Donna Dasher in FEMALE TROUBLE was a great role, and you wore some stunning fashions in that. Now, you said before, the costumes got less fancy as the money ran out during the shooting?

MVP: Yeah, the first costume I wear – that white silk suit? That was made for me. And the others were just my clothes, and ah, the one in the [later] hospital scene is just some scarves thrown together.

JS: You were recognized in New Orleans once on the street for being in PINK FLAMINGOS. Could you describe that encounter briefly?

MVP: Yeah, I was there on vacation.

JS: That was a few years ago?

MVP: Yeah, and I had gone to the racetrack The Fairgrounds – lost all my money, I was walking home [chuckles] and I was just looking at the marquee for the show *One Mo' Time*, and the guy came out and he just started looking at me really weird [laughs]. I thought, "God, what's the matter?!" – he says "Can I help you?" and well, I'll ask how much it is – don't have any **money** to go to it, but... and he told me it was 19 or 20 dollars. And then he says [shouting] **"You were in Pink Flamingos weren't you???!!!"** [laughs] I said, oh, that's why he was looking at me like that. I was kind of relieved. I said yes and he let me go to the show for free, and that night three of us went to Tipitinas to see some live music. He told me that he had seen PINK FLAMINGOS 17 times... when the Toulouse was a movie theatre.

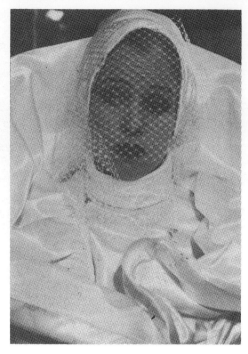

'Donna Dasher'; *Female Trouble*

JS: Are you recognized often on the street, or...

MVP: [Emphatically] No.

JS: That's surprising.

MVP: Well, I don't have platinum blonde hair any more.

JS: Right, that's true. So your natural haircolour was always brunette? But you used to dye your hair a lot, or...

MVP: Oh yeah. Uh-huh. I really wanted to be a platinum blonde [chuckles], but when I was a little kid I didn't know how to do it. So – I didn't know how hair dyes worked or anything, I just knew Clorox had bleach in it? So I went in my mother's laundry room [laughs], and I dumped Clorox all over my hair, and then **boosted** it with Ajax! And so presto! I was **platinum blonde!!!** Well, my parents weren't too **pleased** with the look [laughs], you know, they thought I looked like Kim Novak. And it was, oh – it was really – the ends were all broken up – **smelled** horrible! [Laughs]

JS: Yeah, that's amazing – that was straight Clorox? Or...

MVP: Yeah, **straight** Clorox!

JS: Wow, if you soak clothes in that they come apart, disintegrate!

MVP: I know!

JS: [Laughs]... and then your natural colour would grow back after a while?

MVP: Yeah... and then I'd do a touch-up with Clorox. But that was when I was 13 or 14... then I learned how to use dye properly.

JS: Yeah, you were a blonde in most all of those [films], as "Cotton" and ah...

MVP: Uh-huh.

'Miss Cotton' and 'Crackers' (Danny Mills); *Pink Flamingos*

JS: I guess you knew Danny Mills, "Crackers", back then pretty well.

MVP: Uh-huh.

JS: I guess he's in jail today or something?

MVP: Well, he's in a half-way house, he's out of jail. He's doin' really well.

JS: Yeah, John said in his lecture in Los Angeles about half a year ago, said he was... the prosecutor was trying to get him for LSD distribution or something.

MVP: Uh-huh.

JS: Were any of those people at all like the characters – especially PINK FLAMINGOS I'm talking about – were any of those people at all like the characters they played in that movie?

MVP: [Quiet disbelief]... Are you kidding? [Laughs]

JS: Or should I say were any of them **not** like the... [attempts to repair this line of questioning are unsuccessful as Bonnie drowns them out with incredulous laughter]

MVP: [Laughs die down] Ah... no.

JS: I mean some of them couldn't possibly be—

MVP: No [flat, serious tone].

JS: Because the production values obviously weren't slick or anything, and there wasn't a lot of... you know, make-up and stuff... a lot of the people seemed to he acting naturally... [loss for words]...

MVP: [Laughter of toleration] No, [deadpan response] no-one's like that.

JS: Didn't Danny run a health food restaurant for a while?

MVP: No. His – it's just a restaurant. It wasn't "healthy" [laughs]. The food was pretty good.

JS: Was that a while ago?

MVP: Just before he went to prison. Supposedly they used the restaurant as a front.

JS: So back in 1973 before PINK FLAMINGOS came out, the three of you, John and Danny, moved to New Orleans and moved into, John describes it in *Shock Value* as, "the worst dump" he's ever seen.

MVP: The worst dump?! [Laughs] Well, it, uh... yeah, it was a dump, it was a little shotgun-style house right outside the French quarter... and we didn't have much money. We didn't have any **furniture** [laughs] and we just had a mattress on the floor, and ah... had a little backyard and the hot water heater was **outside**, so the pilot light was constantly going out, and so we never had hot water. And then across the street was this food store that – was always making these announcements about what was on sale, and [laughs] I could hear it from our house.

JS: And you worked in a bar?

MVP: Uh-huh.

JS: Do you remember the name of that bar?

MVP: The Gunga Din.

JS: Wonder if it's still open? Do you, when you go back to New Orleans on a vacation or something, do you still know the neighbourhood you used to live in then?

MVP: Uh-huh.

JS: Everything is still there, the house and everything?

MVP: Yeah.

JS: Do you have fond memories of those months in New Orleans? You were there for about half a year? I guess John went back to New York.

MVP: Oh yeah, we had a wonderful time.

JS: So otherwise outside of that time you lived in the Detroit area, you've lived mostly in Baltimore?

Multiple Maniacs

MVP: Yeah.

JS: You worked on a horse farm? Does your family own that?

MVP: No, a guy I knew from a long time ago was the trainer there. And I got the job from him. It was breaking yearlings and schooling two-year-olds.

JS: When you grew up did you have horses at your house? Did you live on a large estate or something like that?

JS: No. I had a horse but I kept it at a friend's house, about three miles away from where I lived. They had a barn and a... it was near Windy Valley – that's where I got involved with the race horses, they corrupted me. It was the strangest place. It was about a half mile from where I stabled my horse, and that's where I learned how to ride. The trainer there, he owned it... it was a frozen custard store and then up the driveway he had a barn with – his racetrack was really a **ploughed path** [laughs] and ah, he asked me to exercise one of his horses and taught me to ride, put me on a real quiet horse named **Sam Fireball**. And I galloped him every day, and then this other guy that worked at the racetrack showed me how to tie the reins and do all this stuff that you do when you gallop racehorses. It was really fun.

JS: You were really young then?

MVP: —and they had this frozen custard store that he owned, the trainer of the horses, that was just a really strange place. It was a kind of restaurant and they had this man that worked there that made the donuts, his name was "Sarge" and he lived in a shack behind the barn, and he was an alcoholic, and some say he was shell-shocked from the war – something had happened to him and it might have happened on Joe's place because for some reason they adopted him – and then he worked in the store and then he'd go on a drunk. But he made the donuts and the ice cream and he'd usually go down to the store in these blood spattered pants, [chuckles] right out in the open making these donuts in the most awful looking grease... and wipe his nose [chuckles]. And the donuts were delicious! [Seriously meant] He also made ice cream, the health department would close him down once in a while. They had **rats** roaming freely in the back of the store, a **skunk** pickin' through... Sundays they sold pony rides... small ponies Joe had up there. And they had these racehorses.

JS: This was near your house?

MVP: Uh-huh, 'bout three miles. And then everyday at noontime there'd be a big card game... trainers, exercise riders... and, my favourite was Marie Fox? An ex-stripper from The Block [chuckles]. She played cards every day. I learned how to play "Pitch". And then every **night** they had a card game. It was wonderful.

JS: Yeah, it sounds like a lot of people hung out there and stuff, it wasn't just a... So that was where you were first corrupted, and then...

MVP: [Laughs]

JS: You were quite young when you hung out there?

MVP: Uh-huh. About 16, 17.

JS: And then, would you say, well you knew John during this period?

MVP: Uh-huh. I was still hanging around with John then. He would call me at Windy Valley.

JS: Did, ah – did you ever go... go straight after that or has it been a **life** of corruption?

MVP: [Laughs hard] No, I've gone straight! I'm still a racetrack degenerate. An' I played poker last night. Yeah, I realized how well I've learned to play Pitch 'cause – which is kind of unfortunate because now no-one will play with me. And all the characters are gone that played – it's a **regional** game, you know, it's very popular in Baltimore. You probably never heard of it.

JS: Well, I'm not – I don't know much about cards anyway.

MVP: Well, no-one's ever heard of it outside Baltimore, especially **south** Baltimore. It's very popular there. And um... it's really a complicated game, it's... much more complicated than poker. It's a **trump** game? And there's different points and you bid.

JS: So, you go out today—

MVP: Yeah, we go out to – if I go out to play cards everybody will play poker because I play Pitch too well.

JS: And that's Pimlico Racetrack that you live next to now, right?

MVP: Uh-huh.

JS: And you work there, too, right?

MVP: Right.

JS: So you know a lot of people that – racetrack people?

MVP: Uh-huh.

JS: John said in his early – those early films when they had openings, and there was publicity and festivities and... a lot of show business stuff, that you didn't care too much for all the spotlight type of things. Would you say that's true? Would you say you love the life of show business, or you like to live more quietly?

MVP: Yeah, I like – more quietly. I always helped advertise. At EAT YOUR MAKE-UP in Provincetown I gave out candied lipstick... and EAT YOUR MAKE-UP flyers. I always helped out with the publicity, to push the movies, we'd go out in the streets and just hand out flyers and stuff.

JS: Right, that was back when it was more of a basic type of publicity.

MVP: Right.

JS: Certainly it's come a long way, huh? With the Baltimore HAIRSPRAY première – that was incredible. Like John said, they don't even have openings like that in Hollywood any more.

MVP: Right, it was – yeah.

JS: Did you hang out at Pete's Hotel back in Fells Point?

MVP: Uh-huh.

JS: Do you ever go back to that neighbourhood or have reason to go back to that neighbourhood these days?

MVP: Oh yeah. I go back there occasionally on weekends.

JS: Has it changed a lot over the years?

MVP: Uh-huh.

JS: Yeah, I was talking with a black guy outside Edie's thrift shop – which I was surprised to learn was still open – and he was giving me the whole story about the neighbourhood. I guess he's a character that's been hangin' out there for, he claims, 75 years. I don't know, you might recognize him.

MVP: For 75 years!? What's his name? "Hots"?

JS: He's a black guy and he was sweeping up next to Edie's thrift shop.

MVP: Yeah, yeah – does he have a store right next...

JS: Yeah.

MVP: Yeah, that's Hots. He has a stable down the street too.

JS: Oh really?

MVP: He has that store and he runs the stable around the corner... they have the horses for the people who sell fruits and vegetables on the pony carts.

JS: I'm not too familiar with... I've been down there a few times but... but he seemed to be a walking encyclopedia of the neighbourhood.

MVP: Oh yeah.

JS: And I was happy to see that the thrift shop was still open. I had thought it was closed, but it's still open.

MVP: Yeah, Bob Adams has it now.

JS: And Pete's Hotel is **still** a bar. It's run by Greeks now.

MVP: Right, it's a Greek bar. He sold it.

JS: Did they do a lot of renovation or is it still pretty much the same way—

Mondo Trasho

MVP: No, they've changed it around. It's darker, and air conditioned and all closed up, and... that's what I liked about it, because in the summertime you could, uh, it was the only bar that wasn't air conditioned; some of 'em, ah – except on weekends when they're real crowded with body heat – were so air-conditioned that it was actually uncomfortable. So I'd always go over to Pete's to get warm. They had a nice big fan, you could look out onto the street...

JS: Of course that was quite a while ago – that was in the early '70s, right?

MVP: Uh-huh.

JS: These days... what sort of books do you like? The last conversation you said you occasionally borrow books from John's collection. Do you have, ah... gentle tastes in reading, or...

MVP: [Chuckles]

JS: Or do you like sometimes the more crime type...

MVP: Yeah... I like – I love the crime type books.

JS: **Who** is the one you say you don't like at all?

MVP: Your fr— [she's about to say friend!] the one you like so much.

JS: [Laughs] I don't **like** him!

MVP: Those letters! [Referring to copies of John Gacy's love letters I'd sent her that had just appeared in the Chicago *Sun Times*]... and that poor welfare woman! What'd she think!?

JS: Yeah, what a tragic love affair. I mean, she's got ten kids.

MVP: [Laughs] It won't work!!

JS: Yeah, exactly, you feel like telling him – "Look!" You know? I mean, it's true that the Chicago *Sun Times* did **buy** those letters off her, so she had a little spending money for a while. But I'm sure it got **him** plenty pissed. But... no I don't... you know [voice trails off] I don't **like** him. He's...

MVP: My favourite book I've read this year is *Detour*.

JS: Is it fiction?

MVP: No, it's true. Cheryl Crane? Lana Turner's daughter? It's her autobiography and it's really good.

JS: So, I guess... you **did** read some of those xeroxes I sent you?

MVP: [Laughs] Yeah, **thanks** a lot!

JS: You know, a little "light reading"...

MVP: I **told you** I hated him so you send me these letters! I couldn't **wait** to finish *Buried Dreams*! I read *Detour* right after that [laughs]... it was an "up" book by comparison. Even though her life was very tragic. Especially – if you got **raped** by Tarzan. And she became – she has a woman lover and she's been going with her for 18 years? So really it's the exact opposite of her mother, a **stable** gay relationship.

JS: What sort of movies do you like? Are there any that stand out that you've seen recently?

MVP: Yeah – HAIRSPRAY.

JS: Absolutely.

MVP: Before, I saw IRONWEED and PATTY ROCKS [Dead silence].

JS: Okay, I guess the last question is... I just wondered if you ever got to Boise?

MVP: [Laughs] No, I've never been to Boise.

JS: No? Never got to Boise? Never got a crew cut?

MVP: No. Where is Boise?

JS: Boise, **Idaho**.

MVP: I know, where is that? [Laughs]

[Long pause then confused laughter, as Stevenson tries to figure out all possible metaphorical and Freudian meanings to this]

MVP: Is it in the Midwest? Or the West?

JS: Ah – [not sure if she's putting me on] actually I was near there once, hitch hiking a few years ago and I was going to stop in and just go through Boise, completely on the strength of PINK FLAMINGOS' ending. But instead I met somebody else who'd been there so I didn't have to make the pilgrimage.

MVP: [Laughs]

JS: Like John says today, he's shocked by it [PINK FLAMINGOS] himself when he sees it again, how ugly some of the... do you remember where it first opened by any chance?

MVP: PINK FLAMINGOS?... um... Danny and I were still in New Orleans. John left because he was worried about what was happening to it. The distributor had it but it wasn't playing anywhere. It might've opened in... New York?

JS: I think it opened in a gay porno house in Boston.

MVP: Right!

JS: In fact, the guy who ran the porno house [South Station Cinema, torn down in 1987], George Monsour, he's a big film booker in Boston now.

MVP: Right, he was there [at John's 1986 Boston show]. But it didn't – he said it **was** the first place it was shown?

JS: Well, I thought it was the first place in **Boston** it was shown, but that was the first place in the **world** it was shown.

MVP: Oh really?

JS: Yeah, 'cause John, in *Shock Value*, describes it in rather unflattering terms, he says it opened in a gay porno house in Boston – was **all wrong** and the cast got pissed off when they heard about it.

MVP: That's right! And **then** it went to New York.

Chapter Six

AN INTERVIEW WITH MISS JEAN HILL
March 22nd, 1988

After many unsuccessful auditions and at his wits' end for a heavy black actress to star in his next film, DESPERATE LIVING, John Waters was introduced to Jean Hill. He extended his hand – instead she grabbed his crotch – and the rest is history. If the gods smiled when Bergman met Ullman then their lips twisted into a shit-eating grin when Waters met Hill.

John immediately gave her the role of Grizelda, Peggy Gravel's (Mink Stole) psychiatric nurse. Jean kills Mink's husband (George Stover) by sitting on him, and the two fugitives flee to Mortville to escape the flabby arm of the law. Now ensconced in Mortville as subjects of sadistic Queen Carlotta (Edith Massey), Grizelda and Peggy Gravel become lesbian lovers and... well just go see the goddam movie for yourself!!! DESPERATE LIVING was Jean's first screen appearance – a star was born and a million minds were blown.

Jean followed this with a brief but hilarious role in John's next movie, POLYESTER, where she portrays a gospel lady who hijacks a crowded public bus in pursuit of a hot-rod full of juvenile delinquents. She immobilizes the car, blowing out a tire (by biting it), then proceeds to beat the shit out of Stiv Bators.

While not featured in John's most recent film, HAIRSPRAY, Jean has gone on to gain widespread infamy as a greeting card model for Rockshots and Comstock cards, actually sparking a bidding war between the two companies that's exploded in a flurry of lawsuits. At the time I talked to Jean she was featured in the current issue of Jumbo porno magazine. [Her layouts are wholly comprised of chaste if ever so bizarre greeting card stills.] Jean's received a multitude of other offers – not all of them printable – including a role as "Love Judge" in a People's Court-style sex series, and in TWA commercials for wide body airliners.

While most people still identify her as a "John Waters discovery" on a par with Divine and Edith Massey, Jean is an amazing cut-the-bullshit type personality in and of herself, and it's an open question as to who discovered who. It's really a "Tale Of Two Cities" to put it in a theatrical and overblown perspective: John circulated in white (and white trash) Baltimore for the most part and Jean in black Baltimore, otherwise it's inconceivable that they wouldn't have run into each other sooner. Yet, while Jean is linked to John in the public mind, she's fiercely outspoken and if she has a bitch with John she lets him know it full square. Future collaborations are probable but uncertain at this point, although the two remain good friends and mutual advisors and live in the same neighbourhood near Druid Park. Jean's entrance at John's parties always causes a stir.

In fact I first met Jean at John's 1983 Christmas party and it's taken me this long to get the lead out of my ass and get an interview. I was staying in a cheap hotel that night and as Jean and I were given a ride home from the party she told me if I ever came down again to stay with her in the ghetto instead of some old sleazy-ass hotel room.

I finally called Jean at her apartment in Baltimore. She had recently been released from Mercy Hospital after prolonged treatment for blood clots, obesity, high blood pressure, diabetes and asthma. Now confined to the hospital-style bed in her apartment, Jean was nonetheless within easy reach of her phone and what followed as the tape recorder spun and cassettes popped in and out was close to three hours of hilarity, equal parts history, philosophy, story-telling and sex advice, all of it delivered in Jean's animated, bellicose style, punctuated throughout by fits of laughter and demonstrating that her hard-ass spirit was unbowed and that she was still indeed the incomparable Miss Jean E. Hill. Words on paper can hardly do it justice.

Exhortation, Harangue, Manifesto... all these terms apply. She answered all my questions and often went far beyond, leaving me gape-jawed in disbelief. Proper English takes a beating, but what the hell... And never did a hint of self-pity creep through, which is amazing considering she's endured health problems that would have devastated the spirits of an ordinary mortal.

I have tried to leave intact the spirit of her verbal barrage. What more can I say?... Ladies and Gentlemen, Drag Queens and Winos, we now present... Miss Jean E. Hill!

JEAN HILL: Hello?

JACK STEVENSON: Hi Jean, how you doin'?

JH: Pretty good.

JS: Well, I found the magazine [*Jumbo*].

JH: Am I on the front cover?

JS: Yeah.

JH: Am I?!!!!

JS: Yeah, you are.

JH: [Laughs]

JS: Yeah – it goes "Miss Jean Hill, Earth Shaking Sex Symbol".

JH: [Laughs] Aw – that's cute!

JS: And the pictures are unbelievable, they're great.

JH: Somebody else said it's not in poor taste even though it's a porno magazine. That the article is not in poor taste – 'cause I said, "Do you have it?" and he read it to me and I wasn't offended by any of it ...I'm not gonna knock it. I'm not gonna knock it. It got me the exposure, and I got over 75 pieces of mail, and I'm pretty sure if I go back down there there'll be more mail down there.

JS: Some unbelievable pictures, about six pages of pictures.

JH: 'Cause if they keep askin' for these videos – does it mention anything about that video? The "videos" were John Waters films?!! [Laughs] They don't know that, they keep saying "Well, can you mail me one of your videos?"

JS: It says you're in DESPERATE LIVING and it goes... "Famous film producer, John

Waters, who lives near Jean, thought she was good enough to put her in his film POLYESTER and star her in DESPERATE LIVING in which Jean portrayed a psychiatric nurse and appeared nude..." So it says "appeared nude in DESPERATE LIVING" – maybe they want videos of that!

JH: I **am** nude, though. But you gotta wait halfway through the film!!! [Laughs]... 45 minutes for a... for two minutes of my ass rollin' on the bed!!! [Hilarious laughter all around]

JS: And by the time they get that far their minds will be so blown they won't— [ongoing laughter]

JH: I love the article, though! I mean it's not ob – sinful, it seems like it's in good taste in a bad magazine.

JS: You got it. You got the whole thing right there. You're getting a lot of responses on the article, huh?

JH: Yeah, because I got 75 pieces of mail between the – I noticed on each one it was between the 12th and the 15th.

JS: You're gonna get buried in mail. Uh... you say there were some crazy replies?

JH: Oh, but all of 'em were so positive – I thought somebody would write "Why did you do this!" and... I got none of that! All of 'em were cryin' for more!... and some of 'em makin' – three marriage proposals, or be their mistress, and one guy said the thing with the two Cadillacs – I'm gonna definitely call him.

JS: It says in the magazine—

JH: It is a lot of pictures in there, eh? Do they have any Rockshot pictures in there?

JS: It's mostly like the greeting card type pictures, actually they don't have any pictures of your tits or, anything at all.

JH: I gotta see this! I mean I'm wonderin' how this got over in a magazine like this. But it was like everybody sayin', "You gave us just enough, but give us more." You know it's like, "You're teasing us, where can we get your video, where..." I told somebody I'm beginning to enjoy this part of it, because it's like "give us more, give us more!" 'Cause I love that one where the guy wrote on the computer paper, he said, "I don't even want to see the front, I want to see that big ass, that big behind." [Laughs]

JS: Yeah, and you know that was coming straight from the heart.

JH: [Laughs] That's all he wrote on there – "I want to see that ass, that big ass, that big behind." I said, now who is this?! He left his name and address.

JS: Was he one of the – you said you got some letters from some crackers from Arkansas?

JH: Oh! The one from Charlotte, North Carolina was cute, he said... "I'm a white male and I'm from Charlotte, North Carolina and I weigh 140lbs. but I've always had this secret desire to have me a big black mama." ...I'm gonna pull some of 'em out and read 'em to ya [laughs]. Oh some of 'em were just wild! Then I had this staff sergeant who talked about lickin' this pussy – all of 'em talked about eatin' my pussy – I love it! [Wild laughter]

JS: Yeah! Talk about lively mail.

JH: I had more offers to get this cunt ate than the law allows [laughs]. I told John, I said, "Come down here and read this shit!"

JS: Right... they've got one quote in here that says "Jean says that she's had sex with over 4,000 men in her life."

JH: Not thousand, four hundred! [Laughs all around] Four hundred...

JS: Jean, they threw an extra zero on there!

JH: She's got four thousand in there! Oooooohh nnnooooo honey!!!... Yeah, 'cause one guy was sayin' to me, he said, "I know you got hundreds of boyfriends, but could you please clear it with one of 'em so that I could have you for a' evening" [laughs]... he be in Baltimore, he says... [looking through her mail] where is he?... and there's one seemed like Ku Klux Klan, lives in Arkansas. I told 'em I know I have arrived now! [Laughs wildly]

JS: Definitely, this is some sort of peak of... the industry, in a way.

JH: He said, "I have a secret desire to what did he say? He had a secret desire to screw a large black woman, he said, but – how did he put it? Wait a minute. And then he asked me was I "TV Mama"... whoever she is, I don't know.

JS: No, I've never heard of her either but this is hilarious: You said 400 and they just threw a little old zero on the end of it.

JH: Oh My God!... Four thousand... Oh my God!! My friend said I was exaggeratin' with 400 – I said, "No girl, let's go back here and count." She been knowin' me a long time. So I start namin' 'em, I can name the first 65 of 'em. That was the second year I was havin' sex. And then the next year... I started datin' – we used to go down to the Royal Thee-ater, and I used to mess around with those guys – I never went with the stars 'cause I knew they thought that they were lovers, and I've always been fearful of disease. So I would pick like, Tommy Hunt's drummer, or some man that looked like he just needed some self-esteem to stay in the band, or something like that. And those are the ones that I would go to bed with. But I rarely went to bed with a star. 'Cause if he didn't want you blowin' him or doin' somethin' crazy with him – the mothafucka thought he was better than you! And I ain't sleepin' with 'em like that.

JS: Was this a club that used to be open?

JH: No, it used to be a bar – I mean a, ah stage, like the Apollo? Well, this was the Royal Thee-ater and they used to let me backstage, and I used to get my pickin', 'cause I was about sixteen years old. And that was the very first time I ever encountered, ah... gay women. I won't call her name, but she was the woman who used to sing [in a sing-song voice] "There she is, standin' in the rain," and I noticed that she wouldn't let any men in her dressing room, 'cause she said, "Baby, if you want to come in," so I went in – first time I ever encountered dope, too, 'cause she and her friend were sittin' on the floor smokin' dope. Then when I seen these two women kiss I said, "Oh my Gawd!" [laughs] I was sixteen. Thought I knew it all but I didn't know a damn thing but what I read in books... use to read Masters & Johnson's *Sexology* and all of that, but by the time I was eighteen honey, I think I had gone through everything there was to be gone through. I'd go to orgies but I have never participated in 'em because I have this fearful thing of disease or somebody else, it just frightens me.

JS: And that theatre was like...

JH: They used to have people like Dinah Washington, ah... the first person I ever saw on stage down there was Dionne Warwick, "Walk On By", and then the Supremes used to come down there. And I used to tease people all the time and tell 'em Diana Ross was gonna be the star, because she had this thing where it looked like she would put her hands – I will never forget it – up in front of those two girls and stand at least a foot in front of them, and [laughs] I said one of these days she's gonna walk away from 'em, and sure enough she did.

JS: This was pretty much a black theatre. Not many white people down there at this point?

JH: Well, a few of 'em had started comin' down, but you know at the time it was still sort of racist here. But you had a lot of white promoters and white producers, and... they had Fat Daddy Johnson, and then they had another white guy that used to like me. But I never would sleep with him, I'd tease him, always gonna, gonna, gonna, but never got around to it.

JS: Yeah, Baltimore is mostly blacks. What do you think – do a lot of blacks like John's films? Or... do they to "get the joke"?

JH: No, you know when I first started, blacks sort of shunned me, in John's films. Because they said John Waters had never used any black people in his films before. I think he had one, Rod, which was a friend of mine. 'Cause Rod had told me that he was lookin' for somebody. I think Rod was the first one that ever told me that he was lookin' for a black woman to play this role. He said, "Jean, you'd be perfect," so I said, "No, I'm not interested in bein' in the movies," 'cause you know at the time I thought about the consequences. One of the reasons I just stayed away and played "hobby" with it was because, before I went off and had my little emotional breakdown, I always worried about people findin' out my skeletons in the closet. I don't give a fuck no more.

JS: So you didn't know Divine until he, ah—

JH: Nnnoooo! I knew Divine years ago, but Divine and I back then didn't even get along because Divine had lied and said she had had this operation. And we used to go down to Eddie's Bar, and I told the bitches – this was when he was really tryin' to make a mark for himself. And – but I was just an ordinary girl, but... gay guys and white guys – I'm serious used to just love me when I came to this club. And I said to Divine one night, I said [demanding tone] "Old bitch, you know you ain't had no damn operation!" See, I knew the game already. Divine ain't had no sex change, honey. But that's the lie he used to go around tellin' people... and then he didn't like me for tellin' people he – because back then I pretty well knew, Doctor Money... and a few other people who did that here, and then I was real tight with this white girl. One time you had to go to Tijuana, Mexico in order to get the operation, 'cause they weren't even doin' it here in Baltimore in '57, '60 and '61, and this was when Divine was tellin' people that he had gone over there and got this operation and shit like

that. I said, "Bitch, you ain't got nothin' to show!"

JS: So Divine was around back then raising hell?

JH: Yeah, down to Eddie's Bar! And then I didn't see him no more and he went off to New York, and... I still wasn't aware that he was with John Waters. But people used to tell me about John Waters. I did meet Marion Michaels a long time ago, who was really way out and avant-garde. Because at that time, '69, '70, I was goin' for white guys.

JS: And who was this guy you met?

JH: I was goin' with this white guy named "Skip". My mother, whenever the phone used to ring, she'd yell, "Are ya white or are ya black?!" and if they said they were white, she'd hang the phone up... [begrudging laughter]... But then when I got ahold of Skip she used to say, "That man don't want you!" and blah-blah-blah. My mama's a racist woman, 'cause John and all them tease me, said my mother is a black Ku Klux Klan, she'd burn a cross on a white man's lawn.

JS: So John has met her and stuff?

JH: Ooohhhh yes!!! She cussed him out!!!! Talkin' about how he exploited me, and ooooo-weeeee! Oh baby – she can wear white people out! I don't even introduce her! She's nicer now than she's ever been in her life. 'Cause she's learned to accept the fact that these are the people that I like, and this is the way I'm gonna be. But in the beginning, '68, '69, '70 up till '75, oooh my god she was terrible! Ask John about it, [laughs] tell John... "You used my daughter!" – 'Cause I used to tell John, you gotta meet my mother, all she keeps tellin' me is I get used. And then a lot of people have put that in my head. But the, because she – John don't know this, I don't know whether he knew it – I wrote him an 18 page letter. After I found out he had offered one girl $450, another girl – I wound up meetin' these people later on in life... so with me, I think he offered me more money than any of 'em. But two people had also tried to convince me to do this film. I never read it in the papers, I never read it in anything.

JS: And that was DESPERATE LIVING?

JH: Right. So I was stayin' upstairs with a friend of mine, which was Sonny Smith, on the 10th floor, and he asked Sonny, so Sonny said to me, "John is comin' upstairs," and wanted to know about a fat woman doin' a part. So when I came downstairs I immediately liked John, but I didn't know whether John liked me. So he made me so nervous I went to grab for his hand and I grabbed for his dick and shook it [chuckles]. He wrote that in the book *Shock Value*.

JS: Yeah, he said you goosed him the first time.

JH: Yes, honey, I grabbed the meat, and I said, [polite tone] "Hello Mister Waters, how are you?" – 'Cause that's where I always grab guys when I get nervous.

JS: You just grabbed his crotch, eh?!

JH: Ah-huh! [Hilarious laughter all around] I'm famous for shakin' hands with the dick, honey.

JS: Yeah, he said in *Shock Value* that he was totally unnerved by it – a famous first meeting if ever there was one!

JH: 'Cause when Pat [Moran] and them saw me they said, "Oh she don't even need to audition." So I told 'em I was doin' a play down at the Arena Playhouse, and I was really honoured because about eight of 'em came down to see me in this play.

JS: Eight of his people?

JH: Ah-huh, it was him and Judith and John, and Pat, and the next – they took me out also for my birthday to dinner. We went to a bar. I'll never forget it. I said, "Oh, I like him." And then you know you got black people tellin' you, "Oh they used you, they used—" and then I said to myself, "Well I've never been paid anything for actin' anyway," so it didn't make no difference. But see, I always took the stuff for a hobby. Then I can show you some letters where my mother used to write me and tell me, [low, intimate tone] "Jean, you don't need to do things like that 'cause white people will exploit you, and they will do this and that. Just think of what John Waters did. He done made millions of dollars." But see, I understood the business, 'cause I know he hadn't made no whole lot of millions of dollars, but it was just the idea that I was gettin' exposed to thousands and thousand of people at a time, and then... I'm still teachin' school, not makin' no money, 'cause all my money I'm tryin' to take to pay to go to school. That's why I told somebody, "I'm so proud of me I don't know what to think 'cause I never took a school loan out!" One time I borrowed $750, but I never, ever – since I went to college I paid my own way. So, ah, what John paid me was extra money. Then I had my own apartment around the corner... at the time I was stayin' with my mother but I had saved all the stuff up so that I would have a nice apartment, around the corner. So then I said to myself, "Oh my god, this is it." So then I didn't know what to do because I – I didn't know I was gonna have this impact on people. I couldn't go nowhere.

JS: Really?

JH: Nnnooowhere!! 'Cause John had said to me – this is his exact words – I said, "John, when I do somethin' people always remember me." He said, "Oh, child! Don't even worry about it because in a film like this ain't nobody gonna remember you." He said, "You're here today and a has-been tomorrow." He said, "Just think of ..." and he would name different stars. So I took this for granted. God damn! The next semester? They didn't wanna give me any money! "Miss Hill, we need a W-2 form, you're in a movie." I mean it stopped me from getting everywhere. And I tried to explain to people, all I made was $750. "No, Miss Hill, where's the income tax?" So John never sent me income tax forms for it either. And I never argued with 'em about it 'cause I thought at that time that was his responsibility. So in the meantime, my mother pumpin' my head up about that... [slow, ominous tone] "There's no income tax form... there's no John Waters ..." And I was really likin' this guy, I thought he was one of the neatest people because... if he would admit to it, he can tell you he got that word "shock value" from me! And it came from a guy I used to know, he told me, "Jean, you know what? Underneath all that facade that you play, you are one of the nicest, kindest, quietest people, and you're shy." He sat there one day and really told me about me who I knew was me. He said, "But you know what you like to do? You like to shock people." But anyway, to make a long story short, I was thinkin' to myself, I said, "You know what kind of humour it is? It's called "shock value"... and when I seen John had a book with *Shock Value*, I wanted to choke him! Ask him where he got POLYESTER from! I said, "You know what? People are gonna laugh at me but no matter how many millions I make I'll still wear polyester clothes, because the bigger you get they stretch right along with you." I said that'd be a good title for a movie, and sure enough! [Laughs all around]... He used polyester! So a friend of mine who knew me, knew that I talked to John like this – one of my college professors, he said to me, "Keep on givin' John your information – let him make money off of it."

JS: [Laughs]... So you didn't have any problems with DESPERATE LIVING, I mean, it didn't shock you too much?

JH: No, you know, 'cause we had a private screening and I really thought when I saw myself nude I was gonna be embarrassed, and... the whole bit. But I had this secret desire inside, when I first got to 400lbs., 396 then anyway, I wanted to know what I really looked like.

JS: I thought it was a brilliant movie, I think it's his best movie and I...

JH: Well you know what, a lot of people tell me that. John don't realize it but you know what? I knew it was going to be a classic. That's a movie that's gonna go on forever, whether he wants to admit it or not. I have hundreds [of letters] and I'm not exaggeratin', every person has asked me – no, over half the letters – ask, "Where can I get DESPERATE LIVING?" But I – the more I look at the movie, 'cause if you seen the calendar of me, did you?

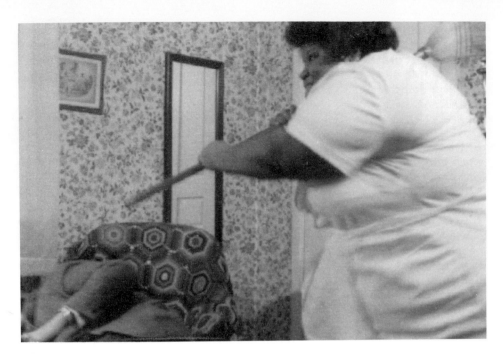

Desperate Living

JS: No.

JH: I'm gonna mail ya one.

JS: Okay... beautiful.

JH: But on – wait till you read the profile, you gonna laugh your ass off. And it says there, "What is your favourite movies?" When they asked me that I said, "Well, I've only gone to see one movie six times, and that's my own." [Laughs] I said, "If you call the favourite the one you seen the most, I guess I would have to say my own movie, DESPERATE LIVING.

JS: You had a brilliant role in POLYESTER, hijacking the bus and biting...

JH: [Laughs] Well he can tell you in the beginning he asked me to be the maid's part. I said, "John, I don't ever want no reference to bein' a maid again." Because you know you can get hooked up in that stereotype stuff, and I didn't want that. I have always had the opportunities to play diverse roles, and... I was worried about bein' a maid in this movie [DESPERATE LIVING], but he **insisted** on that bein' that. Because a lot of people take me – you know in the movie I say I'm her psychiatric nurse, and a lot of people take me for that. You know, as a healthcare provider that came to her house and helped her out or whatever. They don't really look at it as a maid. But a friend of mine who's always advised me and advised me right, he said, "Jean, Claudette Colbert started out as a maid, got," [typecast], he said, "you just don't get caught up doin' maid roles every time. Because the black people, that's where they make their mistakes, they take the same role over and over, and that's how you perpetuate that chain of blacks bein' stereotypical." I have never had to play that type of role – thank god! It was the same way with the cards: they wanted me to do an Aunt Jemima series. I said, "Look Billy, go and get the masters on that," – let him keep it. "Now if ya'all can't create somethin' stupid, wild, crazy, or shocking – I have no interest in doin' nothin' else."

JS: Yeah, that was a—

JH: Because one of the things I've found with me, I have been fortunate enough in my lifetime... and this is what amazed these two people that I work with, they say, "You know we went to the card show and rarely do people call you 'black'." I said, "Because I'm not working to a black audience." When I went up to do Rockshot cards, they wanted mine to be the opposite of Miss Edie's cards to sell to black people. Well, I know black people don't buy that many cards. And then on top of that I said, "Why does this just have to be for black people, why can't I create cards?" – and this was a big argument. So I told 'em if I just have to do black cards, I won't do cards at all. So then they said, "No-no-no-no, we-we-we-we..." I said, "Well ya'all..." that's in my contract, I have to approve it.

JS: And they were wrong too, I mean...

JH: They were very proud, and I am very proud of the work that they did, after we agreed. Because I don't wanna be somebody else! I wanna be me. And I was raised by white nuns, then had the opportunity to come home and live with my mother, and in my work I always want that to show, that I have lived on both sides of the track. And I had an opportunity to see what the rich life is all about and the poor life is all about. And if those things don't reflect it, I don't want to do it!

JS: Have you seen HAIRSPRAY yet?

JH: No, but I will. I like it from what I've seen. I really like it. I helped him with that! 'Cause he called me up and asked me how do blacks look, how do blacks dress, how do... I love John, nobody knows that I really love John. But I've found that people can steal from you in the business. But I'll always give him – not only him, doctors, anybody – that I can clarify there is no difference in the races. It's just that... poor people have the same perpetual ideas. The only thing that I say – and my mother says this, and this is something that I don't usually believe in... she said that if a white man don't make it in the United States, he don't deserve to make it. 'Cause he can change his name, change his looks, but he can still make it. But a black person, people got to get over their colour first, before they will deal with you. You know when I walk in a room I can't say I'm Rockefeller's niece! They would know I'm illegitimate – you understand what I'm sayin'? But you can walk in there and know Mr. Rockefeller's ways and sort of convince them that you're Rockefeller's nephew, and you could get over on that. And this is why I say if white people don't make it, I don't feel sorry for 'em. But black people, you don't know my race of people, I just say that they have been down so long, until, I swear to God in this business I wouldn't take 'em down no further.

JS: So, in DESPERATE LIVING, that was the first movie—

JH: And black people say to me, "John exploited you. You know he ain't never used a black." But honey, I told the little white boy – I'm not rude but it's what I believe in. I believe when you come to me – I didn't go to John – when you come to me you'd think I'm right for the role, this is one thing I brag on – I never had to audition for a job. People send it to me. That's the fortunate thing in this whole business, I never had to write out a resumé or nothin'. So, the little white boy said to me [mock confidential/serious tone], "John Waters is a very famous man, and you are very fortunate to have met John." I said, "No darling, John was very fortunate to have met me." [Laughs all around] He looked at me, he said, "Oh Miss, you're something! Do you know that's a great producer?!" I said, "Well, honey, he came to me so he must have thought I was a great actress." [Laughs]

JS: Yeah, I think he described you as "400lbs. of raw talent".

JH: I looove John. You know what he said to me? When I was tellin' him – I said, "You know, John, with these cards, I bet you I make about $25,000 a year in royalties." He said, "Oh no, Jean! People never make that kind of money." You know how much I made the first year? Eighteen thousand dollars.

JS: For the cards?

JH: Yes! They had to pay me quarterly. They had originally said they were gonna pay me once a year. But then when the cards came out – 'cause everybody laughed in my face – but see, I knew the timing was right because I got to a point, I couldn't go to New York, Washington, nowhere, for people to say, "When you gonna make another movie? When you..." I said, "Well if I don't make another movie I'll make somethin' in another medium," never thinkin' about modelin', modelin' was the furthest thing from my mind. But I woke up one morning at 38 years old, broke, and I said, "Lord have mercy, I gotta make some money." And I called up there and they told me to come up, December the 4th, and I started workin' in February. Now, when the May cards came out – this is a card that will be around forever... I don't know whether you ever saw the one with the bag over my head that says, "Happy Birthday From Your Secret Admirer"?

JS: Ah, no.

JH: I have made over $9,000 from that card. That card stayed number one for... 17 weeks. Now I never knew these things, but I could tell the tension was stirrin' around, and people didn't know – I don't get a swelled head and shit because I'd already predicted it. So this is what they said, when I went up there they had told me I would only make twelve cards. Well, by the time the May issue was out they had started pumpin' me with cards... and calenders, and then key rings. That's when I had this little clause put in my thing that I only make cards. If you want calendars and other things you gotta sign another contract.

JS: So that's good that you've made... and you said one card was your very favourite, called, "I Get Lost In Your Love".

JH: That's one of 'em. I have three of 'em. It's ah, "If You Want My Body I Charge By The Pound," "I Am Woman And Don't Fuck With Me," and "I Get Lost In Your Love". I like those.

JS: So you've made almost more money off the cards than off the movies, or...

JH: Oh yeah – all I ever made for makin' them few movies total, was seven – na, I didn't make $1,000... 'cause John offered me $100 to make POLYESTER, and I told him no, I said, "Honey, you're the one that made me the star." He said, "Well, that's all I have in the budget." So I said, "Get any old fat bitch then." So about two weeks later he called me up, he said, "I had to take some money from somebody else, but I found you $250." So... that's when I wrote him this long, 18-page letter, and he said he swore that he would never speak to me again. 'Cause I told him how I had broke my teeth and had to spend $300, and that I had spent more, and – had never had another new coat 'cause I had gotten too big, 'cause I used my coat and tore it up in DESPERATE LIVING, and used my own shoes – oh child, I went on and on and on and on. 'Cause I was hurt because I had asked John to lend me $500. He said when you want that kind of money you – you ask your parents! I said, "This is what rich mothafuckas say! What? Jean Hill has made it?! Jean Hill now has a little corporation?!"... I don't have a lot, but I'm comfortable.

JS: And you know they can never find another Jean Hill, so they've gotta pay you.

JH: Well, honey, I said to John, "You know somethin'? You lied to me a long time ago." He said, "What?!" I said, "You told me people forget people." He said, "Well, Miss Hill, I didn't know you had somethin' people just don't forget!" And when I was in the hospital – I have won over one hundred more fans.

JS: So when did you go into the hospital?

JH: February 3rd, came out Valentines Day and went right back in on the 20th... and stayed in there until the 14th. No – I came out on the... 12th. I came out two days ... a day before I went to the funeral.

JS: Right, so you were in the hospital in your bed watching TV when you first heard Divine died?

JH: Yep. And I bust out crying, and I had this black woman in there and she couldn't understand why I'm cryin' over this white woman for. 'Cause my head was knotty – I'm tryin' to tell ya, you could never make the association, that I was anybody but a peon in there [laughs]... 'cause I wore sheets... 'cause the doctor would tell how I would dress up in a sheet like a frog [laughs]. I felt fine, though...

JS: So nobody recognized you?

JH: But the doctors, a lot of doctors know who I am. This is another thing that has really amazed me in my career. And this is what I'll tell people... they'll say to me, "Well, I don't know who you are." I say, "Well, evidently you're not a doctor or a lawyer or an educated person, like a college student or something. Because if you were, those are the people that know me. The first day I was in the hospital – here's my hand to god – I had over 150 guests.

JS: So your room was jammed with people?!

JH: Every ten minutes there's... the kitchen help, there's the doctors. I had a doctor bring his fiancée up. He said, "I don't have a card or anything, but can you just sign this medical thing for me? Just so people will know that I know you?" I felt like a real celebrity there. And then I gave one of the nuns, she wanted one of the cards: "Get Well Dammit Before You Make Me Sick". I said, "You really want this card?!" She said, "Oh I just love it!" So I said you certainly may [laughs]. Then up in Intensive Care here was a real joke – four o'clock in the morning I'm layin' down, finally I'd gotten some rest, there's this woman standin' over me, I look up... and it's the nurse. She said, "You don't know who I am! But I know who you are!" [Laughs]

JS: Your personality seems to help you get over hard times.

JH: The doctor told me the minute you start believin' in stuff like that [miracles] and God, you'll forget the medicine. But it's not the truth. I told them in the hospital, and the doctor laughed in my face, but he had to come back to apologize to me. I told David, nobody liked him. I liked him. They said, "Jean, how did you get that man to smile?" He would have to come up to me at twelve o'clock at night, he was tired, he didn't want to talk, but I held this man's attention. "Do you hear what I'm sayin'"? he said, "Let's not go too far off the subject because I got another patient to check on," but we still would go off the subject. And he never got frustrated with me or nothin'. The woman in the other bed said, "I can't stand him!" – the woman down the hall said, "I can't stand him!"

JS: Weren't you actually talking to the nurses about Divine the very afternoon he died?

JH: I had just said that afternoon – as a matter of fact the people that made the calendars was with me 'cause we all was bustin' out laughin' in the thing, they had brought down some gift certificates so the doctors could go and eat dinner, and I said, "I could take Divine's place!" [Laughs]

JS: You said you'd recently seen him on TV and he didn't look too healthy?

JH: No, because when I saw him on *Good Morning America*, his stomach was hangin' and that's what happened to mine... his chest was hangin', and I said to myself, he's got a heart condition, he definitely can't breathe. And see, when you... I'm never gonna let this job get me down, 'cause I ain't in it for the money. I've learned that money don't make you happy. You got to make you happy. And when you overdo anything – and I really felt, and this is my personal opinion, by Divine bein' what he was, which was – I can't say a transvestite... an actor playin', an actress, that's what I call it, he had gone as far with this thing as he could go. And I think this is what his wish was. And this is why he... I have this thing – I have been near death more times than anybody I know, but I have never died. I've never died. The doctor even told me, every operation I have had – now you know, big as I am, 500lbs., goin' through what I went through with a 50/50 chance, but like I told the doctor, I got a nurse, nuns and priests prayin' for me – I'm not gonna worry myself I said, and I haven't made my four million so take me on down [laughs]. And then when I had that gall bladder operation, I had that out-of-body experience, so I had seen more than they did. And I knew in my heart that I wasn't gonna die. But you shoulda seen these people in the operatin' room. I told 'em, ya'all were more scared than I was [laughs]. Because I could remember Dr. Vogler handing the knife to Dr. Vergossa, and they're tellin' me I shouldn't have seen this... My first husband would tell you, I used to tell people back in the '60s, there was a song called [in a singsong voice] "Free looove..." and I said, all of this, we're gonna pay for it one day. I slept with 400 men. But here's how I sleep with a person. Number one: I rarely sleep in the dark with them. 'Cause I like to see expressions, and not only that, I like to look! If my body's too big and ugly to look at, mutherfucka – you don't want this body! Go out the door! 'Cause I'm not sleepin' in no motherfuckin' dark. I don't like to have sex in the dark. If the moon lights up, okay, or turn the light on, or give me a camera, give me something 'cause I need to see [laughs]. Another thing is: if I smell an odour on somebody, they ain't sleepin' with me. Go wash. If they wash and still got it, that person got somethin' wrong with 'em. Another thing about it, if I pull on your dick too much, and I don't think I'm bein' rough and you say "ouch!" – you keep it! And I know you goin' home and sleepin' with somebody. You keep your meat. This is why I don't go with married men. 'Cause honey, I want to believe, even if you got somebody home, that I'm the only one... and that you go home and do nothin' to her [laughs].

JS: Yeah, exactly.

JH: So that's how I told somebody I had the fortune enough to get old without getting venereal disease. And then another thing that I did, I used to screw a lot of guys that were... a lot of alcoholics. Well I wouldn't say "a lot" – at least eight alcoholics. Out of this eight I have brought at least seven out of what I call "alcoholism". One of 'em I called when I wanted to kill myself. You know what that bitch told me?! "I don't fuck with losers – you taught me that." [Laughs] He makes $700 a week now, selling cars for Mazda-Chevrolet. But I don't know – it was this thing that I had about men that I like. I love men, and whenever I saw a good man – but I never fucked with a junky. It had nothin' to do with AIDS at the time. Junkies tend to steal from you, and I like too many nice things in my house. No matter how clean I keep it, I always kept a little oriental stuff, and I don't want that bitch takin' my shit outta the house. So junkies and me never mixed. But an alcoholic, baby! I knew, number one, that he wasn't doin' but so many people, so I take that bitch in my house, bathe him, wash him, and let him fuck! [Laughs]... never went with the stars. Never. Because they're the ones that think they can get anybody, and they catch ya in their thing [long laughter].

JS: Yeah, that's where—

JH: I used to tell people this shit, but they always talkin' about... my sister told me one time, she says, "Keep on..." – and I fucked every last one of my girlfriend's husbands! But most of the time it was when they were separated from her. When Ernst and his wife separated, I went on the bed with him, and I knew he wasn't sleepin' with nobody. When Maxwell left Maxine, I went to – well they didn't "separate" but I knew they weren't sleepin' together 'cause she was sleepin' with my uncle, and he was in another room.

JS: Uh-huh ... so you could hear it.

JH: But if you just take those precautions...

JS: Right, that's some good advice.

JH: Now people might say that I didn't love myself, but I realize now that I was addicted to sex, 'cause if I didn't have sex five times a week, child, I felt like I was nothin' or nobody. But I always was selective. My sister used to say, "Selective with that drunk?" I said, "But I know he ain't been to bed with nobody, honey." [Laughs] And I know when he get up he's goin' right back on the corner and get his bottle [laughs hard]. 'Cause people ain't puttin' up with drunks. But they'll put up with junkies that will rob 'em... knock 'em in the head, drag their friends – ya ever notice that? I can't stand people that take acid and – I can't stand 'em! And the one thing they'll do is they'll take your prized possessions, baby. They don't care, they just gotta take it outta there. But see, an old alcoholic, you can buy him a 59 cent drink and fall on out... [laughs] Cheap thrills, honey.

JS: So you got to know Divine better over the years since DESPERATE LIVING?

JH: Yeah, last two or three years, really, and like I said when I saw him at *Private Eyes*, because even his agent said, "Thank you for coming up to *Private Eyes*." I didn't come there specifically for him 'cause I didn't even know he was gonna be there.

JS: When was this? Recently?

JH: About a year and a half ago.

JS: Was this an act he was doing at a club?

JH: Um-umm.

JS: And you got up on stage, right?

JH: No, I sat up on [stage] – I got the pictures of it. Joe got the pictures, I don't have 'em. But, I sat on the end of the stage 'cause the stage was very weak, baby. I figured if he and I had been up there together we'd have broken it! [Laughs] Because it was one/eighth inch ply-board... but he got to the point I noticed he sweat like a goddam pig on stage. I said he gotta have either a heart condition or the blood pressure's up high – you know once you get blood pressure you're gonna get heart trouble.

JS: Right, and that very day you were mentioning it, and whammo.

JH: But that is what really shocked me, because I said, "Now that I got this, and I'm walkin', I'm ready to take his job." And you know with Edith Massey I said the same thing [laughs], I told John I went to the funeral out of guilt 'cause I thought to myself all I thought about: "It could've been me, it could've been me."

JS: And so at that time [Divine's funeral] you were still quite sick, but you got up and into a wheelchair and got to the funeral.

JH: Yeah, it – I ain't gonna lie, it had not a whole lot to do with respect for Divine, it was just the idea that I wanted to actually see somebody lyin' in their casket where they could have been saved had they just followed simple health rules... I told John one time, I said, "You don't believe this but I'm a very shy person." That's why I said I know John don't really know people. John gets leery of people that love him. And I've heard him say to me, "Jean, I'm scared of 'em!" But I have never been afraid of nobody I've been near... and know that I'm in harm's way with some of 'em – know it. Know that they hate me. But you cannot let that get on your nerves once you decide to go public. You cannot run, you cannot let them bitches tire you out. You just have to ease away. And you've got to stop carin' about what other people say. This is why you need two or three people that love you in your life, that are loyal to you, that will kiss your ass from breakfast, lunch, dinner and supper. And if you can't have those things you move on to the next thing. Because John is actually becomin' paranoid. He don't even realize what's goin' on. But I believe with Divine's death – and you don't need to run from the public, because the public is what's payin' your bills out there for ya. I'm not sayin' you like everybody or you put up with everybody, or you tolerate everybody. But you need to get out there and meet and greet 'em, or if they get on your nerves, tell 'em.

JS: Right, but he still goes out to meet weirdos who come thousands of miles to see him.

JH: You can't hold animosity and fear in your life. I mean there's a certain amount of fear that everybody needs, but never to the point – because sometimes that can cause people, if they react to some of the things you're feelin', they can kill you or harm you, and I don't want that to happen to me. 'Cause see, I've had three people who have told me they were gonna kill me, or rob me, but I just was never rude to 'em. This one guy kept sayin', "You big [unintelligible], you got money!" and he wound up stayin' at my house, and he told me he had killed this guy before – matter of fact he told me he had killed two people. But it didn't frighten me. Because I got to know him real good, and right now if he sees me he says, "Anybody botherin' you? 'Cause you know I don't mind gettin' rid of 'em." When that man raped me – I seen that man walkin' out my back door lookin' for the motherfucker. And I knew who did it, but I said, "If I let you kill that man, it's gonna be on my conscience, not yours." You know in my lifetime I've gotten the opportunity to meet every kind of person that I ever wanted to meet... an oriental, Ku Klux Klan... mass murder killers. I know one guy who's killed six people. He told me, "Jean, when you kill the first one, that's usually the one you remember, but the more you kill, the easier it gets." He says it's the same way with death. Now he told me this when I was fifteen years old. But when my first son died – do you know Michael's been dead since 1962 – and it still, it doesn't traumatize me like it used to, but I'm talkin' to you now about Michael like he died yesterday. But the twins died a year later and you don't hardly hear me say nothin' about it. And I tell people, when people are really close to you: the first one hurts, the second one gets a little less, and I have had two or three people come back and tell me that.

JS: When you went to Divine's funeral, what was that like? You said the priest talked about...

JH: Oh, the minister was wonderful. He talked about the fact that when he first met Divine, and... how Divine and his mother had first joined the church – I think Divine was around seven or eight, and he talked about when Divine wore this red coat and they had to exchange coats. And how so many years he pondered over Divine and how Divine was before his time. And one thing he admired about Divine: he never changed. Because he knew all his life that he was Divine. He knew what he wanted to do and that's what he did... and he talked about the mother being alienated for a long time but these last eight years they got along great. It was like, everything had moved into perspective for him.

JS: This story, when Divine was young and wearing this red coat, now was he like an acolyte in the church or something?

JH: I think he was supposed to speak that day or something. And he [the minister] told him, "You can't wear that red coat before the assembly, it's too loud." So Divine insisted that he wear it – called him "Glennie" – that Glennie insisted that he wear it. So finally the minister said, "Look, if you gotta have a jacket on, your mother and you are about the same size, why don't you put your mother's black coat on and let her wear the red." [Laughs] I know nobody else in the church took it like that, but I said, "That's the first time he went in drag." [Laughs all around]... had his mother's coat on. But they let him speak at the assembly there, with her coat on. And then the minister was talkin' about how for years he pondered over what to do with Divine. But there wasn't nothin' he could do with her – he did exactly what he wanted to do. And John talked about the pranks, and the things that they did. I'm tryin' to think of some of the things that stood out in his mind. And how kind he was, and he said Santa Claus couldn't have been a better person. But he looked life Alfred Hitchcock in his casket.

JS: Did he look peaceful?

JH: Very peaceful, very restful. I mean ya can't look but so good after a whole week dead. And... even the make-up. But that whole silhouette, when he died, it was like – even though it was like Alfred Hitchcock, it was like a star. You understand what I'm sayin'? He could've lost the weight or somethin' and looked like nobody. But you see he resembled Alfred Hitchcock. I wish that I could have got a picture of it. But nobody hardly took pictures in the church. They wouldn't even let the camera people in.

JS: Was it like a movie star's funeral? Or very quiet?

JH: A very quiet funeral, peaceful funeral.

JS: Lot of people, though, right?

JH: It was about three or four hundred people. They filled all the pews up and they was standin' in the back of the church and on the sides, near the back some motorcycle people and the wild lookin' people. But the ordinary people... I think Fran Liebowitz was there. And Whoopi Goldberg sent flowers, Tab Hunter sent flowers. I mean there was flowers galore, you couldn't ask for more flowers. All of the stars sent flowers for her... but it was just great seein'... I don't know nobody knows how I like the transition of life. And I have watched John and his crowd from "just makin' it days" to "arrivin'" days, the following year I met him, to... nothin' as sad as Divine's funeral. But it became sad first when Edith died, but it was like it hit us, 'cause Edith was old, but it hit the basic crowd, like Pat, myself, Judith, Mink, John, and it was like "that could've been us". And the proudest thing like I said, I'm glad it wasn't drugs, I'm glad it wasn't any of the Hollywood bullshit that people think. It was the man seriously ill needing a work-up. A medical work-up.

JS: Yeah, there was no scandal or anything. And when Edith died, did she die in California?

JH: Uh-huh. They just had a service here for her, that people got up and testified, and, they showed a film. But, ah – she was cremated. Ashes thrown over in the Venice waters somewhere.

JS: So you met her first on the set of DESPERATE LIVING?

JH: The first time I met Edith she was down in the hallway, and I was comin' through the doors goin' upstairs to the apartment. And, I seen this little old lady sittin' out there, and she was rubbin' her feet. She said, [extreme Edie imitation] "I haaaate rehearsals." I said it's gotta be somebody that's in one of John's films. So I said, "You goin' to John's apartment?" She said yeah. So I said, "Well I'll be there too." 'Cause that was my first day comin' down to rehearse with them, because he likes to rehearse so he won't have to use a lot of film. But I'm one of them people if you tell me what you want me to do, you won't have to use a lot of film anyway.

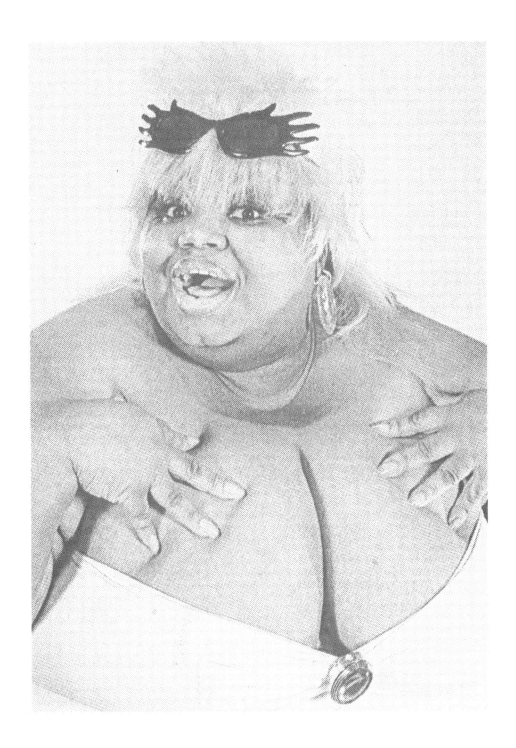

JS: You did some acting before you ever met John, right?

JH: Right, community theatre. And then I use to do children's plays with Wally Sanders.

JS: When you were on the film set of DESPERATE LIVING, do you recall one time when you knocked one of the actors against the wall and knocked him unconscious?

JH: Hm-hmm. 'Cause you know what: I don't act. In my first play, called *Land Of The Golden Apple*, one of my scenes was to push the individual – 'cause I was very mean to my "husband" until the end – well we finally get the children through Apple Valley, and we had searched long enough and hard enough, and then I tell him, "I love you and I'm gonna bake you your own chocolate chip cookies." – well I had to take that part out and tell 'em "vanilla" because it '69, '68, there was still a lot of racism here [laughs]. But, ah, one day we were down at Delaney Valley and they had the stage so slippery, until when I pushed him I had pushed him almost out in the orchestra pit, and the orchestra pit had to be at least six feet down. 'Cause he used to always say, "Jean, don't push me so hard!" I said, "I don't know no other way to do it." Then I was playin' in a play called *Little Ham*, and in order to get the reaction – 'cause see: I love reaction! – in order to get the reaction that I wanted I actually choked this guy with a scarf [laughs]. Every night he used to hate that scene, because it was a woman on one end of the scarf: "No, he's my man!" and I said, "Take your hands off him – he's my man!" – so I'm snatchin' the other side of the scarf. And it's not a reaction, believe me, he's really chokin' [laughs all around]. And then John [Waters] said, "Well, fight, I'm just gonna let the cameras run and you fight." I'm sittin' there, "Now supposin' this bitch can really whip my ass?" Honey, I fought for all I was worth! [Laughs]

JS: And which scene was that in DESPERATE LIVING?

JH: That was the fight scene with the policemen. And I was worried about gettin' out of breath anyway, and then I actually shoved one of 'em through the house and he really went sailin' through there! [Laughs] But I don't "act" when I do those parts. No! If somebody says "slap their face", they get a real slap. When they told me to lay over on Mink, Mink said that she was so scared!!! [Laughs]... she said, "Jean, no one's actin' – all I thought about was your big ass comin' down on me!" [Ongoing laughter] And I'm trying' to raise up on the bed, and the bed would go up in the air!... I don't act! I'm tellin' you, I don't act! Anything you see me do on stage, it's for real. From the grunts to the groans to everything. It's just me. John told me, he said, "Get up there and drive the bus." I got on the bus... can't smile 'cause sometimes I be thinkin' funny thoughts too. And one of the ways that we got the people to react in POLYESTER was, I was on the bus and the brakes went off, and the people said, "Jean, stop the bus!" I said, "I don't know how to drive no bus." [Laughs] They really got John saying, [screams in panicked imitation] "That's what I want, that's what I want!"

JS: And he was shooting all the while! Didn't somebody make you another sort of offer to be in a sex version of *People's Court*, to act as the "Sex Judge"?

JH: Yeah, the "Love Judge", and I'm to determine whether these people should be separated or divorced or stay married.

JS: It would be just like *People's Court* except they would come up before you with their sex problems and then they wanted you to...

JH: Well, basically he said, most of these people are separated because they have sex problems. "My husband doesn't kiss right," or "He doesn't make love right," or... somethin' like that. So I'm to listen to it and determine whether they can resolve it or should they get another bed partner.

JS: And he, like, wanted you to open up full blast on these people.

JH: Uh-huh. He said, "What would you say..." Like if it had to do with kissin' I guess I would say, "Well, let me see how you kiss and maybe I could supervise that." And I asked him what the outfit would be and he said just a regular black robe. I said, "Well, I would have to have a large gavel!" "Oh yes!" he says, "That'd be great!" He said, "They told me that you probably could do that." [Laughs] But he said it would be run like *People's Court*, and the Supreme Court, only it'll be real funny, and these are real people... real people's cases. He said if you need any help we can give it to you but from what I see I you could do it by yourself! [Laughs]

JS: So what are your plans for the future? Probably first just get yourself back in shape?

JH: Well, I hope – I'm prayin' and I'm crossin' my fingers – that by, maybe... six months from now somebody offers me a film role, or I go and make the rest of these all-occasion greetin' cards, or hang that up and then try to get into the movies, or a series or somethin'. But my love is really wantin' to be on the screen. I'd really like to make a couple of commercials. Now the guy from Amsterdam told me that he possibly has a – that wide-body commercial for TWA, he said because they have been negotiating, but he hasn't really cleared anything up with 'em. It's somethin' like, "If Jean Hill can ride wide-body seats, then anybody can."

JS: As far as movies go, I think a lot of people who don't know what John's films are, they think all he does is porno films and you do porno, but it's not that at all. People that don't know John, have never seen his films, have always made that mistake with him.

JH: But he's only made one X-rated film! DESPERATE LIVING. The rest of 'em are Rs. And he asked for that X.

JS: But the films are so wild, and people think that [porno] is the only way things can be wild and shocking, when actually most porno is slow and very standard.

JH: Well, you know a lot of people just don't understand shock humour either. I was tryin' to explain to somebody what it's all about: when a child shits itself and the shit is runnin' out the drawers, nobody says anything – they come in and change the pants. But John would have a grown man doin' the same thing, and hopin' that people find it funny. And nobody says to him, "Come change your drawers," 'cause he would have to change himself. You see what I'm sayin'? A child might eat their own shit, and you would just say, "That's not what you're supposed to do." But for a grown man to do it... And that's what shock humour is to me. It's acceptin' what a child do, or acceptin' something at a certain age, but when you reach another age it's not supposed to be.

JS: Right, and his movies are a lot more shocking and funnier than porno movies.

JH: Right! You know, where would you find a fat woman, nude, in the movies, except in a porno movie? But I wanted to be the first nude person in his film – that was another reason I wanted to be nude. I told him I really didn't care, because I said, as long as it's not pornographic, it didn't make no difference to me.

JS: Right, exactly. And being in this magazine, *Jumbo*, I think people don't really know how to take you. I think you – and all your photos in *Jumbo* are done so tastefully – and strangely – that people just can't understand. I think you blow their minds a little bit.

JH: But they really like it, but it's like, "Tease us with more," or "Where can we find more revealin' photographs?" I said I **got** to see what's in this magazine!

PART TWO

The Day The Bronx Invaded Earth

Chapter One

THE LIFE AND FILMS OF THE BROTHERS
OF INVENTION: GEORGE & MIKE KUCHAR

The sudden death, disappearance or withdrawal of a key actor during the shooting stages of a big Hollywood movie is the kind of patented Industry debacle that drives producers into a panic, capsizes multi-million dollar productions and sends office complexes full of studio flunkies scrambling to manipulate damage control with press and investors alike as everyone involved is eaten alive by heartburn. Tidal waves of alarmist gossip and trade press wash over the bulwarks of such foundering Titanics in a thunderstorm of pulp reportage and morbid speculation... receding to leave behind a pile of bones on the beach that tell the story of "Hollywood's Latest Disaster". Hollywood loves a disaster.

Low-budget Hollywood directors working out away from the glare of publicity are often able – and forced – to come up with cheap solutions to keep their productions going. Bela Lugosi died (1956) during initial shooting stages of Edward D. Wood Jr's trash classic, PLAN NINE FROM OUTER SPACE, and Wood merely grabbed a chiropractor friend to play out the rest of Lugosi's role with his face hidden in the folds of a cape. New York City independent filmmaker, Amos Poe, lost his male lead, John Lurie, well into the filming of his 1981 film, SUBWAY RIDERS. Lurie just disappeared. Poe himself simply stepped into the lead role of the saxophone-playing serial killer even though he looked nothing like Lurie. He couldn't play the saxophone either, so he just held onto it.

Underground filmmaker, George Kuchar, goes one step further when confronted with the normally disastrous loss of a key actor: he writes it into the film without missing a beat and actually finds it inspiring. Instead of substituting a cape-draped face, he substituted his own buttocks – when the Puerto-Rican lead actress refused to do a nude scene in his 1962 film, NIGHT OF THE BOMB, and George filled in as the 19-year-old nude body double.

It wasn't to be the last time an actress refused to shoot a provocative scene for George, but no roadblock erected by feminine modesty could ever impede the overloaded, steamrolling progress of one of his scripts once a downhill momentum had been gained and the brakes had been greased by reams of florid dialogue. No setback was insurmountable.

In fact setbacks could be turned into successes, as George went about the black magic of low-budget filmmaking with the same aplomb of ancient alchemists who set about the business of distilling sea water into diamonds. In his 1987 film, SUMMER OF NO RETURN, George had to make the beautiful lead actress disappear, as he remembers, "because she didn't trust me – she thought I made dirty movies. She thought I was trying to get too much **flesh** from her. So we had her character burned in a fire and put in a hospital, and **that** advanced the plot because now we knew that her beautiful young suitor was to struggle to become a plastic surgeon and fix up her from-now-on bandage-draped face. He had to get money so he delved into the underworld, became a hustler and a drug addict and then had to clean up his act – all to get money so he could train as a plastic surgeon to rebuild her face. So, thanks to her, the plot advanced **considerably**."

Hold Me While I'm Naked

In George's best known film, HOLD ME WHILE I'M NAKED, the lead actress caught pneumonia after spending hours in a drafty shower and left. The scene was filmed and written into the movie to help add drama and direction.

No art form demands as much spontaneous, imaginative improvisation as low-budget filmmaking, and no American low-budget filmmakers are as imaginative as George Kuchar and his twin brother, Mike. Major figures in the American Underground film movement of the '60s, they are the acknowledged pioneers of the camp/pop aesthetic that would influence practically all who came after, from Warhol and Waters to Vadim and Lynch. Their influence is still being felt.

IN THE BEGINNING GOD CREATED THE BRONX
Born in Manhattan in 1942, the brothers were moved up to The Bronx at an early age. There the tenement blocks, the TV-antennae-studded rooftops, the bleak blue winters and the littered streets of New York City's northern-most borough would become their familiar world. A world, that like most adolescents, they wanted to escape. Failing that, they would make it over, colourize it, give it plastic surgery and drape it in cheap tinsel and leopard skins.

The nearby Bronx Park and the Bronx Botanical Gardens offered temporary refuge from the hostile city streets. George would take long, solitary walks in the wilder, more remote areas of the park, off the beaten track, where one could discover idyllic waterfalls and fast-running streams splashing over rocks.

Young George was also keen on violent storms. "Since I was born in a city and lived in a city, New York, all my life, I worshipped nature and storms – anything that disrupted the city in a 'nature way'." Tornados were a particular fascination that would figure literally and metaphorically in his cinema. (In George's 1961 film A TOWN CALLED TEMPEST, there's a remarkable effect of a tornado destroying a town). "I think in the '50s a big tornado had gone through Worcester, Massachusetts, and there was talk about it in New York. It was in the news and for some reason it excited me. The great storm smashing up towns and blowing into people's lives, changing them."

Other less naturalistic forms of destruction were then taking place in the Bronx as whole tracts of land not far from the Kuchar home were being cleared to make way for the construction of the infamous Cross Bronx Expressway. Debris-strewn blocks of abandoned buildings waiting for the wrecker's ball provided illegal recreation for George who would delight in pushing rusty refrigerators out of top floor fire exits to watch them explode in the rubble below.

George's own neighbours were being pushed out of upper-storey windows on the pages of his actively cluttered drawing pads where he developed a comic-book drawing style, and later, a style of painting that might be called "Vulgar Humanism au naturel". Mike also displayed drawing talent at a young age, and likewise eventually took up the painter's brush to create a series of pictures more in the vein of "Mystic-classical". (Mike's apex as a painter would culminate in series of compelling oil portraitures that evoke a satanic eroticism at once evil and pleasurable; muscular, leering jinnees rendered in glowingly bright colours.)

Mom was a housewife, and Dad, as George describes him, "was a virile, sex-crazed truck driver who slept all day semi-nude, and lusted after booze, bosoms and bazookas (having served in the Second World War)."

His Dad's taste in literature and cinema would have a profound influence on George, as he recalls in a 1989 interview. "In New York there were a lot of trashy novels on the bookstands, and my father was into reading trashy novels, or at least novels that were exciting to me – the artwork on the covers. That inspired a lot of imagery in my head. I loved the kind of sordidness of what it was like, evidently, to be grown up. It was a turn-on for me, I'd get excited looking at those paperback covers. And also the comic books. I think they twisted me also. I remember I used to be real disturbed when the heroes were captured, and whipped... and beaten, and my Dad also used to belong to a little film exchange group, he used to bring home the "red reels" – red plastic reels of 8mm pornography. He had some pornographic books stuck away in his drawer too, and when I was a little kid I used to find them, and look, and was amazed and would laugh... these adults. The world of adults."

George's later literary reminiscences of a Bronx childhood would throb with the same lurid, hyperbolic glow that characterized his films. In an excerpt from a 1989 essay entitled *Schooling*, George relates: "Going to elementary school in the Bronx was a series of humiliations which featured Wagnerian women in an endless chorus of: 'Keep your mouth shut', 'Where's your homework?', and 'Spit that gum out!' The male teachers were much shorter than the females and whatever masculine apparatus they possessed was well concealed amid the folds of oversized trousers. After school my twin brother and I would escape to the cinema, fleeing from our classmates; urban urchins who belched up egg-creams and clouds of nicotine. In the safety of the theatre we'd sit through hour upon hour of Indian squaws being eaten alive by fire ants, debauched pagans coughing up blood as the temples of God crashed down on their intestines, and naked monstrosities made from rubber lumbering out of radiation-poisoned waters to claw the flesh off women who had just lost their virginity."

The brothers virtually **lived** in the theatres: seeing everything that came out, seeing the **same** movies over and over ("We saw Douglas Sirk's WRITTEN ON THE WIND something like 11 times when it first came out" says George)... rolling under the seats, climbing through the balconies, making games.

BEDSHEETS, BATHTUBS AND THE BOMB – FIRST FILM PRODUCTIONS

The brother's first introduction to "hands on" filmmaking was courtesy of an aunt who let them loose in a closet full of her 8mm vacation reels which they would watch and edit together in sequences that followed logic.

For their 12th birthday they were given an 8mm DeJur movie camera. They immediately began to stage productions inspired by the epics they saw on the big screen. In a 1964 interview with critic Jonas Mekas, George describes one of these first films. "At the age of 12 I made a transvestite movie on the roof and was brutally beaten by my mother for having disgraced her and also for soiling her nightgown. She didn't realize how hard it is for a 12-year-old director to get real girls in his movies. But that unfortunate incident did not end our big costume epics. One month later Mike and I filmed an Egyptian spectacle on the same roof with all the television antennas resembling a cast of skinny thousands. Our career in films had begun."

In a 1993 interview, Mike reflects on these earliest productions: "I forget what is actually the first one. Some of them we threw away. We did one, THE WET DESTRUCTION OF THE ATLANTIC EMPIRE (1954) [often cited as the first —Ed.], which had a flood at the end. We did matte paintings of the city and we stuck it in a fast running stream and ran the camera in slow motion and it was like a flood. We had some friends dressed up in costumes which were really bed sheets."

These first films were largely improvised. SCREWBALL (1957) was envisioned as one continuous love scene, but that got boring so they had the hero go insane and strangle the leading lady. THE THIEF AND THE STRIPPER (1959), typified a lasting Kucharian penchant for pedal-to-the-floor melodrama: an artist murders his wife after falling in love with a stripper, while the stripper falls in love with a burglar. All die violently as it turns out that the stripper is actually the sister of the murdered wife.

In the meantime "real life" occasionally intruded upon the brothers' activities. In an excerpt from Schooling, George remembers his teenage years and the smoking emergency brake his Catholic upbringing unsuccessfully tried to apply to his sex drive: "Eventually I had to leave the Church as one warm, lonely afternoon I found myself kneeling in a pew praying for wild, disgusting sex. I was a teenager with a heavy inclination to explore my own groin, and the emissions threatened to put out the fire in the sacred heart of our Lord. I looked around me at the elderly ladies scattered here and there throughout the shadowed house of God and knew that they at least were at peace because they didn't possess a big piece that defiantly poked holes in Christian dogma, demanding lubricated shortcuts to the Kingdom of Heaven. I fled from that place of holiness that warm, lonely afternoon and God answered my prayers: a young, suffering Christian was granted wild, disgusting sex. Praise be the Lord!"

Mike and George were both enrolled at the Manhattan School of Art and Design, which specialized in training for commercial art. Mike, who matured faster than George, eventually got his own apartment and adopted a "swinging lifestyle" as George terms it.

If George's teenage years in the Bronx were the essence of adolescent desperation, he did find an emotional outlet in making movies. "I was social making movies. It was my one connection with other people. I used to show my pictures at friends' houses, at parties. I'd go to the house of friends, they'd be the cast and I'd shoot the film. A week later we'd come back with the film developed and show them the rushes and shoot more, then maybe a week after that I'd edit it all together and we'd have a party and show the finished film."

Many of these film parties were held over in Queens, at the house of a highschool classmate who would become their best known "movie star" – Donna Kerness. A dancer and aspiring model, Donna had a way of moving and expressing herself. She had that indefinable resonance on the movie screen. She also had other

---

Donna Kerness   Donna Kerness

more definable attributes: "She had big bazooms," recalls George, "and she had a very nice face. She could **act**. She had a style about her. So I put her in movies. All my Bronx buddies were excited about her – they thought her a great sensation. So I milked her: I went over to her house and we began to put her in bathtub scenes, where she wore a bathing suit, of course – the straps were pulled down. We simulated the tawdry stuff that I used to see on the big screen."

Some of the topical scandals and phobias of the day found expression in the brothers' films. Their 1962 film, NIGHT OF THE BOMB, for example, plays as an 8mm take on the Cuban Missile Crisis that ends in an all-destroying explosion. "When the bomb was supposed to go off, all we did was put chairs on top of the actors as if it were debris – we tried to tangle them up in chairs," relates Mike.

Such violent, apocalyptic endings were common to most of the early 8mm films, like the all-consuming fire at the end of PUSSY ON A HOT TIN ROOF (1961). "All those movies end in fire," recalls George, "horror pictures... the house collapses. We tried to make big spectacular endings."

"The bomb in NIGHT OF THE BOMB," adds Mike, "was a vehicle to use as a spectacular image – people in conflict – otherwise it's hard to make a narrative if something drastic doesn't happen."

The brothers scored these 8mm films with soundtracks laid down on reel-to-reel tapes that ran in loose sync. The music they chose reflected their love of the '50s big screen composers like Bernard Herrmann, Franz Waxman and Alex North, but all sorts of other audio oddities ended up mulched into their soundtracks as well, oddball cuts plucked and pillaged from a vast record album collection they began amassing in their early teens and that they still draw on today to score productions.

The tape soundtracks to some of these earliest films have badly degraded. "It's been many years," says Mike, "they're like mummies now." George recently began transferring some of these 8mm films onto video in San Francisco. The original and sometimes defective soundtrack tapes were in the Bronx in his mom's closet (along with the original prints), so he ended up composing new soundtracks for PUSSY ON A HOT TIN ROOF (1961) and TOOTSIES IN AUTUMN (1963).

These 8mm productions (1954–1963) percolate with the influences of just about everything that hit the screen during this period. Of the Hollywood directors, Douglas Sirk was a major inspiration as were Otto Preminger, Howard Hawkes and

Frank Tashlin to name but a few. Special effects artists like Ray Harryhausen and Willis O'Brien also had a big impact. But just as important, if not more so, were the B- and Z-grade horror and science-fiction films being pumped out by directors like Roger Corman, Albert Zugsmith and Jack Arnold. Studios like Allied Artists, Astor, and especially American International Pictures (AIP) were key to this exploitation boom that would reach a peak of sorts in 1957/58. AIP alone would release 42 pictures over this two year period with titles such as VOODOO WOMAN, THE ASTOUNDING SHE MONSTER, ATTACK OF THE PUPPET-PEOPLE and THE SCREAMING SKULL. Mike and George saw almost every single one as their grey matter grew just about as polluted as the nearby Harlem river.

The brothers' first "public" screenings took place at the 8mm Motion Picture Club which met regularly in the function room of a Manhattan hotel. "It was run by fuddy-duddies," George recalls. "Everybody got dressed up and they showed their vacation footage. There'd be old ladies, and the old ladies would be sitting next to old men, and their stomachs would be acting up and making noises. And the old ladies would get offended at my movies because they were 'irrelevant' I guess. I was looking for... **subject matter**... and I'd pick anything out of the newspaper. That was after the Thalidomide scare came out and ladies were giving birth to deformed babies, and I made a comedy out of that (A WOMAN DISTRESSED, 1962) – that was the last time I was at the 8mm Motion Picture Club, and it was the only time they ever gave a bad review to a movie."

SLOUCHING TOWARD AVENUE A – THE UNDERGROUND UNCHAINED
The early '60s would witness the emergence of the Underground film movement (aka "New American Cinema") on New York's Lower East Side, centred around venues like The Charles, The Bleecker Street and The Gramercy Arts theatres. For a while in 1963 informal screenings were also held at filmmaker Ken Jacobs' Ferry Street loft located downtown between the Fulton Fish Market and the Brooklyn Bridge. At the suggestion of filmmaker Bob Cowan, an actor in the brothers' movies whom Donna Kerness had brought into the scene, Mike and George took I WAS A TEENAGE RUMPOT (1960) and some of their other films down to Jacobs' loft. That was the night the Underground met the Kuchar brothers.

The fey, decadent milieu of the Underground, populated by dilettantes, beatnik intellectuals and gay artistes was spiritually a million miles away from the work-a-day tenement neighbourhoods of the Bronx – not to mention well over an hour distant by subway. This first encounter turned out to be a meeting of mutual incomprehension. Mike and George showed up in suits and ties, and, as George recalls, "There were all these underground people. We came in suits and we showed these 8mm movies, and I guess I was kind of a bit square-looking but the movies took off. I wasn't always liked at that time, I know, because I guess I appeared kind of snotty sometimes to those people. I wasn't, I was just... callously irreverent, maybe? But they were kind of snotty too, some of those people. (In an article on Experimental Cinema appearing in the April, 1967 issue of *Playboy* magazine, authors Knight and Alpert would comment: "The Kuchars take neither themselves nor their movies too seriously. For the most part the Underground is a dreadfully intense bunch of people.")

Jacobs, also a tireless promoter and programmer of underground film, liked the movies and put them into the "circuit" – whenever there was an 8mm show the Kuchar brothers were usually on the bill. Mentor and critic, Jonas Mekas, began to write regularly about them in the *Village Voice* and in *Film Culture* magazine. Mike and George were now officially part of the Underground, a rising movement that had momentum, ideas, energy and a following of righteous supporters on its side, and perhaps most importantly, because so many of the films flaunted a provocative in-your-face sexuality (at least by period standards), it had a rebellious notoriety about it that would trigger censorship, attract publicity and ensure it an audience far beyond its original borders.

The brothers were now exposed to a whole new world of independent filmmaking which they would influence and in turn be influenced by. They saw the films of Andy Warhol, Stan Brakhage, Kenneth Anger and others. "I met Warhol a few times," recalls Mike. "'Hello, how are ya?', and I used to see him coming out of my shows. I would go to see his shows and sometimes he would bring his films into the booth where I'd be, 'cause at the time some of the projectionists were my friends – he had to give directions to the projectionists. And Kenneth Anger, we saw SCORPIO RISING when it first came out... met him a couple times. It was like, 'Oh – we finally meet!' 'cause we'd heard of him and he'd heard of us."

I Was A Teenage Rumpot

"That was kind of an exciting period," says George. "One foot in the lobby, one foot in the street. The street was full of people in business suits, and they'd be coming in, and there's be more... bohemians inside. A mixture."

The early 8mm films were shot on old Kodachrome stock that tended to bleach out, but by 1963 Kodak had changed their 8mm stock to Kodachrome-2 which resulted in a considerably richer and finer image, and the brothers took advantage of it to string out one of their more lurid plot lines in a film entitled LUST FOR ECSTASY, which premièred at New York's New Bowery Theatre (later renamed the Bridge) in the early spring of 1964.

"LUST FOR ECSTASY is my most ambitious attempt since my last film," hyped George to Jonas Mekas at the time. "The actors didn't know what was going on. I wrote many of the pungent scenes on the D-train, and then when I arrived on the set I ripped them up and let my emotional whims make chopped meat out of the performances and story. It's more fun that way and then the story advances without any control until you've created a Frankenstein that destroys any sub-conscious barriers you've erected to protect yourself and your dimestore integrity. Yes, LUST FOR ECSTASY is my sub-conscious, my own naked lusts that sweep across the screen in 8mm and colour with full fidelity sound."

The brothers playfully satirized the Underground in their final production of 1963, LOVERS OF ETERNITY, an overcooked ode to bohemian decadence and artistic angst on the Lower East Side. The film starred several noted underground filmmakers, including Jack Smith and his neighbour, Dov Lederberg. Lederberg was renowned for cooking his 8mm film in the oven until it assumed the texture of eggplant before projecting it.

In 1988 George recalled working with the celebrated and eccentric Jack Smith in that picture. "Jack Smith at the time was like King of Underground pictures in New York. You would think that maybe because he was 'king' he would act like 'nobility',

Mike & George Kuchar, c. 1963

but he didn't – he was crazy as a coot which he probably still is now. [Smith died of AIDS in 1992 – Ed.] I always admired his work, though. And I put him in this picture and he was fine in the picture. Got out of control once in a while, which was fine – let him get outta control. You want to get away from him anyway so let him get out of control so you've got a chance to get away from him."

LOVERS OF ETERNITY was also the last 8mm film the brothers would make before switching to the 16mm format in response to the better detail and clarity they saw that other filmmakers were getting on 16, and the fact that you could put the sound right on the film. Ironically they had inspired other filmmakers to switch from 16mm down to 8mm (Super-8 wouldn't come along until the early '70s). 8mm became more "underground" to filmmakers searching for the ultimate in a personal, anti-commercial form of expression. The home movie was suddenly cool, prompting from the more verbose members of the movement – Mike and George included – satirically pompous manifestos on the revolutionary purity of 8mm film. Jack Smith changed from 16mm to 8mm as well – but only because his 16mm equipment had been stolen.

The brothers began work on their first 16mm production, a black-and-white *noir*-style action drama entitled CORRUPTION OF THE DAMNED (1965). Mike starred, garbed in a trench coat and embroiled in long chase sequences. A marvellously well-filmed brawl in a flour factory calls to mind the plaster warehouse punch-up in Stanley Kubrick's 1955 noir, THE KILLER'S KISS. (The Pacific Film Archives in Berkeley, California, recently undertook CORRUPTION as a preservation project, assembling a compilation print from which they struck a new negative – essentially salvaging CORRUPTION for posterity.)

With their jump up to 16mm, the brothers would begin to develop individual if similar styles and go their own separate ways – although they would always continue

Mike directs Donna Kerness in *Sins Of The Fleshapoids*

to assist on each other's productions when needed. CORRUPTION OF THE DAMNED began in the usual collaborative fashion of the 8mm films, but Mike abandoned it about mid-way through to embark on a colour science-fiction film that he wanted to do, and George finished it. "That movie is 80% George's," Mike estimates today.

The colour science-fiction film, financed by paychecks from Mike's day job as a photo retoucher, was to become SINS OF THE FLESHAPOIDS (1965). SINS would stand as Mike's best-known film and the single most significant and creatively-realized embodiment of the '60s camp cinema sensibility. Pulsing and throbbing with juicy, excessive colours, SINS unfolds while the camera's eye floats indulgently over bright flowing fabrics, jewellery, tropical plastic foliage and platters of glowing fruit that evoke a corrupt paradise. Colour as a plot device, colour as a drug. Colour as sin itself.

"My specific aim was to bombard and engulf the screen with vivid and voluptuous colours," said Mike of SINS in a 1967 *Film Culture* interview, "because SINS is a fantasy of science-fiction. So I tried to boost the colours according to its category: 'fantastic' or 'unreal'. I intentionally used a colour film that when reproduced in the final print becomes 'unnatural' and 'souped- up', especially in the reds."

SINS starred Gina Zuckerman, Maren Thomas, Donna Kerness and Julius Middleman (who later became a cop). Bob Cowan, who narrated the film and picked out the music, submits a jerky, deadpan performance as the lead male robot, and George, made up like a Persian opera butler, steals the show as Gianbeano, evil prince from the future.

The story transpires a million years in the future, after "The Great War" has depopulated the Earth and ravaged the landscape. Mankind, reduced to a debauched

---

Julius Middleman; *Sins Of The Fleshapoids*

few, has forsaken science for greedy indulgence in all pleasurable, carnal sensations afforded by art, aesthetics and lust, leaving work to be done by a race of enslaved robots. One rebellious male robot (Cowan) tires of pampering his lazy masters and murders a human woman after a failed rape attempt, then engages in successful robot sex – the touching of fingers – with a female android. Thus the Fleshapoids join their human masters in **sin**... and also in procreation, as the female android gives birth to a baby robot.

Although SINS is set in the future, there is a classical look to the costuming and set design that foreshadows Mike's fondness of an ancient, muscular, Roman sexuality that he would elaborate upon in later films and in his published pornographic gay comics, and that George did not particularly share.

SINS OF THE FLESHAPOIDS played midnights for 3 weeks at an established theatre on MacDougal street in Greenwich Village and went on to become a widely circulated staple of the Underground. Mike was now able to quit his day job and live for six years off the income of his films which included, among other things, sales of prints to museum archives worldwide and honorariums for presenting his work at University and film society screenings. (This was more a testament to Mike's modest expenses than any great heaps of cash generated by the films.)

Along with Kenneth Anger's SCORPIO RISING (1964) and Andy Warhol's THE CHELSEA GIRLS (1966), SINS OF THE FLESHAPOIDS remains one of the three most influential works of the '60s American Underground, if one of the least self-consciously scandalous. It was never "busted" as was SCORPIO RISING – resulting in a publicized 1964 California court case (Los Angeles theatre owner, Mike Getz, was convicted of "exhibiting an obscene film", a judgement later reversed on appeal, all of this sparked

George as 'Gianbeano'; *Sins Of The Fleshapoids*

by a brief flash of frontal male nudity that seems tame today) – and SINS lacked the aura of fashionable decadence that radiated from everything Warhol attached his name to and that propelled THE CHELSEA GIRLS to heights of notoriety and financial success arguably far greater than the film itself merited. (At a sold-out 1991 screening of THE CHELSEA GIRLS at the Brattle Theatre in Boston, the entire audience left during the unannounced intermission, thinking the film over.) That SINS achieved the influence and success it did without the benefit of the sexual scandalousness or scenester celebrity that so many other underground films exploited, is exceptional.

PROMETHEUS APPROXIMATED – DEVELOPMENT OF THE UNDERGROUND SUPERSTAR

The active and increasingly publicized New York underground film scene was now attracting devotees from outside the confines of Lower East Side bohemia, among them a skinny, teenage would-be beatnik from suburban Baltimore who would frequently bus or hitch-hike up to haunt all the weird joints, catch the "experimental happenings", and shoplift. His name was John Waters.

"**They** made me want to make films, **they** are the reason," says John of the Kuchar brothers in a 1988 interview, specifically lauding SINS as an influence. "I hadn't even seen Douglas Sirk yet – they were the first people that ever idolized Douglas Sirk. They were so ahead of their time. And their films were that lurid colour. They were the biggest influences on me of the Underground filmmakers, more so than Warhol because I saw their films first, and Warhol movies at that time were like SLEEP and EAT... that was before the 'Superstar' thing."

An obvious Kucharian approach to gaudy colour photography and set design can be seen in Water's three colour masterpieces of the '70s: PINK FLAMINGOS (1972), FEMALE TROUBLE (1974) and DESPERATE LIVING (1977). SINS OF THE FLESHAPOIDS had revealed to young John the kind of lush, vulgar look that could be created with cheap, discarded objects and fabrics you could pick up in one trip down to the local thrift shop. And for filmmakers who could scarcely afford the film, let alone special effects, a shamelessly prurient style of cinematography marked by vulgar close-ups, zoom shots and over-saturated colours could compensate nicely in creating a stir.

The brothers also doubtlessly influenced John's ideas about acting. "I have two kinds of actors I work with," said Mike in a 1967 *Film Culture* interview, "half of them overact, the other half can't act at all." There it was in black and white: he wasn't complaining, he was boasting. Being unable to hire professional actors was no longer a drawback, it was an advantage. John often refers to *Film Culture* as his "Bible" – he devoured every word and no doubt read Mike's comment. But he didn't **need** to read it because he'd already seen it work, he understood the chemistry involved and would employ it himself, most successfully in FEMALE TROUBLE where he plays off great "over-actors" Mink Stole and Divine against unabashed non-actors like Edith Massey and Danny Mills. In the hands of a mad alchemist like Waters, the mixture was combustible. If he couldn't turn sea water into diamonds he could at least turn dog shit into gold. And did.

Simply put, Mike, George, and later John, focused on **people** in their films: faces, bodies, personalities, "movie stars", flesh and blood... and more flesh, while eschewing the more experimental, avant-gardist techniques such as montage, found footage, emulsion-scratching and the ponderous if beautiful light show visuals utilized by filmmakers like Jorden Belsen, Bruce Conner, Stan Brakhage and others. Waters would later go as far as to say that it was abstract colours "jumping around" on the screen that killed the Underground.

The three were more attuned with the branch of the Underground that originated with the films of Ron Rice and Ken Jacobs. Rice unknowingly created the concept of the Underground Superstar when he loaded his hand-held 16mm camera with out-dated film stock in 1960 and turned it on former stockbroker and coffeehouse poet, Taylor Mead. Shot amid the fleshpots of San Francisco's North Beach neighbourhood, THE FLOWER THIEF found its audience two years later on the Lower East Side where it became an underground hit. Jacobs, in turn, immortalized the mercurial madness of Jack Smith in LITTLE STABS AT HAPPINESS (1958–61) and BLONDE COBRA (1959–62). These films introduced the concept of plotless, improvised films fuelled wholly by slavish fixation on one freakish personality who inexplicably (and hopefully) resonates on screen in ways that defy orthodox analysis (which is why adjectives such as "poetic" and "lyrical" are used with numbing frequency when describing such films).

The Kuchar brothers would, after their own style, similarly enshrine neighbourhood non-actors Larry Leibowitz and his mom, Francis, alongside unassuming *ingénue*, Donna Kerness, in the chapel of subterranean stardom. Andy Warhol would later inject considerable glamour potential and a narcissistic hipness into the concept for maximum controversy and media impact in a voluminous output of films culminating in his magnum opus, THE CHELSEA GIRLS, where, at the September 15th, 1966 première a 19-year-old John Waters would be a paying customer... no doubt sitting down front.

Waters himself would eventually unveil his own restless stable of Superstars, but unlike his fellow directors in the Underground, he would give much more weight to narrative structure and insist on fully scripted and rehearsed dialogue. Improvisation was **out**.

Unlike most of their compatriots, Mike, George and John never slagged Hollywood. They **believed** in Hollywood. None of them more than George...

SUBWAY AUTEUR: THE SOUND AND THE FURY SIGNIFYING SOMETHING

Fresh from his performance in SINS and with CORRUPTION behind him, George launched into his first 16mm colour production, HOLD ME WHILE I'M NAKED (1966), a 10-minute film that would become his signature piece. An abstract meditation on the emotional and technical traumas of making a low-budget movie, HOLD ME was a deft parody of Hollywood stylization gripped in an undertow of personal frustration and loneliness that was a direct read of George's current mental state. In fact while these short 16mm films from George's mid-to-late '60s period invariably provoke laughter from audiences, George never considered them comedies.

In 1988 George reflected on the paradox: "My movies were playing in New York City once, and this woman I know said, 'let's go to your show – they're having a night of your movies at the Film Forum.' And I said, 'no, I don't want to go because I don't want to relive all the pain.' I realized my career has all been based on pain. Those movies, even the funniest ones, had this horrible pain behind them. And I know exactly why they were made. I didn't want to go because I didn't want to relive that – I didn't want to relive the main motivations of those pictures. (But then I went and there were people **laughing**, and I was even laughing, having a good time. And I forgot about the pain.)"

At this point George was financing his films with "paychecks from hell" that he earned as a messenger for Norcross Greeting Cards in Manhattan. George recalls the place was run mostly by women. They were "Amazons... large, frightening, terrifying Amazons that walked the halls all made up and smelling of perfume. Madison Avenue type women, clacking down the halls. Frightening, terrifying figures. I don't know what was wrong with those women, but... I **do** know what was wrong with those women, they had ulcers, some of them were eaten up alive... they were like men with wigs on. And in fact some of them looked like Glenn Strange, the Frankenstein monster. Their faces were horrid..."

After Norcross, George got a job as a chart illustrationist for NBC's weather show. His daily commutes to work in Manhattan on the subway would spark more of the written imagery that so closely resembles the style and vocabulary of his cinema, as revealed from an excerpt of his 1988 essay, *Early Role Models*":

"It was thrilling to ride the jam-packed subway trains to work in the morning: discreet perverts would reach out for some sort of stabilizing support so as not to lurch over and fall in the rocking cars and they'd grab onto your private appendages. Full-figured senoritas would mash you against metal partitions using flesh of such abundance that no amount of latex rubber could suppress the meat into trim decency. Fights would suddenly break out with alarming ferocity but there could be no room

Eclipse Of The Sun Virgin

for swinging fists and so the squeeze of the travelling mob would suffocate further, violent escalations. In those subway train cars the hot, metallic-smelling air was super-charged with the most primitive of living emotions. We would all spill out of these cars (some of us being pushed or being thrown out) and climb the stairs into the canyons of dark glass and gargoyled stone which housed the machinery of commerce and coffee breaks, industry and indigestion, finance and fiscal flatulence that smelled of syndicated corruption."

The 1966–67 period was a busy time for the brothers as they honed their individual styles and saw their films go into even wider circulation, due to the still-gaining momentum of the Underground which had benefited overall by the amazing success of THE CHELSEA GIRLS.

Of the three films George made in 1967, ECLIPSE OF THE SUN VIRGIN was probably the stand-out. Starring Larry and Francis Leibowitz, ECLIPSE was similar in pacing, length and style to HOLD ME WHILE I'M NAKED but throws up more extreme imagery and ends with George and Larry watching found tracheotomy footage on George's projector. On the surface it plays as a colourful and bawdy burlesque of life, love and supper in the Bronx with George caught between the many-headed hydra of sexual lust and the bony grip of Catholic guilt.

John Water's oft-repeated assertion that "Beauty is looks you can never forget", and that "A face should jolt, not soothe", first articulated in his article, "Casting", published in *Oui* magazine, 1979, was an idea that George was already innocently drawing upon in ECLIPSE where he pays sincere homage to rotund Bronx babes and facially imperfect others. Seen today, ECLIPSE strikes one as distinctly "Waters-esque", but of course it was made in 1967 when John was still sifting for his style – a style that would eventually emerge as much more "set up", exaggerated and intentionally shocking, custom designed for the Midnight Movie market of the early '70s which he aimed to take by storm.

MOVIES OF THE MOMENT – TRUE UNDERGROUND

Mike followed up SINS OF THE FLESHAPOIDS with THE SECRET OF WENDEL SAMSON (1966), casting famous avant-garde artist, Red Grooms, in the lead role. SECRET is a personal story told in the vocabulary of expressionism and pop-fantasy. Entrancing use of dream-like musical collage merges with fluid hand-held camera work to express the inner turmoil of Wendel, who is caught between his diminishing sexual interest in a current girlfriend and unfulfilling gay relationships. As Mike himself declared: "Wendel Samson is a Universe in himself, but perhaps even more complex. The cosmic bubble is governed by the forces of electrical magnetic inertia. He is governed by a need. Unstable. A hunger to understand the impossible. Himself maybe. A quest to find the equation to happiness in a cosmic structure where happiness is not a physical property. He is a star in a cluster of stars. A solar speck in the speckled nebula of souls. A silent phantom radiating in the heavens of shining phantoms. Floating on the islands within islands, in a bubble, fifty million light years curved." Set largely in a series of spare, barren interiors and on a desolate, snowy plain – in contrast to the lavish sets and atmospherics of SINS – SECRET is a surreal, troubled rumination on sexual need and the entanglements of relationships. It remains one of the most uniquely personal and overlooked works of the '60s Underground.

THE SECRET OF WENDEL SAMSON was a very different kind of film than SINS OF THE FLESHAPOIDS, illustrative of Mike's philosophy that to him a film was the unchartable confluence of personal inspiration and all-important chemistry – a creation of the moment unattached to what had come before or would come after.

In a 1988 interview, Mike reflects on his approach to filmmaking: "I can only do a film when I feel really inspired or when I really want to. What mood I'm in determines what I'm going to do. For every film, if the chemistry is just right, then I'm able to make it. It's very hard to make a film like SINS OF THE FLESHAPOIDS again because I don't fall back into that chemistry – where everything comes together. You meet these kinds of people and they're just right to fill the parts for this film that you've always had in mind. I have a few films that I want to do, and they're not really related to each other, but then I'll make them when I meet the right people or discover the right place to film it in. Its a matter of chemistry. Then it works and stands on its own, unto itself. Then life goes on... until something else brings out something that you've always wanted to make. You know when it's right and then you go out and buy the film and make it."

Mike's straightforward approach to filmmaking, obviously antithetical to commercial cinema or the "careerism" seemingly endemic to every form of human endeavour today, encapsulates the transitory essence of true underground. His refusal to work within an identifiable genre and produce films synonymous with his audience's expectations, or films that are at least predictable or "characteristic", is why he never achieved the kind of fame awarded to many of his contemporaries, including George to some extent... and why he was, moreover, one of the very few pure underground filmmakers.

In its truest sense, "Underground" was not a genre – it was an anti-genre. Underground was an image-negative term that refuted, denied and disowned definition rather than created and defined. A thing underground was a thing unseen, without a face or profile, something ominously "other" happening in the darkness. The Underground film movement was never anything more than a collection of individuals who never quite collected. As with any other creative cultural movement with claims to revolutionary purity, be it Underground Cinema or Punk Rock, it is threatened by nothing so much as its own success – the blacklisting of venues, the censorship of the courts and the harassment of the police is nothing in comparison. Popularity breeds pressure. Public demands for follow-ups and remakes from the often more-than-happy-to-oblige leading lights of the movement (who never dreamed of the kind of money there was to be made) suck it dry of any spark or spontaneity as it ossifies into paid entertainment and the Movement rolls over and dies in a cloud of financial squabbling and superficial fashion-plate notoriety.

Only the completely nuts or the completely committed can stay true to their personal visions. There were more than a few of these characters in the Underground – Mike was one. In a milieu overpopulated with spotlight-hogging *enfant terribles*, prima donnas and media-savvy myth makers, Mike never "followed up" and never sought celebrity – he just made his movies.

OVEREXPOSED PERSONAS – HOLD ME WHILE I'M DESPERATE

In HOLD ME WHILE I'M NAKED, George framed certain scenes by turning the camera on his own face from low or straight-on angles, putting his personal stamp on a shot that might be called "house-of-mirrors close-up". Used occasionally in his '60s 16mm shorts, George emerges via these intimate portraits as something of a graceless overgrown goofus with mild acne and hair that "sticks up like a toilet brush", as he himself describes it.

There were other sides to George, however, and a radically different persona is captured in Michael Zuckerman's "lost" 12-minute nugget from the psychedelic underground, SOUL TRIP NUMBER NINE (1969). SOUL TRIP is, as Zuckerman describes it, "a story of burned-out love... taking the viewer to the shadow world of dreams and yearnings that hover in the psychedelic twilight of the turned-on mind. Slowly, as the lovers sink deeper into a drugged state, their unconscious desires rise to the surface. In brilliant colours the images tumble across the screen to reveal the feelings evoked by this, their last trip together." George, smoothly done over in pancake make-up, a Beatles wig and a mod outfit, cuts an effectively dashing and soulful figure as lead man in this non-speaking role. A bevy of topless young women cluster and swirl around him in kaleidoscopic fashion via masterful superimpositions and other hallucinatory effects.

PORTRAIT OF RAMONA, filmed in 1971, signalled a major turning point in his life and filmmaking. George recalls this, his last New York film, in an interview of January 1989: "At that time Mike was friends with this deaf guy. He could speak fairly well but he knew this other guy who was also deaf, I think from birth, and he learned how to talk just by watching people's mouths open or something. Listening to him speak was the most amazing thing, you really couldn't understand it but it was an interesting combination of sounds. And I wanted him to narrate PORTRAIT OF RAMONA. But some of my friends looked at me with shock, like, 'how could you do such a thing?!!'. I actually thought it would be really interesting to hear his voice on the soundtrack. It wouldn't matter if the audience understood it or not because they would be hearing a narrator and they would know the thing is somehow being explained, even though they didn't understand it, and so they'd accept the visual format of the film better."

George unfailingly refers to PORTRAIT OF RAMONA as a "desperate scream for help". It was time to move on to new things, to start a new chapter – to get the fuck out.

It was time to leave the Bronx.

CALIFORNIA (WET) DREAMIN'

In 1971 George attended a film festival in Cincinnati where he made the acquaintance of fellow filmmaker, Larry Jordon, who was at the time – and still is – teaching film at the San Francisco Art Institute. Jordon began in film as a compatriot and disciple of Stan Brakhage but would himself become a major figure in the Underground for works that spanned a remarkably wide range of styles. He would become best known for a series of animated collages, most notably DUO CONCERTANTES (1962–64).

Larry asked George if he wanted to teach film at the San Francisco Art Institute (S.A.I.) as a visiting artist for a one year period. George accepted the offer and packed his bags. He moved out to San Francisco and never left.

George remembers his first student on that opening day of school. The young man had actually beaten him to class and was sitting on a desk in cut-off jeans and sandals, swinging his feet, when George walked into the room that morning at about a quarter to nine. From first impressions this bearded and sandy-haired kid seemed "like a nice, playful person".

The meticulously punctual student that morning was Curt McDowell, and sitting on a desk in film class was one of the lesser dictates of cinema he would go on to break.

Born and raised in Indiana, Curt never lost his Midwest mannerisms. "He was a pumpkin-pie type of person," George recalls. "You know, cooking food, being social, a real Indiana transplant, sewing costumes and telling us stories about his mother... he also was a catalyst; he brought people together and got them involved in situations they normally wouldn't have gotten involved in, sexual and otherwise. Well... like, I never cared for bowling, but when you went out bowling with Curt it was fun. But he was also this kind of lewd, crazy person who went on binges."

Enrolled at the San Francisco Art Institute in the late '60s on a painting scholarship, Curt was turned on to movies by instructor Bob Nelson and switched to the film department. "And so," remembers George, "we began to share each other, first literally then on the screen. He would use me in his pictures, in musicals and stuff like that which gave me an opportunity to sing even though I can't hold a note."

Curt circulated a petition to get George hired on a permanent basis, arguing that the school needed new blood from outside, new influences. George was hired. Mike also began to spend time in San Francisco.

Starting out as a protegé of George's, Curt quickly found his own style and began to incorporate a large circle of friends, artistic collaborators and virtual strangers off the street into the more than 30 films he would make. "He made friends everywhere," recalled companion and lover Robert Evans in 1987, "and he eventually talked most of them into taking off their clothes and appearing in his movies." A host of his friends, including George, Mike and his own sister, Melinda, were featured in his poetic 1975 film, NUDES: A SKETCHBOOK. A stylistic departure from the grainy, rough-hewn pornographic look Curt often favoured, NUDES is a gentle homage to the sensuousness and physicality of those close to him.

Movies weren't the only things Curt got his friends to appear in naked, as his bisexual orgies were the talk of decadent '70s San Francisco, and at least on one occasion threw a shock into the supposedly shock-proof John Waters, who had dropped by to visit Curt and decided to wait it out in the antechamber.

From the outset George would find San Francisco planets apart from the Bronx, especially when it came to the libido. "The City was considered an outdoor bordello at that particular time," he muses today as if looking back at another century. Indeed. San Francisco in the early '70s was capital of the booming hardcore porno industry which native sons Alex DeRezny and Jim and Arty Mitchell had pioneered in 1969, and the gay underground was pulsing with energy. A not-yet-famous Divine could be found holding court down at the Palace theatre in North Beach, starring in stage productions like *Vice Palace* and *Divine And Her Stimulating Studs*, while across town the Castro was beginning to formalize into a major gay enclave. A more low-rent sexuality was coinage of the realm over in the Mission District where a narrow, dank 200-seat theatre stood at the grubby corner of 16th and Valencia Street showing non-stop porno flicks. (In 1976 Robert Evans, himself fresh from a stint managing a porno theatre in Oakland, took over the Roxie and turned it into one of the most visionary indie rep cinemas in the Country.) The hot-house atmosphere of the City was omnipresent and the Art Institute served as something of an organ donor centre for the out-of-control libidos of the artistically inclined.

McDowell was hardly the only Art Institute student bent on exploring the outer limits of erotic cinema. In a 1988 essay entitled *California Concoctions*, George describes a typical period student film and the effect that all of this was having on him: "Young people in this City By The Bay were aiming their movie cameras at exposed chakras left and right as the Sexual Revolution was in full swing at that time. One female in my class was up on the silver screen being sodomized by a latex novelty while indulging in a coke of non-carbonated powder. The person on the other end of that rubberized protrusion was a female classmate of lesbian persuasion obeying the direction of a unisexed university urchin who looked like Hermaphroditos incarnated. ...Eventually I fell victim (happily) to this quagmire of humming and heaving viscosity and embarked on an orgy of flesh-debased delinquency that knew no bounds..."

In the meantime Mike would continue back East through the '70s with a slew of his own films: AQUA CIRCUS (1971), DIDGERIDOO (1972), FARAWAY PLACES (1972), DEATH, QUEST OF THE JU-JU CULTS (1976), and DWARF STAR (1977) among them.

FACTORY OF DESIRE: THE LOW-BUDGET ECSTASY OF THE CLASS FILMS

George's own filmmaking now took two distinct directions: the class films he supervised at S.A.I. and his own personal films.

The class films were cast and crewed with the students who took George's course, many of whom had specifically enrolled at S.A.I. to study film with him, some coming from Europe and Latin America. These class films tested George's resourcefulness since he was confronted on the first day with up to 30 students, each of whom had to be involved in some way and some of whom spoke limited English.

Facing a linguistic gridlock that would give other instructors an ulcer, George leaned into it with gusto and actually sought out students with pidgin-English speaking proclivities for starring roles. "In those days," he recalls, "James Broughton was teaching at the school, and always complaining. He had a screenwriting course and he was always complaining that the class was full of foreigners who could barely talk English, much less write it. And I was always sayin', 'well send them to me!', because I loved these accents – they gave the pictures a continental flavour. They had strange pronunciations of words and they made the screenplays come alive in weird ways."

The budgets were always small for these class films and George's talent for spontaneous improvisation was constantly tested, distilling the productions down to the essence of low-budget filmmaking. He often wrote the dialogue and scripts on the spot, locked in a nearby closet so he could concentrate. Once, lacking dialogue for an actress, he told her to recite some Shakespeare. She did. It worked.

George's approach to directing a student cast was to create custom-tailored scenes and roles that would best exploit the multifarious talents and looks before him, playing to individual strengths and enthusiasms, freeing the energy rather than subjugating it within the disciplined context of polished scripts, storyboarding and rehearsals. It was all about chemistry cooked up between the actors themselves and between actor, scene and setting. It was about spirits, energies, mixtures and unplanned moments captured. It was, again, it would seem, more about Alchemy than anything else.

Instead of trying to compensate for lack of formal structure by coming to class over-prepared as many a nervous director might have done, George turned unpreparedness into an art form and a modus operandi – he leaned into it. "In being unprepared you are never sure of what you're going to do and the sudden chance for discovery and inspiration becomes greater," he would essay. If this resulted in some productions that didn't resemble movies as we know movies from the narrative Hollywood idiom, it **did** result in films that moved with a bracing energy and flamboyance and held together in uncanny ways, geared on moments of hilarity and serendipity. The pacing of the class films would always tend to be uptempo, but from the mid-'80s on they tended to become even more fragmented and episodic as George adjusted to what he believed were the shorter attention-spans of the MTV generation. WE'S A TEAM (1989) for example, is essentially a series of vignettes and rapidly executed skits.

Occasionally George would find himself surgically implanting the plot on the editing table. But then again Hollywood does that all the time, too, usually with a naked intent to cater to box-office (see SLIVER, the 1993 Sharon Stone vehicle) that George would never stoop to.

Lack of funds also forced him into unheard-of technical improvisations. Unhappy with one roll of film that had a kind of orange tint to it because they lacked the right lens filter when they shot it, George gave it to a student who soaked it in a plate of bleach. George declared himself happy with the results: she'd fixed the colour and also brought in unexpected flashes of lavender into the bargain. Another time, shooting outdoors in sunlight too bright for the film stock – even after cutting down on the aperture – they stuck sunglasses on the lens and it worked. "You could see the two lenses of the sunglasses," testifies George, "and we positioned each actor so that one would be in the right lens and one would be in the left lens, and they did their scenes. Everything else around them is bleached, but you can see **them** well enough through the glasses."

A Kuchar class production (photo: David Hallinger)

The constant flow of new students assured that each film would have its own personality, though invariably stamped in the Kucharian mold. Some students would take more than one class and so "stars" would emerge over an "era" of several productions. Sometimes people not enrolled at S.A.I. would drop by and be cast into a film, and sometimes George would cast faculty members, visiting artists or people wandering by who looked right to fit a given role.

THE DESPERATE AND THE DEEP (1975) opens with a striking credits sequence filmed through an aquarium. An enduringly popular film with audiences, this talkie drama at sea was designed and photographed "low-budget minimalist" with everything taking place at night against black backgrounds. The effect of deckside ocean spray in people's faces was supplied by a student off-camera throwing a dixie cup full of water at the actors.

Heated dialogue was needed to fuel these films as well as distract from the down-scale sets and absence of professional effects. George was always more than equal to the task – sometimes crediting his script to a pseudonym when he deemed the dialogue too florid.

One could always count on **action** in these class films as well as an unhinged exuberance, in contrast with George's own usually more contemplative, mysterious or atmospheric personal films. Brawls often erupted in the class films and George himself could occasionally be seen tumbling over cheap furniture and stage sets, as for example in REMEMBER TOMORROW (1979).

SYMPHONY FOR A SINNER (1979) was a long, lavishly photographed colour film generally considered the magnum opus of the class productions. New York critic and co-author of *Midnight Movies*, J. Hoberman, would rank it as one of the ten best films of the entire year, while Stan Brakhage would call it "the ultimate class picture". John Waters, who now visited George regularly whenever he passed through San Francisco, was in envy of the lurid colour photography and wanted George to shoot his next picture (which would have been POLYESTER and didn't happen). It was, said Waters, the look he had craved for DESPERATE LIVING (1977).

Yet perhaps the real gem of George's class filmmaking lies embedded in a relatively forgotten film from the following year, HOW TO CHOSE [sic] A WIFE, the concluding third of which features a bizarre wedding chapel scene complete with stumbling, heavily-pregnant bride and mystic Arab on-lookers engulfed in abashed awe. An apocalyptic earthquake erupts – the ground trembles and the chapel walls crumble and crash down in a hallmark scene of mass destruction. This single scene is more effective than anything to be found in a score of big-budget Hollywood productions, and made for less than anybody working in Hollywood could possibly imagine. George recalls the budget at around $300. Everything was done with inventive camera effects and a keen sense of staging and scoring.

Mike also made a number of class films under the auspices of the San Francisco Art Institute during the '70s: THE MASQUE OF VALHALLA (1972), THE WINGS OF MURU (1973), BLOOD SUCKER (1975), THE PASSIONS: A PSYCHO-DRAMA (1977), ISLE OF THE SLEEPING SOULS (1979); and in the '80s, CIRCE (1984). THE PASSIONS, a chapterized reflection on base human emotions, set amid some marvellous Expressionistic sets and with the feel of live theatre about it, is a stand-out piece, particularly the chapter on jealousy.

George's most sustained class film in a narrative sense would be the previously mentioned SUMMER OF NO RETURN (1988). A year and two films later George would change over to shooting the class films on video due to the rising cost of working in film and the shrinking size of his budgets. It became impossible to conduct a class of 20/30 students all semester, all day Fridays, on budgets of $300. Jean Cocteau once asserted that "the cinema will only become an art when its raw materials are as cheap as paper and pencil." Apparently Kodak wasn't listening.

WHITE ELEPHANTS ON LSD – PERSONAL FILMS AND COLLABORATIONS
The fresh currents of inspiration George encountered in San Francisco stamped his own films with a distinct personality from this point on, although his general style would forever carry the imprint of his roots in what might be termed "Bronx hyper-reality".

Completing THE SUNSHINE SISTERS in 1972, George then moved on to his GONE WITH THE WIND – or what he terms his "white elephant" – the 1973 black-and-white production he would entitle THE DEVIL'S CLEAVAGE. Consisting of a series of episodes that would total 21 hours, THE DEVIL'S CLEAVAGE was a recreation of '40s and '50s black-and-white melodramas that weaves between heartfelt homage and deft parody, playing on references from Hitchcock to Preminger. Curt McDowell excels in the male lead as the putz sheriff spouting bald Kucharian dialogue with an hysterical deadpan delivery.

In return for Curt's help on THE DEVIL'S CLEAVAGE, George assisted Curt on his 1975 feature, THUNDERCRACK! This would be their glorious gift to posterity – the world's only underground porno horror movie. George titled and wrote the film, did lighting, made up and costumed lead actress, Marion Eaton, and acted in the role of "Bing" – the psychosexually troubled gorilla keeper who attempts suicide by crashing his circus truck in a thunderstorm. Rumour had it that George wrote the script during a thunderstorm in Nebraska while tripping on LSD. Actually he wrote the 192-page script during a prolonged stay at an Oklahoma YMCA where he used ballpoint pen to preclude erasures and the spectre of eternal rewrites.

George wrote the part of Bing, as he recalls, "for someone a bit more aesthetic looking – in an Austin, Texas kind of way. I'm sort of bulky but they asked me to do it. Unfortunately I never had time to memorize my lines, which was a great source of embarrassment since I wrote the damn thing! But it seemed to give the character a little edge." To say the least. George's performance is one of the most maniacally possessed in all the annals of the Underground and ranks alongside his role as Gianbeano in SINS OF THE FLESHAPOIDS as his most twisted screen appearance.

In a 1989 essay entitled *Reflections On Lighting*, George describes his make-up work on THUNDERCRACK! lead, Marion Eaton, reminiscences which quickly suck into a dizzying whirlpool of colonized Bronx recollection: "The main actress on the set had delicate features and gentle eyes until I got my hands on them (I was also the film's make-up and hair stylist – going under the pseudonym of Mr. Dominic). Mr.Dominic is sick... recreating for the motion picture screen the women he viewed in his youth: tremendous creatures of endless fascination. Women garbed in fabric coats of dreary tone who straddled the vacant lots of the Bronx, urinating on a kaleidoscope of broken beer bottles. Females who descended between the stone columns of edifices constructed to house the denizens of a naked city revelling in its own shame. Descending the steps with their cheeks all rouged in oval splendour, the circular patterns in the poodle-fur shawls that draped their shoulders glistened all black and dead in the sun. Ladies who watched television in the morning with hideous, shrunken men articulating from the screen in a desperate attempt to sell cardboard eyebrow stencils to the frustrated and the frumpy. Mr. Dominic sick? Perhaps he is just temporarily regurgitating the visions of his youth: seeing in the black rainbows that arc above the eyes of that lost race an archway to the magical kingdom of Maybelline and its colourful treasures. Maybe that can explain the splash of candyapple red that spills way beyond the contours of lip to lap at chin and nostril alike."

SPARKLES TAVERN was Curt's next feature film and would employ many of the same actors that had appeared in THUNDERCRACK! McDowell wrote the script, reports George, while high on LSD in Yosemite National Park. George was cast to play to role of "Mr. Pupik" – a mystical stranger with intuitive powers and Dadaist mannerisms who peddles bizarre but effective remedies for personal troubles. George was required to sing, execute arcane dance steps and play the saxophone (or at least the "air saxophone"). A one-of-a-kind role to be sure. Filmed in 1976, SPARKLES lay unedited and unreleased until 1984. Three years later, on June 3rd, 1987, Curt McDowell would be dead of AIDS at age 42. (The original negatives of both THUNDERCRACK! and SPARKLES TAVERN have since been lost or destroyed, apparently due to oversights by the Curt McDowell Foundation.)

CALIFORNIA ABNORMAL – INVASION UFO
George's 1979 film, BLIPS, would initiate a six-part UFO series inspired by UFOs he was spotting at the time. He elaborates in a 1988 interview: "In the mid-'70s I found out that UFOs are real. Whatever they are – I don't know what they are. But there was a big rash of them and they were in California, in San Francisco. I happened to fall into the mess... or mystery, by viewing what were UFOs. They were of different colours and they came in a series that lasted about a year and a half. Also in different sizes and shapes... and they have strange mental effects on you. They interact with you in a **personal** way, although I can't see how extra-terrestrials would have that much interest in you. But from the stories you hear and my own personal experiences, it's very **personalized** and **bizarre**. I began to investigate it in the films."

Set in several barren, debris-littered rooms, BLIPS plays out as impressionistic soap opera, equal parts PHANTOM FROM SPACE and *Waiting For Godot*. Bewildered, frightened and yet somehow **energized** after a spate of UFO overflights, a group of neighbours find their nerve coils reverberating with anxiety, compulsion and sexual hunger as they fight against – and submit to – the strange electricity in the air. George was more concerned with portraying the psychic effects UFOs had on people, on their libidos, their zeitgeist, than with the over-worked science-fiction images of UFOs delivering mass destruction and millennial doom, and special effects are at a minimum.

The UFO sextuplet continued with THE NOCTURNAL IMMACULATION (1980), YOLANDO (1981) CATTLE MUTILATIONS (1983), THE X-PEOPLE (1984) and ASCENSION OF THE DEMONOIDS (1985), which stands as George's last personal film to date. The films occasionally strayed into other areas of parapsychology as well.

George received his only funding grant for ASCENSION OF THE DEMONOIDS ($20,000 from the NEA), and so, freed from the usual financial binds, he was determined to have a good time and make a "spectacle" awash with "tons of colour" and dazzling superimpositions and other camera effects. It was supposedly the last of the UFO pictures, the big, colourful mural at the end. "And I wanted to look away from the subject," George relates in a 1988 interview, "so the movie looks away from the subject towards the end. In fact it completely drops the subject, basically... goes to Hawaii and examines the scenery, forgetting about what had previously happened or what the picture was about. That was my intention. I wanted to get off the subject."

George submitted another inspired acting performance in the 1984, black-and-white feature, SCREAMPLAY, an unjustly overlooked ode to silent movie-making that featured some astonishing montage and superimposition. Successfully cast against type by Boston-based writer-director Rufus Butler Seder, George plays a dour, reclusive superintendent of a courtyard motel with convincing menace and foreboding – a persona in fact recognizable, at least from a distance, to anyone who has seen George sullenly loping down Mission Street to his 19th Street flat where he lives today.

These days Mike splits his time between San Francisco, where he shares the 19th Street walk-up with George, and New York City where he works in-season at the Millennium Film Workshop. He periodically tours his films in Europe and the U.S. and hires on as cinematographer with independent Dutch and German film productions. In December of 1993 he premièred his new video feature film, *Purgatory Junction*, at the Millennium to a full house. Mike has also given a name and enduring inspiration to the New York City underground punk band, The Voluptuous Horror Of Karen Black,

George at an art opening

---

fronted by nude, body-painted lead singer Kembra Pfahler and her guitar-playing Japanese husband.

George, with over 60 films and 100 videos[1] now to his credit, has a somewhat higher profile and was the subject of recent retrospectives at The Museum of the Moving Image in Queens, New York (summer of 1993) and at San Francisco's palatial Castro theatre which staged a joint George Kuchar/Curt McDowell retrospective in November, 1993. George also continues to teach guest film courses and workshops at Universities and film foundations around the country but seldom travels abroad. He works almost exclusively in video today.

Since the late '70s, George has been a regular May visitor to an unremarkable little roadside motel in El Reno, Oklahoma. He's become friends with the motel owner who now picks him up at the airport. With each visit he produces a *Weather Diaries* video as he kills time in El Reno, films daily existence, clears his head of psychic flotsam accumulated in San Francisco and waits for tornados to strike.

The tornados, still...

Has it ever happened?

"When one finally came," laughs confidante John Waters, "he ran and hid. I'm not sure – he might have been joking."

[1]Videos made by George since 1984 include: *Video Album 1; Greetings From Boulder; Caged Culture; Precious Products; Reunion In Los Angeles; Xmas; The Weather Diary 1; Xmas New Years; We, The Normal; Thanksgiving With Mom; Video Album 2; Evangelust; Low Light Life; Studio 8; Orbits Of Fear; 1980-Seven; Screening Workshop; Video Album 3; The Weather Diary 2; East By Southwest; Motivation Of The Carcassoids; Calling Dr. Petrov; The Warming Of Hell House; The Weather Diary 3; Rainy Season; The Creeping Crimson; Mecca Of The Frigid; Cult Of The Cubicle; The Weather Diary 4; The Muffled Darkness; Return To The House Of Pain; Video Album 4; House Calls; Video Album 5: The Thursday People; The Celluloids; Jane's Visit; The Hurt That Fades; George Kuchar Goes To Work With Today's Youth; Scarlet Droppings; Weather Watch; The Gifted Goon; Portraiture In Black; Nirvana Of The Nebbishites; Going Nowhere; Pilgrimage; Graffiti Junction; The Deafening Goo; Artists In Residence; Come Forth Julyowa; A Passage To Wetness; Gastronomic Getaway; Impaction Of The Igneous; The Story Of Ruthy; Kiss Of The Veggie Vixen; The Redhead From Riverside Terrace; Holiday X-Mass Video; Indian Summer; Ann Arbor; Edible Atrocities; Award; Interior Vacuum; Chant-N-Chew; Snap-N-Snatch; Point-N-Shoot; Indigo Blues; Kitchen Etiquette; Snake Goddess; 500 Millibars To Ecstasy; The Migration Of The Blubberoids; Big Ones Hurt; The Cellar Sinema; Fill Thy Crack With Whiteness.*

Desperate Visions 1: Camp America

Chapter Two

THE GEORGE KUCHAR INTERVIEWS

Part I: What follows is an interview George taped for us while staying in the Reno Motel in El Reno, Oklahoma in May 1988. We had supplied him with several pages of written questions. May is the peak of tornado season in Oklahoma. George is a regular guest at the Reno Motel and the setting figures prominently in his Weather Diary video series as well as his film, WILD NIGHT IN EL RENO (1977).

JACK STEVENSON: Describe where you are at the moment, the decor of the room, what activity you are engaged in: drinking? eating? smoking? How do you feel about this interview, talking to yourself into a tape recorder?

GEORGE KUCHAR: I'm here in Oklahoma, I'm at the Reno Motel here in Oklahoma – maybe don't mention the place... I don't know **why**, but ah, maybe... don't get anyone else trapped here. I'm sittin' on the sofa, which they had re-upholstered in kind of a... Virginia design, Virginia water-wheel? On a **mill**. The kind of activity? I'm just sittin' – I thought of doing this because I'm gonna fall asleep. Not that it's late, it's just that for some reason I get hit with tiredness here in the middle of the day, and then in the middle of the night I wake up. My hours are all screwed up. Anyway, I wasn't drinking coffee, I was drinking "Postum", because I had already had two cups of coffee – that's enough for me, two cups of coffee today. I feel okay about this interview... talkin' to myself, I'm used to that, I talk into a video recorder all the time, so... I'm constantly acting, in fact I'm here working on *Weather Diary 3*. I turned the air conditioner off in this room and put it on in the bedroom, it's a two-room "suite", let's call it, because it's kind of hot and humid out, and I don't want the buzz of the air conditioner, the **roar** of the air conditioner to interfere with the interview, so...

JS: Now, you started making films at about age 12? Back in the 1950s? – with your brother Mike?

GK: Now I did start making movies with my brother when I was – before I was a teenager. And people seem to nowadays "admire" or "respect" or "envy" somebody that was a teenager in the '50s. Of course it was a usual time of pimples and gang wars, and... other kids beatin' you up, and – I don't know, feelin' like you had to go out on dates and stuff like that, so it was a typical... hell period. I wonder if kids got it better now? I don't know, I see the kids in San Francisco: they're kind of awful. But that's because they copy the adults that are out there. And the adults are terrible. So, I started makin' pictures when I was... ah, a pre-teen.

JS: Where did you show these early films and what was the reaction?

GK: Now when I used to show my pictures, I used to show them at friends' houses, at parties. You know, I'd go to a friend's house – they'd be the cast and then a week later we'd come back and they'd be developed, and we'd show 'em the rushes and then maybe a week after that I'd edit them, and come back and show 'em the thing and we'd shoot some more, and then we'd have a party and show the final finished

---

film. I used to show them in Queens, and they were regular 8mm. But I used to work in **cassette** at that time, they had 8mm cassettes, only they called 'em "magazines" [metallic magazines] in those days. They weren't plastic, they were made out of metal, and they fit into a DeJur camera, I had a DeJur 8mm, magazine load camera. And, ah – then I used to show 'em at an old fuddyduddy club, the 8mm Motion Picture Club. In New York. It was run by fuddy-duddies; everybody got dressed up and they showed their vacation footage... and there'd be old ladies there and there'd be old men, and the ladies'd be sitting next to the men and their stomachs would be... acting up, and making noises. And the old ladies would get offended, and... you know, people would get offended at my movies because they were "irreverent" I guess. I was looking for... I don't know... **subject matter,** and I'd pick anything out of the newspaper, and at that time – I remember one time the Thalidomide scare came out where ladies were taking Thalidomide pills and giving birth to deformed babies and I made a comedy out of that, and that was the last time I was at the 8mm Motion Picture Club, and it was the only time they ever gave a bad review to a movie.

JS: Where are these earliest films today? Like THE NAKED AND THE NUDE ('57), and PUSSY ON A HOT TIN ROOF ('61), etc.?

GK: Now those early films are... I think they're in my mother's closet in the Bronx. The originals. I have copies in San Francisco, I made copies. Some of the copies are good, some of them are not so good. They just made an untimed print of all of them. Ah... the originals are still in my mother's closet, I think they're still holdin' up. The **soundtracks,** unfortunately, are falling apart. Although some are still there. But they're beginning to flake off the tape, the magnetic particles are flaking off the tape. So, I probably gotta get that fixed sometime.

JS: What was your childhood like? You used to **live** in the movie theatres, eh?

GK: My childhood? It was... well I guess... torture, except I was a nature lover, since I was born in a city and lived in a city, New York, all my life, born in Manhattan and then moved to the Bronx at an early age so, I worshipped nature and storms... anything that came into the city and disrupted it, in a "nature way". I liked sunsets, and the colours of the sky,... a different series of weather events. And going to the park 'cause I did live near the Bronx Park, and the Bronx Botanical Gardens and they had waterfalls, and water running over rocks. And there were animals in cages – I didn't much visit them, that was sort of the boring part of the park... the **wild** part was a turn on for me as a youth. And... I was a tortured youth I think. Miserable a lot. And I took solitary walks. But I was "social" making movies. It was my one connection with other people. The fact that I was able to interact with them, and we were all doing things together. I had friends, but I wasn't that much of a party-goer. I used to go to movies a lot. That's for sure. And I loved going to the movies, my brother and I used to go spend hours, whole Saturday afternoons seeing pictures over and over again. We had our favourites. Got to know movie film scores and who the composers were. In fact I would go to the movies just because a particular composer was on. Bernard Herrmann was in his heyday. And Franz Waxman and Alex North and all of them were... grindin' out stuff. My brother and I would sit through movie after movie, sit through the **same** movies, and WRITTEN ON THE WIND we used to go, I don't know – I've seen that eleven times when it came out... and spent a lot of time in the movie theatre and made games, used to crawl under the seats, and... well, it was a house of activity – a house of activity.

George directs Florraine Connors in *Corruption Of The Damned*, 1965

JS: Didn't you shoot most of those first movies on Bronx tenement rooftops?

GK: I did shoot a lot of early movies in the Bronx on the rooftops because we needed bright light. We didn't have light at that time, in the beginning, you know – artificial light. We weren't into that yet so we needed the sun. And we needed black backgrounds so that you couldn't see that we had no sets. This way you could **invent** – see the black background and maybe invent in your mind an imaginary set. And that was a current trend at that time, on television they used to have the actors act with just a step ladder and a black backdrop. I guess it was avant-garde at that time in TV of the '50s. And so, I carried it over into film, but the pictures were – would begin bright but then get darker and darker as stratus clouds would move in. We were always making pictures when a warm front was approaching, and the clouds would thicken and thicken and so by the end of the 50-foot reel of film you couldn't see the finale, it was just too dark. The camera only opened up to... F-2 maybe? Couldn't squeeze a 1.9. And so the pictures got murkier and murkier and darker at the end.

JS: So what if you had grown up in Los Angeles or... Orange County? Or Yugoslavia? Would the inspiration still have been there?

GK: Well, I don't know about growin' up in L.A. I probably would've drove, be drivin' a car by now. Had a tan. I don't know... I didn't get to L.A. until... late '70s? Mid '70s? I don't know where my inspiration would've been. In New York there's a lot of trashy novels on the bookstands, and my father was into reading trashy novels, at least novels that were exciting to me – the art work on the covers. That inspired a lot of imagery in my head. I loved the kind of sordidness of what it was like, evidently, to be grown up. It was a turn on for me, I'd get excited looking at those paperback covers. And also the comic books. I think they twisted me also. I remember I used to be real disturbed when the heroes were captured and whipped and beaten and... I don't know... strange experiences that might have warped me.

JS: You were reportedly first introduced to the New York underground when Bob Cowan suggested you bring your films down to Ken Jacobs' Ferry Street loft where it seems a lot of good shit was going on at the time. Do you remember vividly those days?

GK: Now the early days, I was making 8mm pictures, and I did meet Bob Cowan, and I was making 8mm films with him. I met him through Donna Kerness, she was my big star, we went to high school together. I started putting her in movies – she had big bazooms. And she had a very nice face, and she could **act** – she had a style about her. And so I put her in movies, and all my Bronx buddies were all excited about her. She was a big sensation. I had regular Bronx buddies – they worked either in the Post Office or they were furniture polishers, or they were going into the Air Force, or, later became transit patrolmen on the subway. And, ah, they really got excited about her and thought her a great talent, so... I **milked** her. I went over to her house, and we began to put her in bathtub scenes where she wore a bathing suit of course, the straps were pulled down. We simulated the tawdry stuff that I used to see on the screen. It was very nice, I met a lot of girls that way, she had girlfriends that were dancers – but I didn't particularly care for them, they were snooty, a lot of them. Except for Donna, she was kinda down-to-earth, and probably troubled also. So, we got along well, but it was only via pictures. We got along in personal life, also, but personally we, ah... well I never used to get involved with anybody personally making pictures, it was always "make the picture". And ah, well that later... changed. But then ya have to, I don't know... you get tired of doin' one thing all the time, you know. Now Bob Cowan took me down to Ken Jacobs', and we went to the loft there, my brother and I, I remember we came in suits, and these were all the underground people. But we came in suits and we showed 8mm movies, and I guess I was kind of a bit square lookin', but the movies took off. Ken Jacobs liked them and played them the other week, and Jonas Mekas came and he wrote about them in the *Village Voice*. And then they began to be on the "circuit" – whenever they had an 8mm show, my brother and I, our work was on there, and it was shown to the public, and I got to meet a lot of the other underground filmmakers. Some are dead. A lot of them are dead now I guess. Ron Rice died early... Warhol I met a few years later when I was doing 16mm. Dead. Who else? Gregory Markopoulos went to Europe... oh I don't know, a bunch of people. And I used to **see** movies, the Brakhage movies... Kenneth Anger movies, SCORPIO RISING when it first came out. That was kind of an exciting period. It seems like a past life. One foot in the lobby, one foot in the street. The street was full of people, they'd be in business suits and they'd be comin' in, and there'd be more... bohemians inside... it was kind of an interesting time in New York. And I do remember them vividly. I wasn't always **liked** at that time, I know. Because I guess I appeared kind of **snotty** sometimes to some people. I wasn't, I was just... callously irreverent, maybe? But they were kind of snotty, too, some of the people.

JS: It seemed like a great time to be alive and working with film, like the whole "underground" movement was taking malformed shape. John Waters always mentions HOLD ME WHILE I'M NAKED as an early influence on him when he was a no-good teenager coming up to New York City.

GK: Now it was kind of an exciting time, and there was – of course we had been making movies way before, 8mm, and our friends were paying attention to it. And now this underground movement, got to meet a lot of other people making films. And then we saw these 16mm movies and said, "Oh, wow, you can see so much more detail, you can put the sound on the film also"... and 8mm didn't seem like too big of a deal. I had to get a new projector so I said maybe we're gonna rehaul and just get 16mm. It was nice to be in New York at that time. Although New York ain't always that nice to be in. But when you're **there**, it'll probably eventually get **worse**, so, enjoy it now, then forget about it, leave it, you know. Yeah, HOLD ME WHILE I'M NAKED was my most popular film. I think it took about six months to a year to catch on, and then when it caught on it was played a lot. I had liked it myself very much. But, ah... I never met John Waters in New York, you know. I met John Waters later, in San Francisco.

JS: Is there anything similar going on today? Anything that can be called "underground" any more?

GK: Yeah, there's plenty of that going around. But you gotta be in the big bucks a little bit now, to afford that damn film. Of course you can make it in Super 8. There's tons of stuff goin' on. People workin' and makin' real, ah... trash. Interesting trash, and making kind of elegant stuff. And then of course there are people making kind of "politically correct" stuff, and... that kind of trash, too. So there's still a lot going on, a hell of a lot going on. In San Francisco a lot. And New York. New York you're supposed to kvetch a little more than San Francisco. New York is always kvetching, kvetching, kvetching! At least that's what the filmmakers there tell me.

JS: Did any of these other early NYC filmmakers like Jack Smith or Warhol or Ron Rice influence you or was it mostly the stirring Hollywood epics?

GK: Now I got influenced by everybody. And probably a lot of my work has scenes in it lifted from other things because, ah... they just imprint on me, and then when it comes time, just cough it up. Sometimes I don't even know I'm doing it. Anything will influence me. Therefore... I think it's fine. Just keep watching things and doing things and getting involved in things, it all influences you and you don't dry up. Cough it up,

George in his own *Hold Me While I'm Naked*

you cough it up in your work. Of course the Hollywood stuff influenced me a lot, but then also Warhol, **Jack Smith**... all of it.

JS: You knew Jack Smith – he was in your 8mm film THE LOVERS OF ETERNITY. What is he like and where is he today?

GK: I did know him a little bit when I was in New York, because I made a movie, my last 8mm movie at that time, with ah... Dov Lederberg who lived next door to him. Dov Lederberg used to make 8mm pictures, and he used to take the 8mm film and put it in his oven and cook it. It looked like, ah,... texture of an eggplant, when you projected it, you know the emulsion was all cracked. And he lived next door to Jack Smith. Of course Jack Smith at that time was like King of Underground pictures in New York. And you would think maybe because he was king he would act like "nobility," but he didn't – he was crazy as a coot which he probably still is now. I guess you can call him mercurial? And I don't really relate to him too much, goes up and down too fast, too high and too low probably. I always admired his work, though. And I put him in a picture, and he was fine in the picture. Gets outta control once in a while, which is fine – let him get outta control. You want to get away from him

The young George Kuchar

anyway, so let him get out of control so you got a chance to get away from him.

JS: You worked as a messenger for a greeting card company back then. What was that like? Did you lead a "normal existence" – whatever that is?

GK: Now I did work for a greeting card [company] in New York, it was Norcross Greeting cards. And it was mainly run by women, although Mr. Norcross was the big deal – I never met him, though. But it was run by women. And they were... amazons. Large, frightening, terrifying amazons, that walked the halls all made up and smelling of perfume. Madison Avenue type women, clacking down the halls. Frightening, terrifying figures. I don't know what was wrong with those women but... I **do** know what was wrong with those women, they had ulcers, some of them were eaten up alive... they were like men with wigs on. Wigs and make-up. And in fact some of them looked like Glenn Strange as the Frankenstein monster, because, the faces were horrid. It was – severe amazons. I worked at that job many, many years, and then I left that job – thank God – I can't remember how. And I was leading a normal existence, that you come home with a big cake, after work you come home with a big cake, you have a big meal and then you come home with a big cake, you eat it and you bloat, you get fat. Look like 40 when you're only 25. And that's... the normal existence.

JS: From the Bronx you ended up coming out to San Francisco where you now teach at film school.

GK: From the Bronx I came out to San Francisco, because I met Larry Jordon, teaches film in San Francisco, I met him in Cincinnati. It was some kind of a festival, and I stayed an extra day and we flew kites together in Cincinnati, and he asked me if I'd ever like to come to the San Francisco Art Institute to teach for a summer. I said yeah, I went, and then, I guess... I was a "visiting artist", or I was something. I came there and they hired me. I did a summer course maybe? I can't remember. But the students, and my very first student, Curt McDowell, circulated a petition to get me there. They said the school needed new outside blood, or someone from New York, so I got on the payroll, at the Art Institute.

JS: Were there any scandals or infamous episodes or wild times in between, that the prurient voyeuristic scum that comprise our readership would be interested to know more about? Or any shameless dirty secrets, very personal, about **anybody else** that you can tell us?

GK: Well at that time... [thoughtful silence]... I don't know, there was, of course. But the shameless dirt never comes out until, like, you're in your thirties. It's there, it's forming. But it's never that **dirty** I think when you're in your twenties, at least in my time. It was developing, a developing dirtiness that exploded, I guess, when I hit 33.

JS: In the early 1970s in San Francisco you became good friends and a collaborator with Curt McDowell, right?

GK: Now Curt McDowell was my very first student. In fact he was sitting in the room when I came in, sitting on the desk I remember, it was ten to nine, and there he was, and he looked healthy... he was swingin' his legs, sittin' on the desk... and... he... [voice trails off] I don't know how much I should go into this. Well, he was a strange person. Strange in a way... ah, maybe I ought to turn off the recorder [laughs].

JS: Didn't he shoot THUNDERCRACK!, the hilarious porno flick with people incessantly talking as they fuck? What about that movie?

GK: Curt McDowell had at that time been going to the Art Institute, he was originally a painter and got interested in film via Bob Nelson, who turned him on to film. He saw some movies and then switched to the film department. Curt McDowell's main calling in life... God gave him a calling in life, and that was to make pornography. Sex pictures. He was mainly interested in homo-erotic, and **men**, he loved buns, men's buns, and he loved that kind of stuff. That was his calling in life, and his early pictures he would do it in a round-about way and he'd also throw in women so it would be a more... rounded picture. He was interested in heterosexual sex, watching it. He was interested in heterosexual men humpin' them. He was a strange person. Sometimes he had very low self-esteem, but he used to... get, I think, power by eating men. And, I guess it was a form of probably, sex magic. And he was a very loving and a very giving person. Like he was very, very giving. And I'll always remember him, the image that stays in my mind of Curt McDowell is him one time when we went to the North Country by the beach, and he was standing in a field of flowers with his pecker dangling out. He was shirtless and his pants were unbuttoned and his pecker was dangling out and he was smelling a flower. It wasn't a hippie type image, it was just, I don't know what you'd call it, it was just... weird, but sweet. He did have a strange... sharp edge to him at times. Probably a lot added to it... drugs maybe. But, he was a very giving person. He gave a lot, let's just say that. He did work on THUNDERCRACK!. That was funded by two other guys, John Thomas and Charley Thomas, they were the producers. They were rather handsome guys. Charley, I always remember him – he always sweated under the armpits, his armpit area was always wet. And he was very stocky and kind of muscular. And John had a bit more of an elegant face, although he had a little problem with his back – he was stooped over, and then he went for rolfing and they straightened him up. But they were rather handsome guys, contemporaries to Curt, they were students and I was their teacher. And, I think their dad used to own

Burger King, or something like that, then he sold it. So they had a lot of money and they were dabbling in the arts. It was sculpture and painting, and then they were doing filmmaking – they had money and they bought a lot of equipment. I guess Curt asked me to write a screenplay of THUNDERCRACK!. I labelled it THUNDERCRACK!. He wanted me to do a sex picture – all kinds of mixed sex in it. And, I wrote it, and he wanted to make it because he made a lot of money on another film called LUNCH, that he starred his friend in, Mark Ellinger, who later did the soundtrack for THUNDERCRACK!.I remember I just saw one shot of LUNCH, and it was Ellinger ejaculating, and he squirted clear across the room... almost practically missing the head of the girl who was lying down whose name was Wendy. Wendy was kind of a chunky girl, built like a "brick shithouse" or maybe built like a refrigerator. She was a student also. Those students used to make sex pictures, because in those days it was fashionable to show your chakra. So, those were the '70s.

Anyway, Curt asked me to make this movie, and he was sure we would make money because LUNCH was making money. And I had a feeling, no... usually whatever I work in doesn't make money, would be a disaster. Sure enough, the picture never made any money. I think the audience was repelled by it, the porno audience. Ah, they didn't want to see black-and-white I hear, and they don't like talking, and they go to see specific sex acts. I think if you mix 'em up too much they get turned off. It offends them. I don't know if that's still true today. But the picture got very good reviews in the magazine *Sight And Sound*. John Russell Taylor, I remember he had a whole thing, he wrote about John Waters, he wrote about the **trash** movies. And he called that one a genuinely erotic and genuinely frightening picture. That was a very nice review. The picture was later cut by the producers – it played at Filmex, Buck Henry liked it a lot. The other judges wanted to turn the thing off after 15 or 20 minutes. But Buck Henry said, "If you turn this picture off I'm leaving the film festival, I won't judge." So they sat through the whole thing and it got on. Thanks to Buck Henry that picture was – we had a big L.A. première in Century City. Very nice. I look at it as my big Hollywood première where we arrive in, like, a limousine, and there's search beam lights outside. So, I did that already, I don't feel I missed out on anything. Thanks to Curt, the Thomas brothers and Buck Henry. Curt found the picture at the end was too `sour or something. Or maybe... one of the gay actors wound up with a girl? A gay guy – I don't know what it was. I guess it was like a "bitter-sweet" or sad ending, and he was more into sex as a jubilation or something. But, ah, I felt... the thing was tragic. And I guess my view was sex as **horror** in people's lives. **Obsessions** they have, fetishes, urges that they don't know where the hell they got these but they can't understand it and many times they can't control it, so it becomes a horror in your life. So that was my outlook on the thing, my outlook on sex. Of course as I look back on the film now I realize I was in serious trouble, probably. There was something **wrong** somewhere, but, ah... I don't know, you just forge ahead.

JS: What was Curt like? Describe some of his other films – I know nothing about him.

GK: Curt had... appetite. Insatiable appetites. Some of them I guess were spurred on by various substances. And others... your libido sometimes goes crazy in this [California] area of the country – know what I mean? He was originally from Indiana, that was a turn on for him because of all the guys smoking with their rolled-up shirt sleeves and stuff. Well, he was hungry. And he also did very good artwork, he was an excellent artist, a wonderful painter. And had a wonderful sense of smut cinema, I guess. Actually he loved **zooming**, his movies always had a lot of zoom shots and they were kind of over-exposed and he loved raw-looking stuff because he was turned on by pornography, and he incorporated all pornographic movie techniques into his pictures.

George Kuchar

George awaits a tornado in El Reno

That was his calling in life. He had a sister, Melinda. And Melinda finally wound up on the West Coast. And, well he used to use her as bait to attract the men. She was a very voluptuous girl. And they'd be shooting footage of her with Arabian... grocery clerks, you know, three of them, they're all humping away, and Melinda's there, the object of their... affection I guess, and they'd be squirtin' all over her. So, Melinda had her San Francisco experience. She's still there, she's a mother now. She married kind of a nice looking guy – at least he was nice looking when I saw him which was maybe 10 years ago. But I think he has troubles. He's a Vietnam vet and he flies off the handle now and again. But she's got two or three kids now. Lives across the Bay.

JS: George, you've always had a deep love of tornadoes. In A TOWN CALLED TEMPEST (1961) there's a great special effect of a tornado destroying a town, while the more recent *Weather Diary 1* [video] seems centred on tornado lust and longing.

GK: Yeah, I did like storms, and **twisters**, tornadoes. I don't know why. I think in the '50s a big one had gone through Worcester, Massachusetts. And I guess there was talk about it in New York, and it was in the news, and for some reason it excited me. The great storm smashing up towns, and blowing into people's lives, and changing it. Not so much that I was interested in the carnage, but the fact of... whirling clouds and big winds and stuff like that. It was weather on the rampage, it was nature unleashed, nature loosed. It was dramatic. From all descriptions the sky is a weird colour, the clouds are **boiling**, and etc., etc. It struck my fancy. And I think most people that are interested in meteorology are fascinated by that particular character in meteorology, the tornado.

JS: When you first met John Waters, didn't you get together and talk about tornadoes?

GK: Yeah, John Waters came over to the house and I showed him my tornado books – I collect literature on tornados. Any visual material I can get. We discussed this. He's got some of the books.

JS: You shoot a lot into TV sets. Plus you seem to like to **spy** on, watch, observe people... sometimes from behind the curtains. This sometimes gives your work a voyeuristic feel. In previous interviews both Rosa [Von Praunheim] and John have said they possess voyeuristic inclinations (me too!) Society in general seems to treat this tendency as some evil or perversion or character flaw. What do you think about one of the most important issues of our day – voyeurism?!!

GK: Voyeurism? Well... you know I was a voyeur way back because nobody used to look at me, so I'd be looking at everybody, you know, look at people, and nobody would really pay any attention to me so it was like being invisible. So I'm very comfortable with voyeurism. I used to go to motels and put the drinking glass against the wall and put my ear to it and listen and hope there was some action in the next room. And sometimes there was, and it was sweet to listen to a couple exchanging talk, and how they got around to the intimacies. It was something very interesting, something very – touching – I thought. It was also something very exciting. My father, who was a truck driver, used to belong to a little film exchange group, he used to bring home the "red reels", red plastic reels of 8mm pornography. And I remember – I think it was via my father I got interested in pornography 'cause he had some pornographic books stuck away in his drawer, and when I was a little kid I used to find them, and look, and was amazed and would laugh... these adults, the world of the adults. And then later when I was older, in my twenties, and he would bring in those movies – 'cause I had an 8mm projector, and he would want to borrow it, and I said I'd like to see the movies, so he would leave them with me after he was finished lookin' at 'em. I would get a chance to see pictures. But I was very much repressed, ah, very much... secretive, and... probably... well, I was hungry also. It's getting dark here, I think I may stop this and start tomorrow. But, ah, last word on voyeurism – I guess 'cause I was invisible anyway, nobody bothered lookin' at me – I was not that attractive, I was... kind of quiet, bland dressing, hair stood up... in fact I looked like that character in ERASERHEAD only a skinny version with a skinny neck. Ah, but my hair was the same – it stood straight up, the type of hair the wind blows and it just sticks up, like a toilet brush. And that's why I like so much the David Lynch movies, because ERASERHEAD was like my New York living experience, and the new one, BLUE VELVET, is exactly like my California experience. That's it in a nutshell.

[Next day] Alright Jack, it's a new day, and I'll start answering from page 3, question 20, "Do you like your job today?" I do like my job today, in fact... I don't really like saying I like it because sometimes i feel if I say I like it I'm not really doing that good of a job, 'cause I think there has to be a certain kind of **tension**, teaching. But I am pretty lucky, because, I thought about it last semester – which ended a few weeks ago – because we're working on this movie SUMMER OF NO RETURN, it's a "teenage picture". The male lead was extremely beautiful and so was the female lead, they were like real movie star material. I found myself on a makeshift bed with most of the cast, and I looked around at them in various stages of undress – they were in various stages of undress 'cause we were doing a sleaze scene, the students wanted to do a sleaze scene. And so I said "fine, let's have a sleaze director" 'cause I don't want to be blamed for these sleaze scenes. And a girl said she would do it, but then she told me when it came time that day that she was tired, she didn't get much sleep, she'd been taking too many drugs, so she was going up to the library to rest. So I said fine, so of course I was the sleaze director, and... I found myself on the bed lookin' at these beautiful skinned people. Life had not smashed them, they were like wonderful things of beauty... great, ah... living things of beauty. And really I guess arousing, but when I'm with the Bolex, you can get aroused now and then but not that much, you know what I mean? – it's the picture, you think of the picture. And suddenly I realized how lucky I was, that this was like a dream come true: I was in California surrounded by semi-nude beautiful people. The male lead was extremely beautiful and he was layin' right there in front of me, and they were tellin' him to pull his underpants down more, and I... thought this **is** a dream come true. So, the job is pretty good. [Tape runs out.]

Okay, here we go, Side Two. I was talking about this personality split the character was supposed to have in SUMMER OF NO RETURN... straddling the fence – one side of the fence was the seedy side, the other side was yuppie heaven I guess. And the character was walking on this fence. Falling over onto the seedy side, then managing to scramble back to save his girlfriend who was... hurt in a fire. She had her face scarred. You see we had to get rid of her because she didn't trust me, the actress – she's a very nice girl but she thought I made dirty movies. And she thought I was trying to show her underpants. And I said, "I'm not interested in your underpants, I'm really not, if you don't believe me, take 'em off – I don't care." So, she thought I was tryin' to get too much... **flesh** from her. Whereas the male lead, he was pretty much all for it. He knew I had an eye for... this type of beauty. I knew that we were creating a sex symbol, a new sex symbol was being created. He was to be a new one and she was to be one. But she balked at it and he didn't and that was fine with me, we just had to put her out of commission, because, ah, I didn't know quite how to work with her any more if she didn't **trust** me that much, so we had the character burned in a fire and put in a hospital, and **that** advanced the plot because we now knew that her beautiful young suitor was to try to be a plastic surgeon, fix her face up. And he had to get the money so he delved into the **underworld**... became a hustler, was addicted to drugs, then had to clean up his act, all to make money and to clean up his act to fix her face. So, thanks to her the plot advanced considerably.

JS: What's your advice for a kid who wants to make movies? Go to film school or do it on your own like you and John Waters did?

GK: All I can say is, this is a kind of strange transition time. If you have money, go ahead. Best of luck, make your movies, and... have a nice time. But if you don't have much money I'm afraid you may want to pursue another medium. There's many things out today, and many things in plastic that are lightweight – I'm talking video cameras, Camcorders. I bought a Sony 8mm video Camcorder three years ago, because I was having difficulty financing pictures. It's outrageous now, the cost. It was always kind of high but you were able to do it. Now I'm afraid it's... they've discontinued stock like crazy, and the cost is preposterous. So... I hate sounding negative, but – if you've got money go right ahead, 'cause it's great to get your dreams and fantasies on the screen. Now of course I'm talking in terms of 16mm movie making. You can work in 8mm, and I'm sure you can still finance **those** things. But every time I go to a Super-8 festival at the school it's like demolition derby. They put it on the projector, the projector's rippin' 'em up, the splices aren't working, the **sound** goes out, and it's truly disaster time. The projectors all seem like meatgrinders. And there is great hurt to the filmmaker. They see their work butchered while the public views it. Butchered on stage. So I'm sure if you have nice equipment, go ahead and do it. But... I think what's happening now, electronically, pay attention because it may save us... and I'm talking about... how can I phrase this? I don't want to sound negative, but negative does enter into the picture because you've got to shoot negative nowadays. They don't want you shooting reversal film any more. You have to shoot negative stock. And that'll cost you I estimate $40 every 2½ minutes. That includes buying the negative, getting the work print and stuff. Forty dollars for... 100 feet. And what's that? 2½ minutes? You'll throw away two thirds. So, with this already you might as well be in the big time, and thinkin' about Dolby sound, and – maybe you better look for a job in commercial movies. Because they're doing very good work in the commercial movies and they got all the big technological advances. I guess what I'm getting down to saying, this is a transition period. Please be careful. And please look around at the electronic media, what's happening in the electronic media. They're doing a hell of a lot. Sorry to sound this way, but don't get into trouble. You've got to get into something that's not gonna be a 40lb. monkey on your back, it's **gargantuan**, whatever's gonna be on your back. So, lighten the burden, see what's around.

JS: Are you "famous" today? Recognized?

GK: I'm not famous. Well, visually once in a while somebody spots me who's seen my movies. Usually they spot me in some place I don't want to be spotted, like in the dirty bookstore. Although that doesn't happen too much, it used to happen in some seedy houses I used to frequent. That was always a bit strange. You didn't know if you should twist your personality back to your, what you were supposed to be instead of what you are now. But... I have a **reputation**, 'cause I've been at this long enough, like 30 years or something, grinding out stuff, so... I guess I have a reputation in certain circles, like movie circles, which would be the festivals... in Athens, Ohio, and places like that. And perhaps also in other "spheres" that widen out, sometimes in Los Angeles. But I can still walk the streets unobserved and no one pays attention, nobody really cares, either. My friend, Virginia, went down to L.A. She said, "In the underground film world it's what you **made** that makes you important, what you made in the past, and in the commercial film world you're only as good as your last picture." See, she had gone to the Art Institute and now she went down to L.A. and she's hardcore junior executive with Bud Yorkin Productions. And she said that, and I think there's wisdom in those words... I think. (She's now laid off from her job, though.)

JS: Do you think **technically** video will ever replace film? Will "high-definition" video soon be perfected and shown in theatres, making celluloid obsolete?

GK: I don't know. I **like** film, I like big pictures, I like going and I like seein' big pictures, and I like Dolby sound. I like going to the movies. But I'm not a real... in other words I don't **battle** for motion pictures any more. I see no reason to put up a boundary, 'cause I like going to the movies and I like watching television. Sometimes what disturbs me is I've found that a lot of people in the filmmaking community were very provincial and bigoted and narrow-minded, and this was in the supposedly avant-garde. And I can understand if you go to school and you were trained in motion pictures, or trained that this is an art form. But if the thing gets so damn expensive that you can't afford it, and you're paying big companies like Kodak tons of money, and you're paying other places tons of money in order to rent machinery so you can edit your sync-sound pictures – when you eventually did try to get sync-sound equipment. And then you go to labs where you're paying high cost to make colour prints of movies that have no colour in them because you couldn't afford the stock and therefore you had to scrounge around and get outdated film stock, and yet you're paying high prices to get a colour print... I think it's like, come on, you should be fed up already. And if this is what's happened with movie-making, the hell with it. There's a lot of things out there in the world. I also like watching television. I was raised on television, and... I enjoy painting and I enjoy writing. I'm not gonna get stuck in one thing and then go down with the ship when the ship appears to be sinking. Or maybe it should be sunk already. Maybe, let it go down, you know. Certainly, putting I didn't know how much money into movies, and trying to make talking pictures also, and you get soundtracks nowadays with reversal prints that you can't hear anything – you made a talkie that's completely unintelligible. After a while you can get completely fed up. So there's a lot being done. See, in 16mm there's no technical innovations being done any more. In other words stock is being cut, you can't get the kind of stock you used to get. The technology is all going into video and they're getting some amazing things. Pictures, in the big commercial pictures, they're doing wonderful things with technology. You know, they got the Dolby sound, THX sound, they're also thinking of changing the shutter speed, make everything more realistic, and stuff, so there's advances in that, but you need a lot of money for that. I'm afraid if you want to be – I'll use the word "personal," or an **artist**, so called, an artist using a medium, if it gets where you can't afford it, I see no sense in going with it. Sorry to say that. Of course you can work in Super-8 and 8mm, and I worked in 8mm and I had a really good time doing it, and also in Super-8. But I also wanted to make pictures with sound. And, things on the market today, where you can get sound and pictures together, electronically, and you can edit in the camera... you can undermine this whole system that's been built up on money, because movies mean money. You hear the magic word "movies", it's money, and costs are escalated. Movies mean you pay a lot of money, you know what I mean? Movies are also big things on a big screen and you get a big reputation at a big festival, and – bigger than life. So, I don't mind shrinking it, pulling the plug and shrinking it down, boob-tube size. Maybe it got a little too big for its own good.

JS: What do you find are the **aesthetic** differences between film and video?

GK: They are different, of course. One is smaller and the light is coming from the back, unless you have like in a movie, "rear screen", you don't get that kind of effect. Also it is small, and it's a **despised** medium, video, 'cause it's related to the TV which is a despised medium. I got attracted to video because it **was** a despised medium, and because film got to be too puffed up financially for me. So, I thought it might be interesting to try something new in a different medium, maybe it would change my approach and subject matter. Because in film I worked in a certain kind of language and it was kind of a short-hand. Film, I tried to squeeze the essence out of each scene because each scene was expensive. I don't really know if that was on my mind while I was making it, but I did know I had a certain language in film. And that was like, do away with extraneous scenes like coming and going out of doors and telling people where you were and who these people were. Just have them go around doing their business, and their business, while you're photographing, should be very high key, at that moment. Emotional peaks. So that became my movie style. And in video, I look at the medium or the tape as not something small and cheap although that's what it is, it's really cheap stock but it creates pictures and it's just as valuable to me as a roll of film, it's just in 8mm, it's smaller. Therefore, there's nothing that's that expendable. See, when you make movies you throw it away. You take strips of film and when you're editing you're eventually sitting on a pile of film, it's all your rotten scenes are at your feet and you're steppin' all over them and you're keepin' just the cream of the crop, which may be out of 100 feet is maybe... 20 feet? You're lucky if it's 25. Sometimes you get three sequences out of a 100-foot roll – maybe it'll go from the floor to the ceiling, and meanwhile you're sitting on a mountain of film, you threw it in the garbage. So the material itself never really mattered to me. It was eventually just put on a projector – you didn't look at the material – and thrown onto a screen and you saw that. And the tape to me is the same way. I look at it as – you know, it's **stock**, and, ah, you slip it into your cassette player and it gets thrown onto a screen, and the screen's a hell of a lot smaller, but, it's fine with me. I will always enjoy going to the movies and I love going to the movies. And I enjoy making movies... I don't know if you can use the word "enjoy". There are many stages to go through, and there is great enjoyment, and great work. Like, I love the work. But... you see, I made a lot of movies and I don't really know how I made them. I don't know how I put all that effort into making them. And I've been sidetracked so often, I've been hit with such terrible vices... that I don't know how I managed to pull off the pictures. But, for some reason, maybe in order to overcome my vices, or, maybe that movie-making **was** a vice on my part, I was able to turn out these things and go through all the steps that you have to go through making a movie. And I would wind up in the editing room and say, "I've been here before," and these were like great markers of my life, this was the "editing room". And it was like, "my life either had significance?" or it was like, "I'm alive again and I'm here in the editing room and this is the final stage." And then you go into the lab, you bring it in, you get your movie and there's the première and people look at it and... of course it's like, how did this horror ever get made? So... making movies is a very peculiar thing. But if I have difficulty... am paying $600 or $700 for a 20-minute movie, you know, that gets shown on a screen and gets pooh-poohed because it's either not "politically correct" or, for some other reason. And I could make something that's even more offensive for $6 or $8, and that's so offensive it would even offend the filmmakers – because I'm workin' in **video**. I would option for the more offensive medium. Makin' movies, see, sometimes you see a very beautiful person. And the first thing that comes to my mind is I want to make a **movie** of that person. I don't say, "I want to make a **video** of that person." I **would** say that if my camera broke, my Bolex, or if I didn't have access to any film. But in the classroom, when I see a beautiful person, I want to make a **film** about that person. 'Cause I like putting gauzes... ah, cheap – it's a black cloth on the lens with a rubber band, and creating these, what look like 1940s movies, or movies of a beautiful Hollywood style, and blowing these people up bigger than life and making them into gods and goddesses. And I think in the movies that's a wonderful way of pushing them on the public, and infusing the public with great objects of desire, and **dreams**, and things of great beauty... living human beings of beauty. So, unfortunately in a lot of underground pictures and, art school films, if you have people in your movies you're considered... not very avant-garde. They're very "anti-human". They're more like... conservationists, probably. Hate the rotten people that pepper the landscape in the park, make all the filth amongst the trees and nature, you know the bears walk around and they're okay, but people stink. So, in a way, I say if I really want to create a star I want to do it via movies. But video's fine too, in creating a, ah, god or goddess. For the masses!

JS: You say you've fallen from favour, or "fallen from grace" with the film people since your recent conversion to video? What sort of flack have you caught in this newly erupting holy war?

GK: Well I know when I started making video, I did in a way disappoint, or **anger** some people, or they thought I was making **crap**. Of course I was beginning making video so I was just trying to develop my style, get a feel for it, and learn how to edit in the camera, and do everything in the camera. And very few people encouraged me. But there were those people who did encourage me, after seeing some work, and told me

Mike, George and Mom

to please go on. Which I would have **anyway**, but, ah, very few people did encourage me. Very few **filmmakers** encouraged me.

JS: Would you ever want to shoot a big-budget 35mm feature movie? What does it strike into your heart, the idea?

GK: What it strikes in my heart? Well... I don't have very good working habits. When I'm working on a movie, I sometimes only work... 4 hours a week? I'm not really very good at **meetings**. I don't like getting together with a bunch of people and we discuss the project. I do that at school 'cause we got sometimes 28 people in the room, that's our cast and crew. And I explain the project and we get feedback, and I like doin' that, but that of course only lasts about 15 minutes, and then we get right down to working and see how we can bring this, ah... subject, or theme on the screen. Or bring these performers that we think are nice looking onto the screen. And then of course the movie develops its own style, when you see what you have and you see the limitations, and you work with the limitations, the style begins to develop. So sometimes meetings mean absolutely nothing to me because when you actually get right down to doin' the damn thing it's a totally different story. So we have a fast meeting and a general idea, and we think we want the picture to look a certain way. And so we do it, but then of course it can detour into other areas. So, I'm afraid of working on a big picture, I really wouldn't want anyone to sink their money into a project of mine and then **lose** the money, so, my working habits are not that good for the big-time, 35mm production.

JS: Do you ever get homesick for Queens (sic)?

GK: Now, getting homesick for the Bronx, I may get sick for the Bronx, like a certain area of it, in other words the **land**, maybe the rolling landscape which is wooded. There are sections like that in the Bronx. Or the look of the clouds, and that certain kind of feel to the air, and that shade of colour that would be "Bronx sky". Ah, that would perhaps make me a little homesick. As for anything else, no, it's all changing, you know what I mean? I don't have that many friends there in the Bronx any more. I have my mom and when I go there I revert back to my old self, I lay around and say, "What's to eat, Mom?" And... I get back my old self and it makes me stronger for a while. But then of course I've always gotta leave home, and I go... into the world that I have to **deal** with 3,000 miles away. In California. And that sort of changes me a bit.

JS: Are you still in touch with any of your early stars? Where today is the ravishing Donna Kerness?

Donna Kerness, 1993

GK: I am still in touch with my old movie stars, like Donna Kerness – she's in Texas. San Antonio, Texas. She had married the guy who she was in the shower with in HOLD ME WHILE I'M NAKED. They had a very tempestuous marriage, with three children, I think. Or two. And, I think when he eventually threw an open container of lye at her, I think that was the end of the marriage. And divorce came, and then she got a job in a... discotheque or cocktail lounge, where she wore scanty clothes and did belly-dancing, for jocks. Texas jocks. Then she was **kidnapped**, I hear, or there was an attempted kidnap, and she was in the papers and stuff – I don't really know the details of the story. But, she got away from that, and now she's settled down. She married a kind of heavy-set man who looks very comfortable and nice, and they're living in San Antonio, Texas. I write her now and then, and get letters from her also.

JS: How do you get along with Mike [Kuchar] today? Where is Mike?

GK: Now I get along with my brother Mike very well. We have our ups and downs, and once in a while it's turbulent, most of it is my fault because my brother is much more even-tempered. I mean he's got his ups and downs, but I'm more... jagged-edged sometimes. He's smoother. And much more leisurely. We get along fine though.

JS: You made a movie in 1986 called ASCENSION OF THE DEMONOIDS.

GK: Yes... that was my only – no, I was funded one other time – but that was my big N.E.A. funded picture. I got $20,000 to make that picture, which is hard to believe. $20,000 is an awful lot of money. I got it in two $10,000 instalments. And I finally opened – I had a bank account, finally. That was able to last. So I put the money in the bank, and then I took it out to buy the film stock, to buy all the props. I went to Woolworths, and I went to boutiques and head-shops and bought all these little items 'cause I wanted this to be a spectacle. I wanted to make miniatures, and also have space ships in it, Big Foot, etc. So, I wanted to do all the special effects by myself, I didn't want to have a crew. So I did them in my... bedroom. With these little dolls and miniatures, and attachments for the lens, to make sparkle effects, etc. I like that movie because I said with $20,000 I want to have a nice time. With my last picture, before that, THE X-PEOPLE, I enjoyed making that also, but I couldn't really get a fine print of it. I spent $700 to get an awful print out. You couldn't hear the sound, it was like there was a waterfall in the background, there was this horrible roaring hiss. And, the colours looked like they put the strip of film onto a mimeograph machine, and just gave it one print and sent it out. It was an atrocious thing and yet it cost $700. So a filmmaker friend of mine complained to the lab, he saw how distressed I was when I viewed it on his projector. And the lab brought me down, fixed me up. They said, "Of course you know we can't do reversal film any more, as you know we can't get good prints." And they re-did the whole thing for me in an inter-negative without charging me the money. Very nice of the lab. Thank you, lab. So after going through that, suffering that, then suddenly getting all this money I said, "Wow, I don't have to worry, I got money now. I won't shoot a negative now because I don't wear gloves when I handle film." I like to actually handle the actual film stock with my fingers. Get a lot of myself onto the film. So I work in reversal, and then with this thing I was able to make an inter-neg from it and not even worry, then make beautiful prints from that, where the colours come out **strong**. I was able to do that since I had the money. And also I said, "I'm gonna have fun on this picture" – I do have fun on the other pictures also – but this one especially, I'm gonna make it like a big unusual treat. Tons of colour. And superimpositions, because I had been working in video already and I couldn't do superimpositions in video – you press the button, you get the image and the sound exactly there, which was... fascinating to me. But this, now, I said, "Wow! With film I can run it through the camera three or four times, so I'm gonna make this my big superimposed movie." So, I turned that into the way it looked in ASCENSION OF THE DEMONOIDS. And then my friend, David Hallinger, who was acting in it – his girlfriend lives in Hawaii. I had the money so he asked me if I ever wanted to come and shoot there, he was going there to visit her, and I said fine, and I went there and I got a **tan**... ate good food, went to the beach, swimming, snorkelling (first time in my life), shot our footage... and, was able to shoot in Kodachrome which was $50 every hundred feet. 2½ minutes was $50 – I think $25 to buy the film and $25 to develop. No worries – I had $20,000.

JS: Has it played in many theatres?

GK: It hasn't played in that many theatres. It's a strange picture in that you have to relax when you see it. It was the last, supposedly the last in my series of UFO films. And I wanted to look away from the subject, so the movie looks away from the subject toward the end. In fact it completely **drops** the subject, basically... goes to Hawaii and examines the scenery, forgetting about what had previously happened or what the picture was about. That was my intention. I wanted to get off the subject. So the movie was constructed in that particular way, and also it was a movie focusing mainly on colours, and... attractive combinations of colours.

JS: ASCENSION OF THE DEMONOIDS dealt with the cults and true believers waiting on signals and visitors from space. Do you find these people of interest?

GK: Now the subject of UFOs, flying saucers, had greatly interested me. All my life I have been interested in them. It's like Halloween – you want to believe in the witches and the ghosts, and you read so much about it and you think it would be nice if it's true. Well, in the mid-'70s I found out that the UFOs are true, they actually **are** UFOs. Whatever they are, I don't know what they are. But there was a big rash of them and they were in California. And in San Francisco, I happened to fall into the mess... or the mystery, by viewing what were UFOs. So they came in different colours, they came in a series that lasted about a year and a half. And also different sizes, shapes... and they have strange mental effects on you. In other words, they're not just phenomena out there that don't seem to relate to you. You can actually communicate with those things, whatever they are. This was a big revelation for me, because if these things actually did exist, what else was around that was not supposed to exist but also was for real... in some fashion. So I got interested in this whole para-psychological... UFO... monster, Bigfoot area of life, etc. And all these weird rumours. So I investigated it and the investigation is still going on. It's been over ten years. The movies I made, there's about 5 or 6 of them, deal with different aspects of the enigma. ASCENSION OF THE DEMONOIDS was to be the big mural, at the end, after going through the other movies and hearing about the rumours, and hearing about strange visitors and strange craft and strange animals, and other things associated with the UFO mystery... you finally get to see everything in a big, wide, broad mural, which focuses in here and there in bright colours on certain aspects of it, and pulls back and you see more. The whole UFO thing is a thing of great interest for me. It still is. I find it very fascinating and potentially explosive. It'll probably change our views when we find out what the hell they really are. It's an important thing, even though it sounds like comic book material. But it's really **weird**. I find the people who are waiting for space visitors, I find them sweet. They're gentle people and I too would like to believe in space people, and – in fact it may be true, maybe that's what they **are**. But they seem to be something else, something much stranger. 'Cause they interact with you in too much of a personal way, I think. I can't see how an extra-terrestrial would have that much interest in you. Plus they seem, while very much advanced, they seem very old-fashioned. And from the stories you hear and from my own experiences it's very personalized and **bizarre**. It's a bizarre, archaic mish-mash that's totally new or baffling.

JS: Do you trace your artistic technique back to the Surrealists? The Russians? The...?

GK: I don't really know. There **is** one thing that greatly affected me. I remember when I was in... elementary school, we had to read the literature, some of it was a little high class literature. Short stories. Then there was one short story, I forget what they called it, but it was **absurd**, an absurd story. And it told in great detail – it was this dramatic story of how this woman came down the staircase, she was dressed for a party, and she had doilies hangin' from her ears on strings. That sort of attracted me very much. The fact that such a revered form of expression like writing, **literature**, was actually composed for this ridiculous kind of tale, or this story that had ridiculous elements in it. This revered medium was used for a totally preposterous tale. Not a preposterous tale – the tale was rather mundane but a preposterous **rendering** of a tale... I think that greatly affected me. Suddenly it seemed all alive. It's the same thing like classic cinema. There's a great classic cinema and I enjoy it very much. It's **heavy**... it has significance, and it's a joy. It has value. But I also like the junk, like you don't know why these people made it, and why did they ever get these actors that are so lousy? and the special effects are hideous. Why was this thing made in a medium that can be so pompous at times? Or so "revered". And I think that's also what attracted me to film.

JS: As for "comedy"... there is a lot of sterile, soulless one-dimensional comedy coming out of Hollywood and the studios today, facile, shallow "light entertainment", "trend movies" that you forget as soon as you walk outside, production line product. Your comedy seems to draw or twist from deeper, often darker urges and experiences like failure, frustration, death, jealousy, ugliness, out-of-control sex, slavish blind belief... Is there a connection?

GK: You know, when I'm making a movie I never think of my movie as a "comedy". It's always a "movie", and even though there's funny things in them – in fact the whole thing may be funny – it was never attempted to be a comedy. Not that it was an unintentional comedy or unintentionally funny, it's just that it's... usually about horrible... feelings, or feelings that either I had gone through, or urges... but it turns out in this way it's transferred into this medium in this style, which is... funny. Or it turns out funny. In fact, when my movies were playing at the Film Forum in New York, a lady that I knew from Los Angeles – she was a friend of David Hallinger – she said let's go to your show, they're having a night of your movies. And I said no, I don't want to go because I don't want to relive all the pain. And I realized my career has all been based on pain. And those movies, even the funniest ones, had this horrible pain behind them. And I know exactly why they were made. And I didn't want to go because I didn't want to relive that. I didn't want to relive the main motivations of those pictures. But then I went and there's people **laughin'**, and I was even laughin', havin' a good time. And I forgot about the pain.

JS: You draw comics, don't you?

GK: But yeah I did draw comics because I met Art Spiegelman and he invited me over to his house 'cause he found out I knew Ken Jacobs. So I went over, I knew he was a comic editor – he asked me to do a comic and I did and I had a comic career that went on for, I don't know, maybe two years. And it's printed, so it's in existence, and, I don't know if you can get copies now but go to comic book stores and look for Short-Order Comics, and they also did one, a big format comic, *Arcade*. I did some work in *Arcade* comics.

JS: What do you cook up when you're at home? Any recipes for readers out there? I hear you once made spaghetti and didn't have any spaghetti sauce so you used mushroom soup. George, is this true?

GK: Now as far as cooking I don't remember ever using mushroom soup with spaghetti. It's probably true though. When I was trying to begin to cook I would make weird mixtures.I have no real recipes. My brother cooks much better than I do, and he stays at home and **cooks**. And sometimes he makes very good stuff, but sometimes he makes awful spicy garbage. Greasy junk. Like eggplant that would wreck your system. He's had guests over and the pain evidently registers on their faces just before they have to go to the bathroom. Sometimes they're rather distinguished or continental people and they eat his food and then splatter up our bowl. They have to run to the toilet and really let loose, so that it splatters on the rim of the bowl. So his meals are not always that good either.

JS: Didn't you once do an interview with Al Goldstein of *Screw* magazine?

GK: I don't think I ever **did** do an interview with Al Goldstein of *Screw* magazine. I did used to **buy** *Screw* magazine, I used to read it for the ads in the back, sometimes I used

to answer the sex ads in the back. This was in my youth. And I met... strange people.

JS: You say the British Film Institute loved your *Weather Diary 2* video, that only a handful of people have ever seen yet. What's it like and why do you think they liked it?

GK: Yeah, I sent the BFI my *Weather Diary 2*. They like it very much. They liked it better than ASCENSION OF THE DEMONOIDS, which I sent them a video copy of. I think if they had seen ASCENSION OF THE DEMONOIDS on the big screen they would have thought differently, because **physically** it's quite an overwhelming picture. But they liked very much the Americana in *Weather Diary 2*, which is a **lonely** work. With *Weather Diary 1* I went out more and I interacted with the people around the motel. And I was a little more friendly, the **dogs** I met were friendlier. And in *Weather Diary 2* it was me alone in the room trying to keep things going... when nothing was happening. It does... get the feeling of this place here, this motel in Oklahoma. I think they liked the Americana part of it and also it was kind of a tribute to Jim and Tammy Bakker – I used to watch them on cable television here in the motel room, and... I liked them because they were real "show biz" people, and made-up, and they were fun to watch. So this was a little tribute to them after their fall. Their fall was fun to watch, and I think it made for good television. Good news headlines also.

JS: Give your instant response to these words:

GK: *Sex:* Well... sex is a fun thing, it's an escape thing. It's not really fun, but it's fun to think about. And it's fun to try to use it as an escape. *Death:* I don't really know what death would be like, and it'll probably happen soon enough, or, maybe too soon, and I don't want to think about it... I do think about it, though. And I do hope that I die in a – not in a circumstance that... I would rather not be dead in. *Douglas Sirk:*

Douglas Sirk was a big inspiration for me. I used to go see his movies and they were movies made by adults who seemed to know what they were doing. Douglas Sirk and his cinematographer and the script writers and actors were like adults working in a beautiful form: the Hollywood motion picture. And the narrative kind of Hollywood approach, and they were making beautiful works. So, Douglas Sirk was a big inspiration for me. In fact, I could've met him one time – he was in the San Francisco area and my friends were going to lunch with him and they asked me if I would like to come and I said sure, but that night I was workin' on one of our class movies, a real schlocky class production, and I was up all night and I didn't get finished until eleven o'clock, and then I didn't go to the lunch because I would've been too bleary eyed. It really didn't matter probably because Douglas Sirk at that time I think was losing his vision. But they apologized from me to him, and he said, "Movies are more important than lunch." *Pornography:* I used to enjoy going to pornography. I enjoyed going to pornography when it was hard to get – to see pornography. But when it's easily available you don't feel the urge so much to go and see it. That's why I think pornography should always be around, so that you don't feel starved. I think an element of pornography is boredom. 'Cause boredom will help you conjure up... sexual feelings? Or, you're so bored you can only think of sex to try to stimulate yourself. So I think boredom is a part of pornography, in film anyway. *Freak Shows:* I haven't gone to any freak shows, but come into my neighbourhood in the Mission District in San Francisco – you don't have to pay money to see a freak show. *The U.S. Naval presence in the Antarctic:* **somebody's** got to be there, I suppose. *The death of a butterfly:* I haven't seen a butterfly die in a long time. **Moths** I've seen die. So... *Pizza:* I love pizza, and I hear it's good for you. So after I work out I try to keep my body in shape in case I get called on to do any nude scenes. After a workout I go get a pizza 'cause I hear that it builds your body up. *The National Debt:* I... don't know what that is. *Sharks:* I saw last night on the TV JAWS 2, and it was very suspenseful. They took their time trying to make the characters seem like real people. So when that big shark, which looked real most of the time, came after them there was a lot of suspense. *A vicious hail storm:* There was a vicious hail storm in the next county here. I took video pictures of the thunderheads blossoming. The hail was as big as softballs in Oklahoma City. And it came in on 80 m.p.h. winds and stripped the leaves off the trees. Somebody took a video of it, it was quite impressive. It looked like a giant, noisy blizzard. *Mother:* My mother's getting better. She went to the hospital, she had her pancreas taken out and then they also accidentally threw her teeth out. But now they got 'em back in her mouth, they made a new pair. *Angels:* Angels probably do exist but they may not dress the way they do in the religious literature. I think they probably wear suits, and, ah, they do walk around, and, they're interchangeable with demons. I think it depends on... I don't know what changes 'em into a demon, but I think that angels change... *Beautiful music:* I don't know... I like all kinds of music, and the thing is... I used to buy these records, joke records. They used to be symphonies that were off key, and they'd play classical pieces of music. But after awhile I would get into the record and I would accept it that that was the way the pieces of music were. The way they were composed, the way they were **supposed** to sound. So I stopped buying those records. *Beautiful dreams:* I **have** beautiful dreams, I used to remember them, I used to keep a dream diary. They were rather interesting dreams – some of them used to come true. Then I used to train myself to stop and actually try to see what exactly was in the dream, and there would be like this frozen silence. As you look around the room, and it would seem like a real place. I was aware of myself lookin' around the room and gazing at the furniture, and the lights. But then I stopped, because I was paying too much attention to my dream world, and I think the real world was slipping away.

JS: Last question: Quickly sum up your philosophy of life, art, creation, eternity...

GK: I don't know if I have a philosophy, I just want to get **through** it. In other words, I would like to get through it and do what I'm supposed to do. So every night I pray that... I do what I'm supposed to be doing, because I don't want to waste the time, or not do what I'm supposed to be doing. So I do pray that I am going ahead on the road that I'm supposed to be. What will happen with eternity, I don't know. I read books about weird things, other planes of existence... people that died and came back. And I have friends that died and then came back, and they said it was pretty nice, dying. Seemed like a nice place, so, ah... since I have first-hand information of people that did die already, I don't know if I should worry about it that much. The end.

Part II: What follows is a monologue George taped in January 1989 in the comfort of his own apartment. George talks about past film and video productions, the pidgin-English-speaking stars he has propelled to underground stardom and his constant battles with bottom-of-the-barrel budgets.

GEORGE KUCHAR: I'll talk about a **new** film... we're workin' on a picture now – in fact it's all **finished**... the class ended three weeks ago and we got out the remaining footage. It takes two weeks to develop – we send the black-and-white to Los Angeles, the only place that develops the black-and-white reversal. I wanted this movie to be like *Loveboat*. It's a *Loveboat*, only it's, ah, bound for disaster. The ship is full of disturbed characters. And they have romantic problems, and other things – addictions and stuff. And the ship goes down but there are survivors, three particularly nice looking survivors, two men and a girl. And they make it to an island. We shot this picture in Studio Eight, it's an all-indoor picture, but occasionally they went on location. I sent them out to the Fisherman's Wharf, where they shot a big ocean liner. And then they went on their own to the beach, they found a deserted beach and they were washed up on the beach, and they did some nice scenes. One girl in it, she particularly liked this guy and she asked if I would write in a kissing scene. I said I didn't blame her for liking him, he is really nice looking – he had beautiful long hair. So I wrote them in a big kissing scene and we photographed that, she had a wonderful time with him – she wound up on the beach with him and they did like a FROM HERE TO ETERNITY scene with the sea rushing over them... and they were rolling and kissing. I think the water was **frigid** but they managed to come back looking like they had gone away for a **week** to a vacation paradise – they came in all rosy-cheeked with so much colour and life in 'em. It was wonderful to see the young people **beaming** like that.

We had our problems with that picture... we shot in colour and sometimes the colour was **daylight** colour film, but we were shooting indoors – I didn't want to go outdoors and they didn't have any blue filters to put on the lens to make the colour look better so we tried putting blue gels on the lights, but they weren't the proper temperature to make it look good so the film had a kind of orange tint to it. I was kind of depressed about one roll, and I saw one of the students, she made a film and she **bleached** her film – she brings in a jar of bleach, she puts it in a dish and she throws her film in there. So I said, "Listen, you think you can do anything with this footage? I'm unhappy with the colour." So I gave it to her, and she poured her bleach on a plate, and she put the film in there and it was in there two hours. Then she took a look at it and said, "It's not **unrolled** good enough, it hasn't done much," so she made the film looser on the roll, threw it in for another half an hour, and then she took it out and said, "Looks better – the colours are better now; you got flashes of lavender coming in..." and other types of colours. So I thanked her, and I have the film in a trash bag. It smells so horrible, I don't know – it's not a bleach smell, it's something else mixed in with the emulsion or something and it's a horrible stink. So I put the whole film in a trash bag. It's just a pile of film. And, um, I'm gonna unwind it, clean it... I think we **saved** that sequence. Another time we went outside and we were shooting with 4-X high speed black-and-white reversal, I think 400 ASA, and we went outside and it was a bright sunlight out there, on white concrete. We couldn't cut down the aperture enough, and we had no... no way of getting around it so we put sunglasses on the lens. In other words, it's supposed to be a vacation cruise so we actually stuck sunglasses, so you could see the two lenses of the sunglasses and we positioned each actor so that one would be in the right lens and the other would be in the left, and they did their scene, and everything else around them is bleached, but you can see **them** well through the glasses.

Desperate Visions 1: Camp America

This is a vehicle for a guy in the class named Peter. He was in another film that we did a year ago. Peter Van Lengen is his name, he's part Mexican and part somethin' else... or at least was born in Mexico City. Anyway he was in a previous film we did about a Sasquatch and he played a doctor who was trying to operate on a ballerina that he kidnapped and intermingle her with a Sasquatch or something to make some sort of hybrid. But it didn't work out, as the character fell in love with her, and eventually it turned out to be like a Romeo and Juliet tragedy. But, he was always able to read his lines in a very straightforward, serious, underplayed manner which I found charming. I realized that he had a future in these types of movies. So I wrote him a real big part as the captain of this Loveboat, Captain Steele. And I tried to give him, also, a more romantic overtone to his characterization. Hopefully this will put him back on the screen in one of our productions. One of our... "grade Z" productions, maybe? The budget was $1,000 for this one. Looks like it'll be a half-hour long, black-and-white, **and** colour. I felt like shootin' a lot of black-and-white and then every once in a while we had colour film so we had to shoot colour, so we'd just shoot colour sequences. Evidently these colour sequences will just burst on, with no explanation. But... what does it matter? We're just scrapin' the bottom of the barrel as far as stocks are concerned. But we've had **luck** with this picture, and nothing has been terribly **ruined**. Except one scene we got out. I saw a note from the lab, and also an extra roll of film came – four hundred new feet of film! And we had sent them two hundred feet. And they gave us four hundred new feet of film and a note, and the note said that they were sorry they had ruined our two hundred feet! Something was wrong with the chemicals or something. And I said, "Oh God, they **ruined** it?!" But I put it on the projector and there was an image on there, but they actually **heightened** it. They heightened the film by – it was supposed to be a grubby scene that took place in the boiler room of the ocean liner and they put all these blotches on it, so it actually intensified the sequence, so not only did they make the sequence better but they gave us four hundred extra feet. Which I was very grateful for. So we had luck on this picture.

One of the guys in the class just made a suggestion that one of our leading ladies, named Amy, should do a wet T-shirt scene. So of course I approached her – I said, "Amy, how about your wet T-shirt scene next week?!" And she said, "No way! No way am I gonna do a wet T-shirt scene!" So, I tried to coax her, and every session she'd come in with a little tighter blouse on. And I thought maybe she was warmin' up for it. And then it was time and I said, "Amy, it's time for the scene 'Wet T-shirt'" and she said okay, and so she had on her T-shirt, and I felt in the back and she had a brassiere on, 'cause I felt the buckle of the brassiere. I said, "Amy... ah, you gotta take the brassiere off." And she said, "Oh no! No way! No way I'm takin' the brassiere off!" But I said, "Look, if you do that, if you take the brassiere off and do the wet T-shirt scene, I'll do a **wet underpants** scene." And she still said no, you do your wet underpants scene, I'm not gonna do it. So... she wore this kind of brassiere, it wasn't like a real brassiere, it was like stretched... percentage-of-latex-and-something-else kind of material, and so when you did squirt water on it you could see the formation of the breast. And she had to do an exercise sequence 'cause she played a character similar to the one... Julie? on the Loveboat? She conducts exercises, she's the cruise director of activities. So she did her exercises. Actually the sequence turned out really well. And then she said, "Alright, now you gotta do your wet underpants scene." I said, "No, no, 'cause you cheated – you wore that bra." So this picture's gonna be edited pretty soon. It's a lot of footage – I had to lug it from the school, it weighs a ton. It's already in the house.

The picture we did two semesters ago, the one before SUMMER OF NO RETURN, was this movie called INSANITORIUM. That was done all with outdated film.

All the colours are **mauve**, and green. Not too much colour in that thing. We got one print out of it and then made a video copy. And something interesting happened in the video copy; the video transferring machine couldn't quite read the tones of the picture because they were so faded and so the thing turned out looking **solarized**. It had trouble reading the quality of colour and the exposure, 'cause the picture was also underexposed. So some scenes have this electric colour in them, surrounded by this drab, um... tonality. So it looks more science fiction-like in the video copy. We had problems with that thing, too. I wanted the president's [the president of the Art Institute] secretary to play a role as a woman who runs this hospital-type facility that has the Sasquatch in it, and they're doing all these occult and scientific experiments in there. So I asked her to come about two o'clock, after her lunch period, and I waited and the woman didn't come. She's a nice woman – she does extra work, she's in her late fifties? Maybe. She looks very good, though, she's got red hair... she used to do extra work for movies that came to town. In fact, she was an extra in a Billy Wilder movie, and she said he was very nice to work with. Anyway, I had to do this scene and I couldn't just wait around, so I had Peter – who was doing the scene with her – act with a stand-in. Unfortunately the stand-in was much shorter than the president's secretary and had the wrong hair style... and was also in all the wrong positions. But, ah – 'cause when the secretary, Harriet, came in, we just shot her in extreme close-ups so you couldn't tell where the hell she was, and we just put the script in front of her and she just rattled off the lines. In a way, I guess she was a little humiliated, some of the dialogue was a bit on the **harsh** side. But she was a trooper, she went through it, and in fact the rough parts made her eyes water! And so there was more dramatic tension in the scene. Anyway, you see this big face, and then you cut away to the medium shot and you see this little midget – he's talkin' to this little midget – and they're all in these weird positions. Her head's supposed to be down on the table, and... it's obvious it's a cut-away. But the effect is – the overall effect is kind of interesting. So, I was very happy also with that motion picture, which is thirty minutes long.

I don't know who will ever **see** these pictures. I don't know, I occasionally bring 'em around. There's only one print of each 'cause we can't afford the prints. They cost... almost the whole budget just to print the thing. So we always try to have a benefit show; I show my movies and we invite the public. And try to scrape up money so that we can print the movie... in some form. Of course we've been making these things over the years – many, many years, and so it has a big changing cast, with every once in a while one person coming into prominence over several pictures 'cause they happen to take my class again. And so we do have certain **stars** in those pictures. They go way back... and sometimes when there's a visiting artist at school we incorporate them into the picture. Besides Rosa Von Praunheim, who was in one of the movies, Joyce Wieland, who is a Canadian artist – she does paintings, quilts, movies, she does a bunch of things, and she used to be married to Mike Snow. She's in one of the pictures. In fact she has a major role, she's the person who ties the whole picture together, she plays a Mother Superior. Sort of a twisted hellbent Mother Superior. We took advice from Marlon Brando – we heard that when he does his lines, they're actually pasted on his co-star's face. So we just wrote the script on a piece of paper and pasted it onto our regular star, Joana Zegri, who was the queen of these movies for several years. And, just positioned her so you see the back of her head and Joyce just looked her in the face and just read off from the piece of paper that was blockin' her face. She was quite good in the part. Now, her ex-husband, Mike Snow, was in one picture that had to do with a female... sex... ah... what the hell do you call them? A Dr. Ruth. Although, this was before Dr. Ruth came into prominence. And this was about a sex therapist who instead of getting her information from books, went out on location in back alleys and other places where things were happening and got first-hand experience in sex matters! Mike Snow was in that, he played some musical instruments in the beginning of that picture. And the students liked it very much because he had a little combo, he made a little combo with the students and they played jazz and stuff.

Then we had, in a much earlier picture, Cary Medoway. He went down to Hollywood and made a picture called THE HEAVENLY KID. Which I think bombed. Anyway, he was in one of our movies, he played a... it was an Egyptian – that's what he played. But he had a turban, with a feather in it. And he was on a ship transporting a mummy to Egypt and fell in love with this girl, and the gods were angry; the mummy comes to life. It was a rockbottom picture. The actual really bottom-of-the-barrel type production, where we only had two hundred dollars to make the 16mm film. Or two hundred and fifty dollars. Ridiculous price for the budget. I didn't want to make any big elaborate sets 'cause we had a picture done before that had big sets up. So, we made the scenes take place at night on the deck of a ship, and in the dark little cabins below. So it was just a black background. Somebody had a dixie cup and was throwin' water across the actors, so you'd see this water goin' by so you'd have the feeling they were on a ship. It was actually very successful, the picture, somehow it struck a chord and became a rather entertaining and successful picture. By successful I mean people that looked at it enjoyed it. Another person that worked on that movie was Meno Meyjes who later went on to work with Spielberg and who had written the screenplay for THE COLOUR PURPLE. He was from Holland. In fact, his friend who was also from Holland, this rather statuesque girl, became my agent in Europe. Babe Van Loo. She was queen of those class productions for many, many years, because of her strange accent. Not only did she have a Dutch accent but she had a lisp. I **think** it was a lisp. People said she talked a little like Elmer Fudd. And so all of her lines were charged with this kind of strangeness. It was a great joy to write dialogue for her. Now in those days James Broughton was teaching at the school, and, always complainin' – he had a screenwriting course and he was complainin' that the class was full of foreigners and they could barely talk English, much less write it. And I was saying, "Well, send them to me!" because I used to love these accents – they gave the picture a continental flavour. They had strange pronunciations of words and they made the screenplay come alive in a weird way. So... I always encouraged the foreigners to please be in our pictures.

In fact, many, many years ago I was workin' on a picture, PORTRAIT OF RAMONA, my last movie in New York. And at that time my brother was friends with this deaf guy. He could speak fairly well, but he knew this other guy who was also deaf, I think from birth, and he learned how to talk just by watchin' the mouths open, or somehow. And so listening to him speak was the most amazing thing, you really couldn't understand it, but it was an interesting combination of sounds. And I wanted him to **narrate** that movie, PORTRAIT OF RAMONA, but... some of my friends looked at me with **shock**, like, "how could you **do** such a thing!" But I actually thought it would be really interesting to hear his voice on the soundtrack. And it didn't matter if you understood it or not. Because in our latest class picture I thought of narrating it in German. Because I don't know how I'm going to put it together. I think it's going to make... some sort of sense. In fact, I know it will, it's a series of big scenes on a boat. But I thought that if they heard a narrator and if it was speaking in German, they would know that the thing is somehow being explained, even though they don't understand it, and so they'd **accept** the visual format of the film better. Even if they didn't understand the language that was trying to explain the plot.

Now a couple of years back we worked on another film, also, based on the life of Lupe Velez, the actress who went to Hollywood, made several films, then fell

Shooting *Evangelust*

in love with Tarzan. Then eventually committed suicide. We had a big **Icelandic** girl playing Lupe and she was always getting annoyed at me 'cause she thought there were too many love scenes in the picture. I don't know **why** she would get annoyed. I would be **happy** if I was in scenes like that. Usually. So she was getting annoyed so she would refuse to do scenes and we had to get stand-ins, and the only ones who didn't complain about doin' those scenes were other guys. And so they would do her scenes, and eventually she didn't want to do scenes so we just had three different guys playing her, these parts. And they did all her raunchy scenes... with each other... [voice trails off] other guys...

Sometimes I do those student productions in video. One time the budget, a few years back, was cut to three hundred dollars. The school was having financial troubles. And I didn't want to start a movie with that, I didn't want to be three months with the students on three hundred dollars, not with the prices that were out in those days, you know. This wasn't that long ago. So I decided to do a video, do a Video-8. The school had a video camera. And it was looked upon as a great shame: here he was, the final humiliation, degraded to using video, workin' on the student productions. We had about twelve students. Most of 'em were cranky, but there were a few good ones, and I decided since video was kind of a soap-opera medium, we'd make a soap opera about a hospital. And we called it *Calling Doctor Petrov*. I decided to incorporate film in it, by, we sent a crew out to shoot exteriors. When we had that developed we brought it in and projected it on the walls, and had the actors standin' front of it. Then we also took black leader and scratched in it – like there was a lightning storm? – so we had a slide projector projecting a cloud background and then a movie projector projecting scratches on black leader that were in the shape of lightning. Then there was another projector with patterns going on the actors. And so we had this like multi-media show going on, and we were taping in 8mm video. And so, *Calling Doctor Petrov* is full of special effects of that nature. Nothing was post-production, everything was right there in the studio, on the set. I actually thought it was kind of a good production. Some of them were kind of mad, I guess, that we were shootin' in video. But there were some good students, and the happy people were the people that I brought in from the outside world... bring in to do scenes, and they were sort of excited about the whole project. We finished it, played it and it went over like... kind of dead. But then it caught on a year later, there was great interest in it. And it went to Germany, some guy in Berlin. He took it over. His name is Alf Bold. He was crazy about it, so... It has a **life** now, *Calling Doctor Petrov*.

We did another one, which was a big dense soap opera, based on the Jim and Tammy·Bakker scandal. It was about the Christian network, and it was very **foul**... I wanted everything foul in it, the language, it's got a lot of four-letter words. And a lot of foul visual material hits the screen. That was an interesting project because it was a crowded class. I went in there and it looked like thirty people. Thirty loud people. And I really didn't want to have a full class because I was warned by my chairwoman that by taking in more people I was depriving some of the other people of students. And so I felt guilty and stuff like that. But then when I saw that there were these loud people in the class I didn't want to be alone with them. So I decided it would be better if I **buffer** the whole class with just a ton of people. So whoever came up and asked to be in it, I said, "Certainly you can be in it." And I wrote them a note and they went to the registrar and got into the class. And so we have a big production with a lot of people. And they were having fun being foul. They really got into it and had a great time. It's called *Evangelust*. It's never premièred, I don't know why. I show it occasionally. Occasionally I go to a different school and make a production there.

This past summer I went to the University of Wisconsin in Milwaukee, and was there for a month to teach video. And I brought along my Sony 8mm Camcorder, and they had half-inch machines there and we made a production called *The Motivation Of The Carcassoids*. It's about a doctor who has a cellulite practise, he sucks cellulite from the bodies of his patients. And it got out of hand it got kind of murderous. There were some errors and they had to dispose of the body, and then it just accumulated, the atrocities accumulated. And the doctor had a bad drug problem. There was a lot of subplot involved in it. I also went to Cal. Arts and made a production about an associate professor at an art school who has a skeleton in his closet. It's a living skeleton, because he's still carrying on the way... he shouldn't be. We also made this big soap opera called *The Hurt That Fades*. I wanted a very Hollywood production. I credited a fake scriptwriter by-line of Edna Levinsky that wrote *The Hurt That Fades*, 'cause I had a feeling that I had over-written the thing and the dialogue was much too florid. And I thought let's blame somebody called Edna Levinsky for that. And I also went under an alias for that 'cause I had an assistant called Scott Shelley so it became "Directed by George Scott", which was me and my assistant.

1) REFLECTIONS ON LIGHTING (Excerpt)

When I was assigned to light a pornography film, the first thing I did was to blast their buttocks with a high intensity light source as there is not much to concentrate on when you are up close to an exposed rear-end and consequently you search its meagre features for protruding hairs or skin eruptions. This does not always inspire eroticism and so I made sure that the buttocks were over-exposed... technically speaking. As we all progressed on this pornography film I noticed that the general level of acting was much higher when the producer came onto the set, early in the morning, with a bag of donuts for the cast and crew that was fresh and direct from a bakery. When it was packaged crap off a grocery shelf the morale dropped. Drooping is the bane of pornography pictures. The main actress on the set had delicate features and gentle eyes until I got my hands on them (I was also the film's make-up and hair stylist – going under the pseudonym of Mr. Dominic). Mr. Dominic is sick... recreating for the motion picture screen the women he viewed in his youth; tremendous creations of endless fascination. Women garbed in fabric coats of dreary tone who straddled the vacant lots of the Bronx, urinating on a kaleidoscope of broken beer bottles. Females who descended between the stone columns of edifices constructed to house the denizens of a naked city revelling in its own shame. Descending the steps with their cheeks all rouged in oval splendour, the circular patterns in the poodle fur shawls that draped their shoulders glistening all black and dead in the sun. Ladies who watched television in the morning with hideous, shrunken men articulating from the screen in a desperate attempt to sell cardboard eyebrow stencils to the frustrated and the frumpy. Mr. Dominic sick? Perhaps he is just temporarily regurgitating the visions of his youth; seeing in the black rainbows that arc above the eyes of that lost race an archway to the magical kingdom of Maybelline and its colourful treasures. Maybe that can explain the splash of candy-apple red that spills way beyond the contours of lip to lap at chin and nostril alike. And what of the men of that bygone era? The deep, dark, wet mystery of their armpits and the tiny sparks of light that flashed on grease-coated hair? Men who swam nude in city rivers, the water not yet tainted enough to blotch the whiteness of temperate zone flesh. Flesh that hung over trousers in an unabashed display of delicatessen living. Fingers all yellow and brown with the smell of nicotine and that clamping vise of white enamelled teeth... chomping, chewing... on toothpicks and pierced earlobes; the drab monochromatic shades of their uniforms contrasting sharply with the lightning-white flash of bleached underwear. How could such a creature of filthy promises possess such white underwear?

2) DEVELOPING AN AESTHETIC

You must acquire a finely tuned appreciation of cinema. Don't look at the classics all the time. The classics will be with us till the moon turns blue. Seek out, rather, the neglected works that reveal the world of movies in a bright and blistering light. I write "world of movies" and not "world" period because if you wish to see the world revealed – go out and look at it! Why anyone would spend time in a dark theatre searching for reality up on that screen is beyond me, we should go there to forget about reality. People say that black-and-white movies are more realistic than colour ones simply because black-and-white is not realistic at all and therefore what they are really saying is that they want fantasy disguised as realism by sucking the colour out of it. People suck: they suck in beverages with straws while watching films, suck in their breath when the action gets hot and heavy, suck in their tummies to resemble Charlton Heston, etc. Well, all that sucked in air has to come out sometime but our society frowns on its natural expulsion in theatre lobbies and that's why you see all those folks exiting cinemas with intense, facial gymnastics, they are trying to hold back ninety minutes worth of sucked in air! Be free to release that air along with your time and money when you go to a movie. Realize that what is seen on the screen is a phoney rendition of real life with glamorous dieters playing saints and sinners. Realism only comes to the screen when the film jams in the projector and the image begins to bubble. An instinctual fear of the dark manifests when the projection light fails... heightened by the little, furry things with long tails that scamper beneath the seats. The electrical nature of sex becomes apparent as the hair on your neck bristles when that pervert to your left makes knee contact. In these moments of truth, cinema reveals her face of realism. But, she is a two-faced creature, the other countenance being a rainbow palette of dyed coiffures, pancake make-up and pancake bloated guts crammed into costumes designed by cock-eyed midgets. Superstars who beat their children with wire coat hangers and then peddle soft drinks potent enough to rot their dentures. Aging women taking endless enemas so as not to wind up in horror films. Virile he-men doomed to an excruciating regimen of exercises to keep their sodomized posteriors picture-perfect. EST trained actresses showing the world what it is like to be liberated and free of cellulite. Alcoholic celebrities who barf up their past in book form so that all can marvel at the hideous mess that has been cleaned up by a Christian re-birth. Harpies with herpes who rip apart, in print, plump fornicators whose every performance they slander with typeset Ju-Ju curses. Innocent children who sing and dance down the yellow brick road to drug addiction and toxic box office poisoning. This is the other face of cinema... the side that sells tabloids and makes legends, a trillion dollar heritage of human refuse devoured by a cyclopean eye designed to entertain, to titillate with tit, to teach. **The** art form of the 20th century.

3) SCHOOLING
Going to elementary school in the Bronx was a series of humiliations which featured Wagnerian women in an endless chorus of, "keep your mouth shut," "where's your homework," and "spit that gum out." The male teachers were much shorter than the females and whatever masculine apparatus they possessed was well concealed amid the folds of oversized trousers. After school my twin brother and I would escape to the local cinema, fleeing from our classmates: urban urchins who belched up egg creams and clouds of nicotine. In the safety of the theatre we'd sit through hour upon hour of Indian squaws being eaten alive by fire ants, debauched pagans coughing up blood as the temples of God crashed down on their intestines, naked monstrosities made from rubber that lumbered out of radiation poisoned waters to claw the flesh off women who had just lost their virginity. When three hours were up we would leave the theatre refreshed and elated, having seen a world moulded by adults, a world we would eventually mature into. At home, supper simmered on the stove, smoking, bubbling and making plopping sounds as blisters of nutritious gruel burst just like the volcanic lava in those motion pictures. Oh how I wanted to grow up real fast and be one of the adults who sacrificed half naked natives to Krakatoa or dripped hot wax on a nude body that resembled Marie Antoinette. Not only were these pictures teaching me about geology and geography, but they were an introduction to giants of history and the joy of creative sculpture. Religious instruction was supplied once a week by the nuns of a Catholic complex who took students from the city school system into their classrooms every Tuesday afternoon. I loved it, being taught by a pale figure shrouded in black who spoke of life after death and told us not to use purple ink in our ballpoint pens as it was the colour of the devil. This was information, that to me at least, seemed of vital importance. Every Sunday morning I went to mass and inhaled the pollution of our lord as frankincense poured forth from swinging urns to soften and mute the tortured features of crucified plaster and bleeding replicas of unviolated

women. Eventually I had to leave the church as one warm, lonely afternoon I found myself kneeling in a pew praying for wild, disgusting sex. I was a teenager with a heavy inclination to explore my own groin and the emissions threatened to put out the fire in the sacred heart of our Lord. I looked around me at the elderly ladies scattered here and there throughout the shadowed house of God and knew that they at least were at peace because they didn't possess a big piece that defiantly poked holes in Christian dogma, demanding lubricated short cuts to the Kingdom of Heaven. I fled from the place of holiness that warm, lonely afternoon and God answered my prayer; a young, suffering Christian was granted wild, disgusting sex. Praise be the Lord!

4) EARLY ROLE MODELS

As a youth I yearned to emulate the heroes and heroines of my particular space-time continuum. It wasn't an easy thing to do in those days as television was in black-and-white and the role models exhibited lacked the neon brilliance of today's electronic idols. There was a noon-time show experimenting in an early colour process which featured Yma Sumac but nobody emulated her unless they feared bombardment by cosmic radiation, hoping that all those metal trinkets would repel the deadly rays. Sometimes I found myself wishing that I was like one of the sons on the Ozzie and Harriet TV program, a beefy boy who slept in pyjamas and went through life with half closed eyelids. My eyes were kind of stunted and shrunken behind eye-glasses and I couldn't afford to shrink them any more. As for pyjamas, I got fed up wearing clothing twenty-four hours a day – my body having rebelled in a violent display of red and white boils. As for my parents, well: My mother was a witch (literally) hiding in closets from booming thunderstorms having once seen the devil (in the form of a rat) run into a haystack that a youth had sought as shelter from a coming tempest. Immediately after the devil-rat entered, the haystack was hit by lightning and the boy incinerated. The horror of that spectacle has survived the decades... the sound of any grumbling cumulo-nimbus sending her into a panic. My dad, now deceased, was a virile, sex-crazed truck driver who slept all day semi-nude. He lusted after booze, bosoms and bazookas (having served in the second world war). I, as their son, George, was a gangling youth whose hobbies and mannerisms hinted at a future of dark perversions and grotesque obsessions. They fought (alas, in vain) to reroute my path through life but soon realized that their dilemma was already quite well documented in the *Frankenstein* sagas that played on the television every weekend. Out of wedlock they had created a monster – a two-headed one as I'm a twin – and even the holy sanctity of marriage could not undo the horror they unleashed in the tri-state, metropolitan area.

My twin brother, Mike, matured more rapidly than I and he left me festering in a subjective tar pit of self-abuse and too much chocolate-mocha cake. He got his own apartment and cultivated a swinging life style. I was swinging at my parent's house... on the end of a rope which consisted of entwined strands of guilt, gluttony and gargantuan guts. My best friend in those days was a young Jewish man who was obsessed with cannibalism and bodily mutilations. I'd walk over to his house to view artificial, decapitated limbs and grimacing skulls still in possession of their eyeballs. His mother would make us hot Ovaltine and only once did she object to her son's morbid interests – this occurred during a period of horrific murders perpetrated by someone the press had labelled "the torso killer". The fiend left his victims without arms, legs, or heads. One night she looked out the window and saw her son returning from a walk with a grisly bundle – he had found a battered mannikin torso lying in a vacant lot and was bringing it home as a prop for his 8mm productions. His mom realized the potential for neighbourhood vigilante activity if anyone else spotted him entering the house with this thing and so my friend was appropriately chastised in heated Yiddish.

My other friend in the Bronx worked for the Post Office and collected Barbra Streisand records. His sister became a dope addict and his dog died of rectal cancer because his family hated to take the pooch out for a poop. This friend became prematurely bald and then bought a wig that looked like it was made from the hair on the legs of a horse fly. With that thing on his head he became so horrible to look at that I stopped coming over to the house to see him. I hardly ever met anyone in the Bronx streets who wanted to be my friend. If someone did approach it was either to beat me up or else hand out Jehovah's Witness literature.

My main activity on Friday or Saturday nights was searching for new churches with confessionals that had not yet reverberated with the sounds of my sins. At that time the local churches in the archdiocese had their clergy completely glutted with my whispered transgressions to the holy rule. Eventually I took a subway to another borough in search of virgin ears to singe so that the priests wouldn't feel they were victims of *déjà vu*. Before I had gone through all five boroughs of that monster metropolis my faith crumbled into dust and cigarette ashes... sparing me all that extra subway fare.

Forgive me, dear reader, I have painted a grim picture of my early years in the big apple. There were blinding flashes of great happiness amid the gloom and doom. Unfortunately I was sometimes the only one who thought so as guests who came to see where I lived made harsh, biting remarks, commenting on how the borough of the Bronx resembled a mixture of Miami Beach and Nazi Germany. Of course, their insights were quite true, but this was my home and home is where the heart is. My own heart beat fast at the rolling surface of the land which dipped beneath the surface of Harlem River and then rose in a majestic mound before submerging more extensively under the Hudson where it met the wall of solidified lava known as the New Jersey Palisades. To the east the great Atlantic Ocean spawned storms that roared up the coast causing the window pane in my living room to bulge inward with alarming convexity while outside the metal sheeting on the apartment building was being ripped off and whipped through rainsoaked streets like giant razor blades. Nature swirled past we people of the Bronx as we sat, lay, or squatted in our dwelling units – making whoopee or chocolate chip cookies – living, learning, and lumping it. Making films was my life and the people who befriended me became the leading ladies and men who populated my productions.

In order to finance these motion pictures I had to enter the Manhattan job market. It was thrilling to ride the jam-packed subway trains to work in the morning; discreet perverts would reach out for some sort of stabilizing support so as not to lurch over and fall in the rocking cars and they'd grab onto your private appendages. Full--figured senoritas would mash you against metal partitions using flesh of such abundance that no amount of latex rubber could suppress the meat into trim decency. Fights would suddenly break out with alarming ferocity but there could be no room for swinging fists and so the squeeze of the travelling mob would suffocate further, violent escalations. In those subway train cars the hot, metallic-smelling air was super-charged with the most primitive of living emotions. We would an spill out of these cars (some of us being pushed or thrown out) and climb the stairs into the canyons of dark glass and gargoyled stone which housed the machinery of commerce and coffee breaks, industry and indigestion, finance and fiscal flatulence that smelled of syndicated corruption. Up in elevators we would go – as if to heaven – not realizing that the next step was a purgatory of clattering typewriters and tortured executives who screamed in fury as their insides were being eaten away by excess stomach acid. Lunch time came and every grill in mid-town Manhattan would sizzle with greasy slabs of meat... some of this meat sitting on stools at the counter watching their brethren fizzle and fry. Chinese restaurants administered massive doses of monosodium glutamate in a desperate attempt to curb caffeine jitters. Construction workers could be seen sitting on cinder blocks watching the secretaries stroll by while their hero sandwiches bulged with swollen sausages; sausages which threatened to squirt juice into the first mouth that clamped down on them. In no time at all the hour was up and you had to digest that mess in a fluorescently lit working space, the purplish pulses from the elongated bulbs causing the varicose veins on your co-workers to pulsate repulsively.

Things slowed down as five o'clock approached and the concept of a time warp was no longer an abstraction but a living reality as you witnessed the stretching of space-time without benefit of drugs. You need only glance at the clock to see that it was not moving normally toward the desired numeral. As if in a fever or trance, once again you find yourself crammed into a subway train only this time nobody is grabbing for your manhood, all life has been squeezed out of the beast that lives in us all and it must be resurrected by the six o'clock news, news that will tell us who got pushed down an abandoned elevator shaft after being manicured by a chainsaw. Slowly yet surely we will feel a stirring within us but for most it will take something pharmaceutical to bring it completely out, it'll take an Ex-Lax tablet.

Chapter Three

AN INTERVIEW WITH MIKE KUCHAR
October 22nd, 1988

JACK STEVENSON: What are you up to these days? You're recognized as one of the best underground filmmakers of the '60s but it seems you've been keeping a low profile for the last twenty years or so.

MIKE KUCHAR: No, not really. I have been making films actually. Last one I did was – well, I did three in 1984. This half-hour one and these two kind of picture poems in 1984. So it's been a four-year lapse. I do have shows, but I guess they're not publicized. I was making films through the 1970s. They haven't been **comedies** that much, but, ah ... maybe **that's** the reason, you know. But I've never lost my interest in it, I've been having shows. Like last year I had a couple of shows here in New York, both of my old work and my recent work. I had one at the Los Angeles Film Forum last month... But no, ah, I still been makin' films. I'm not really in the limelight, but that's alright, I don't care. But I have been having shows around.

JS: You teach film now?

MK: I'm doing a six-week course here in New York, at the Collective, a basic filmmaking course. And also last year, a six-week dramatic narrative class, where I made a film with the students. And other things are coming up.

JS: You're based in San Francisco now?

MK: No, now it's kind of like goin' back and forth.

JS: You yourself never had any formal education in film though, right?

MK: No. No, I haven't. It was kind of like a fun hobby. It's always been that way. Whatever I learned I learned by my own working in film, through the years. So I'm sort of like "self-taught" or whatever, I had to learn. I learned by just working on my films.

JS: You used to do erotic comics or illustrations. Do you still do that?

MK: That's what I did when I was in San Francisco recently, I had to do a 42-page kind of comic book. Erotic nature... always falls into these kinds of things. They always ask me to do erotic stuff – that's okay, I don't mind it. Yeah, it was okay. I had no other job at the moment and that kind of helped me get through a couple of months. I got twelve hundred dollars for it. It'll be comin' out right after Christmas, it'll probably get in those more high class gay-lesbian bookshops. It was a nice job, and at least it got me – gave me a creative outlet to express certain attitudes, and got me back into drawing. I do like to draw and paint – not just film.

JS: Going back in time, your movie of '65/66, THE SINS OF THE FLESHAPOIDS, was probably your most famous film of that period. How do you regard this film? Fondly?

The young Mike Kuchar

MK: Oh yeah. Sure. It's a complete entity unto itself. I hope that's like with every film. For every film, if the chemistry is just right, then I'm able to make it. It's very hard to make a film like that again because they don't fall back into that chemistry. In other words, when the chemistry is right I make the kind of film that I always wanted to make. It was my most successful picture as far as financially. I think it came out too when the camp sensibility was beginning to emerge – it came out right at about that time. There was a need for this kind of camp sensibility. The outside world took it well.

JS: By "chemistry" you mean...

MK: Where everything falls together. You meet these kinds of people and they're just right to fill the parts that – this film that you've always had in mind. That's what I find with my work. I have like a few films that I want to do, and they're not really related to each other, but then I'll make them when I meet the right people or discover the right place to film it. It's a matter of chemistry. Then it works, and you know, it stands on its own. And then... life goes on... until something else brings out something that you always wanted to make and then you know when it's right and you go out and buy the film and make it.

JS: That's what separates independent films from the film "industry".

MK: Yeah, right. You know, I have to finance these myself, and put the work in it, and I can only do these when I really feel inspired or when I really want to. And to do what I want to do... What mood I'm in determines what I'm gonna do. And sometimes when I do one thing, the next film I usually do something different. Maybe that's another reason why I haven't got a "name" so much now, because you never can tell what I'm gonna do next. So there's a loss of identity, you know what I mean? In other words, you can't really expect the next film to be like THE SINS OF THE FLESHAPOIDS type thing. Because I can't do that, I'm not that way. If you do it where your films have a certain thematic unity, or a certain attitude throughout the whole thing, then you get a kind of a "following" – they know what to expect.

JS: Sort of like John Waters, in a way – people know, or thought they knew, what to expect from him.

MK: Yeah, right. And that's fine and all, but it's just not me, it doesn't occur to me to do that. I just go about my own whims, you know, for better or for worse. I don't care. But then again, I have a lot of people that like these other films that I do, so...

JS: So each film should be taken on its own.

MK: Yeah. But again it's like, sometimes I could do an abstract film, or sometimes I do these kind of short, hopefully poetic kinds of films, then I might do a comedy. But it depends on how I feel, and also what I had already done. But I've still been making films, so I didn't drop out after the '60s.

JS: Do you look back with any nostalgia on those times of the '60s?

MK: Oh yeah, sure I do. They were nice times. Especially for filmmaking because it was much more inexpensive to make films then. I resent some of it now, because it's become kind of like a rich person's hobby. I feel bad for the people who are interested in film now, I feel a little bad because it's become so expensive. But then my last films I made, I made with all out-dated film. I got hundred foot rolls for a dollar each [laughs]. 'Cause I got kind of mad, I said, okay, I just want to make films like the way I used to make 'em. So with these last films there was a little colour loss, but I said, "I don't care, it's either that or no film, period." But I found that I had some stories to tell, so as long as you're able to tell the story, what does it matter that there's a little colour loss? So what? It's the story that's most important [chuckles]. So that's what I did, so I still keep my eyes open to make it a budget that's my type of budget.

JS: Right, a low budget.

MK: Yeah, low budget.

JS: In a 1967 issue of *Film Culture* there's a quote, you said you have two kinds of actors you work with: "Those who can't act at all and those who overact." Do you still believe in the use of non-actors?

MK: Ah... yeah... but [back] then it was what I only had to work with. Actually, my last picture, a half-hour film, two people were actors and they liked my work and they said, "If you have a role let me know, I'd read the script, I'd like to do it." So my last film I used actors – that was real nice... so, it was depending on who I had to use, who was around, and most of the time it was non-actors.

JS: So you don't deliberately chain yourself to any one philosophy.

MK: No.

JS: Now, Donna Kerness was in some of your films, too.

MK: She was in a lot of our films, both my brother and I... we met her in school. She's real good, she liked dancing, she was very much into dancing, so she had a very nice way of moving... we made films but they were more like parties and means of expression – she'd be able to express herself and we'd be able to express ourselves. She was very good in films, and she liked films very much.

JS: She's probably the best known star of those early films.

MK: We saw her at a high school reunion, about four years ago... after not seeing her for about ten, twelve years. She looked fine, still looks fine. My brother wants to put her in another movie... I don't know... she seems game for it.

JS: Those early films of the '50s, like A TOWN CALLED TEMPEST, and those that you did with George, do you still show those occasionally?

MK: Yeah... we get good turn-outs, because it's like a novelty, something unusual – 8mm – it's so antique now. I don't know what it is, maybe it's the fathers and the mothers also used to like the pictures and told their kids to go. But, a lot of new people – I had a show at the Collective, it was like sold out. A lot of young people there, they really enjoyed it. I didn't know, I was up in the projection booth struggling with this old projector. But when I came out... they really enjoyed the films, I felt glad. That was about five months ago or something. But the format, just having a show of old 8mm films from the '50s and '60s, people are interested.

JS: How did your film style differ from George's back in the early days? Those collaborations.

MK: They weren't too different, our styles blended well together... but as we went on we each got our own... his films are not like mine and mine are not like his now – he's got his own personality, I got mine. Sometimes we still have shows together, 'cause of the name, the "twin brothers".

JS: Right, exactly – "The Kuchar Brothers".

MK: Yeah, right... but our films really are different. It's like... another person, another temperament. He does a lot of turgid dramas and all [laughs], sometimes I don't, ah... some of mine are kind of meditative, they're quiet, they're... kinda like poetic, and, ah, different. Even technically, too. They're a bit slower. There's a different temperament involved.

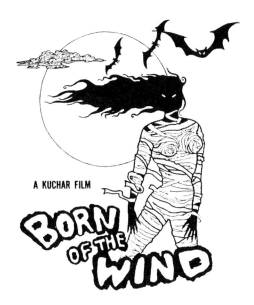

A KUCHAR FILM

BORN OF THE WIND

JS: And then you started making your own films at a certain point after you branched out into 16mm?

MK: Yeah, we had our own projects to work on, so we just shared the equipment, really.

JS: SINS OF THE FLESHAPOIDS was your first movie on your own?

MK: Actually no, back in the 8mm it was BORN OF THE WIND. That was the story of a scientist who brings a mummy to life... a half-hour 8mm film... it was my story, sorta my idea – kind of very romantic, with camp elements in it. Very lush. SINS... was my first 16mm film. Actually we began together on a project, a 16mm film called CORRUPTION OF THE DAMNED, but then I sort of abandoned it 'cause I wanted to do this kind of colour science-fiction film and George picked up and finished CORRUPTION OF THE DAMNED, which he actually did 80 percent of it. So that became like his first picture. Ever since then we sort of, ah, each have our own projects in mind. And we'd just pool together our money and share the equipment.

JS: You helped Rosa Von Praunheim work on his film RED LOVE (1981), which he says you did very good work on. How do you remember that film?

MK: Well, I like to travel, I really enjoyed Germany, and I love cinematography, so... and anytime I'm behind the camera I enjoy it 'cause I love to photograph people, do lighting, whatever.

JS: That was a very beautiful, lushly shot film.

MK: And the pay was good [laughs]. And I made friends with a lot of the crew and some of the actors, which I then saw afterwards – 'cause I had a tour a couple of years after that in Germany, where I brought films... it was a tour arranged by a museum in Frankfurt, and I caught up again with some of the actors, they came to my show and it was really nice. Rosa wasn't quite sure how he was eventually going to finish the picture so a lot of it ended up on the cutting room floor. It don't matter. But a lot of the scenes I took wound up on the cutting room floor. But I got paid to do it so it don't matter.

JS: Yeah, it was rather a schizophrenic film...

MK: Well, eventually it turned out to be, 80 percent of it was this video he shot of this lady trying to make up for her sexual escapades, that she didn't do earlier in her life. That he did completely after all this other footage, and it was like **dumped** in... but that happens, you know... I knew that probably might happen – that's okay. But I had a good time, goin' around Germany, like I say. And the pay was very good. To me it was sorta like a vacation.

JS: He always mentions being inspired by the Kuchar brothers' films.

MK: That's nice, it was nice he wanted me to come in and shoot, so it was fine.

JS: Was there a mutiny against Rosa on the set of that film or something?

MK: Oh yeah... [laughs] well... the thing was it wasn't turning out and then he called George to do the film, and George hates travelling and didn't want to do it. But he also had a job and I didn't. So he said, "What about Mike?" and I said I would, and that was great. But... ah... it wasn't a happy set. He was nice to me because everything was turning out fine, but, ah... he really was kind of groping, he really didn't know what he was looking – I don't know if I should tell you – you gonna **write** all this?! [Laughs]

JS: We did a pretty big interview with him in our last issue, I know him pretty good so I'm not gonna try to create any big upheaval or anything.

MK: [Laughs] Yeah, there was gonna be a big mutiny, the main actors were gonna walk right out, yeah, sure, there was a big fight right in the middle of everything, yeah. And then, ah, well... he had a way of... whenever he was there on the set they would forget their lines because I presume there was beginning to be an animosity growing. Well, I mean it wasn't a set, if I – it wasn't a set [laughs]... that I would have if I was making a film – it would definitely not be that kind of a set [laughs]. But that's between him and them. The leading lady said, "Look, I'll stay on the set if he (meaning me) continues to be assistant director and photographer, and lighting man." So it got to that point. But that was nice, I was sort of like a glue to hold the production together [laughs].

JS: Who is the evil twin, you or George?

MK: "Evil"... I don't know...

JS: That question just popped into my head, I don't know what it means.

MK: Yeah... ah – he has a life of his own and I have mine though sometimes we live together, we each go our own way. This way then you can live together. You know what I mean? We have things to talk about, but otherwise we do have our own lives... keep a certain distance... makes it easier and okay.

JS: Do you have any projects coming up?

MK: Ah… no… I have nothing that I'm itching to make at the moment. So, really, ah… no. I **think** I'll make another film, I'm not really sure [laughs]. I'm not thinking about it.

JS: You've financed all your films yourself, right?

MK: I financed them all myself, it always winds up…

JS: But you made a little money on SINS OF THE FLESHAPOIDS… do you still get any residuals?

MK: Not too much now, but it certainly paid its way back then, many, many times over. And I still have shows, and the artist fee they give me, it's nice, and… I never expected any money anyway when I started making films, so this is kind of like a slap on the back.

JS: So you could never see yourself makin' a big budget Hollywood movie?

MK: Well… ? No – not to go out, like, and push for it. If somebody ever contacted me and said they'd finance me, then fine – I'm all for it. But I'm not… I don't have the… I don't care about going out and pushing for it. Whatever I really wanted to make, I went ahead and made it. With whatever I had to work with. So I don't feel stifled, I don't feel like I haven't made a mark anywhere – I made some mark **somewhere** I guess, I don't know. And I do have a kind of a following that did come up, ah… so it's like whatever I needed to do I somehow managed to do it.

JS: You have a following out there… does that surprise you?

MK: It's nice… that, ah… every once in a while I get asked to play films, and that's nice. Sometimes I have a show in front of five people, that's kind of nice [laughs]. I feel good about it. It's intimate and I rather enjoy those shows. Sometimes it's even better than a full house. Then at times you **get** full houses. Even if sometimes I'm asked to give a show in a place that only fits eight people – that's fine with me [laughs]. I like showing, actually, at ripped-up little joints, joints with ripped-up sofas… the films feel at home there [laughs]. I feel at home in places like that. It's not like intimidating or…

JS: Did you meet a lot of the other New York filmmakers back in the '60s? Like Warhol or Jack Smith?

MK: Yeah, sure. I met Warhol a few times… "Hello, how are ya?" and I used to see him coming out of my shows. I would go see his shows, and sometimes he would bring the films in, 'cause sometimes you have to give directions to the projectionist who… and at that time some of their projectionists were my friends. And I met Kenneth Anger, met him a couple of times. That was, ah, we say, "Oh – we finally meet!" 'cause I'd heard of him and he'd heard of us. An interesting thing about Warhol was that one evening I was walking home late at night and I had a vision in front of my eyes, and I saw a woman with no face… in other words there was a woman but there were no features, and she was shooting him. And it was a "vision", like late at night, you know, and the thing was I felt the **passion** that she had. It was like I was suddenly possessed by this, like, vision. And then it left, it was just like a few seconds – it was very disturbing so I got it completely out of my mind because I wanted to forget about it… this whole scene that I saw in front of me. And then the next day, an uneventful day,

---

but then my brother came in and said, "Did you hear Andy Warhol got shot?!" I said, "Oh no – this is incredible... 'cause I had this terrible vision the night before, and I saw this woman with no face and she was shooting him," and I felt the thrill like, of pulling the trigger. But I saw it in front of me, this vision – just grabbed me right by the throat. It was like supernatural... it was really scary. I was really shaken. But here's the thing – then the next day I heard the news that it was a woman, and then they mention the name, and then I said the **name** is so familiar. Then I realized that about a month before I had the vision we had both received a script in the mail. Somebody had mailed us a script and it was **her**. She had mailed us a script wanting to know if we were interested in doing this film of her script. I wasn't – I was working on a film, my brother was working on a film, and I never **met** her. I didn't know what she looked like. But I remembered the name – I put it back in another envelope, readdressed it and said, sorry, I'm not interested in doing it. Obviously she was sending the script around to have filmmakers work on it, and she probably sent him the script and he said, "Well, let's get together and meet," and somehow he would up with her, and... she shot him. But the vision I had of her was accompanied with this... I **felt** her complete hatred and thrill of pulling the trigger. I remember, it was late at night, I was walkin' home through a park. But I never liked to talk about it 'cause it was – I felt like I was "in" on it, or something, you know what I mean? I not only saw it but I felt it.

JS: And everything changed after the shooting, Warhol became more reclusive and Paul Morrissey took over the filmmaking, still in Warhol's name. In a 1980 interview Morrissey described it as "an ill-wind that blew somebody some good."

MK: I always liked THE CHELSEA GIRLS, that's a real good one. That's Warhol's, completely. And Warhol would come up at his shows and just give the projectionist little key notes on how they should project that movie, which was a double-screen thing. But he was never saying like you **had** to be here or there – he was very open, so the projectionists could actually intellect their own creative impulses on when to turn up the sound or whatever. In other words, there was a lot of elbow room, which was kinda nice.

JS: I guess those days are over, though. I mean, it seems there were a lot of good things happening in those days. Those **were** the days of "Underground Films" and in fact, when I talk to John Waters today he speaks of it as a specific period that is over, most definitely.

MK: Yeah, now it's like a lot of, ah, art schools and colleges, now they've incorporated film as part of the art department. And now there's a lot of students making films and it's sort of gone into that. A lot of films are being made, and students are making them in film classes. And I guess some of those underground filmmakers become film instructors at some of the fine arts schools. They sort of filtered in there. Most institutions and museums now have an understanding of independent film production. An awareness of underground or independent films has been incorporated into the mainstream of film exhibition and whatever, you know, and it's carried on into the classrooms, too. It depends on the school, some focus on the academic or industry side, others on the more fine arts side. Depends on the school.

JS: But back in those days the people who were making films **weren't** students, like you guys, John Waters, Andy Warhol, Jack Smith, Kenneth Anger...

MK: That's right, just people who just made films, just all of a sudden took it upon

Donna Kerness (foreground) with Andy Warhol and Factory acolytes

themselves, you know, dropped either the paint brush or writing and went into film, yeah.

JS: And I think that "movement", so-called, opened up independent films, like today with David Lynch or David Cronenberg, where it's not just industry films. It opened it up – it wasn't all just Hollywood films after that.

MK: Yeah.

JS: You teach film courses you said.

MK: Every once in a while I do, I don't do it often.

JS: Do you think film **can** be "taught"? How do you approach...

MK: Well, to me the most important thing is to be inspirational. I think inspiration is what it all comes down to. If I can be inspirational... and also, not to have the students feel intimidated that they have a big obstacle as far as technicalities, 'cause it really isn't. It's just imagination, really, and a kind of a spirit that one should go about one's work and – that's really the most important thing in one's work: the spirit. I mean, if I could be inspiring to somebody – not that I want them to make films like mine, you know, God forbid [laughs] – but if I can show that you can make a film if you got an idea and you like working with the camera, and don't worry, just go about it any way you can. Because it is the spirit that is most important in the film. And try to capture that spirit so other people feel it. That's all. And not to be intimidated by technology, because it's all an illusion, really – you can get something to look very, very good using very little.

JS: And you can spend vast amounts of money and get nothing.

Mike pictured in 1988

MK: Yeah, because it can be completely empty and lacking in spirit, and it's a complete waste of money, so money's not the thing. You get an idea, there's many ways to do it and you can cut a lot of corners. Gear it to what you can afford. There are little tricks, and you can do it. I mean you can buy a light meter for five hundred dollars – you can also buy one for fifty dollars – you can get stuck in a big budget racket. It's all just a racket. You can do the same kind of films for like ten times cheaper also. If you're resourceful and you see a way.

JS: Kenneth Anger says his whole life has been devised as a means of avoiding a regular job. Did you ever work a nine-to-five job?

MK: Yeah, I've done it. The longest I ever did it was six years. I was in the commercial art field. That was right after school. That's what I made SINS OF THE FLESHAPOIDS on. It didn't cost much anyway. Then I left it after six years, thinking that I'd probably have to go look for another job in a week or so. Then the films started bringing me some money so that kept holding me off getting work, then I actually retired for six years on my films, because museums bought them and whatever – that was kind of nice. Now, every once in a while, I do have to support myself. Temporary jobs or whatever, teaching or illustration jobs. Or also sometimes just a real schlop job, but I know I'm gonna get out of it, just have to weather it out until something else breaks, or save up enough money to take a vacation [laughs]. But a filmmaker, a painter and a writer – they need time to daydream. Plus with daydreamin' you need a lot of time, free time, you know. So it's very important [chuckles] to incorporate that in one's life. 'Cause that's the only thing you're really interested in: your own visions, your own thoughts. Your own work. The other stuff is just there for a paycheck.

JS: Did you ever get any grants?

MK: I got a grant once – 1985. I got three thousand dollars. I did a poem series, I did these kinds of meditative landscape picture poems. I did one on the forest, one on the sea and one on the mountains. So I went to Asia and I photographed the Himalayas.

Chapter Four

IN PRAISE OF GORGEOUS DIALOGUE
The Marion Eaton Story

"...like Gertrude Lawrence returning from beyond to re-make THE GLASS MENAGERIE for John Waters," marvelled a young Los Angeles film student in 1980 after seeing THUNDERCRACK!, the infamous (and probably world's only) underground bi-sexual porno horror film, from 1975. "Uncannily reminiscent of Joan Crawford's performance as a suspected psychotic axe murderer in STRAIT-JACKET (1964)", went another published comparison.

Such spangled tributes are unlikely to win an actress an Oscar nomination, although in any case Marion has had to be more concerned with what the vice cops thought of it all. While leading-lady film stars of today are lavishly feted and serenaded at spectacular opening night galas, Marion spent the night of her première throwing up in a toilet.

Is there no justice?

Although THUNDERCRACK! remains her best known film, it has today entered the realm of the classic *"film maudit"* – a work that provokes and intrigues but is rarely actually seen. It is not out on video and is only rarely booked theatrically on the shrinking repertory circuit. Only four 16mm prints of the film exist, each edited into versions of markedly varying length, and the master negative has either been lost or destroyed. The one print known to exist in England can't be rented to cinemas on the Continent because the Brits are afraid customs officials won't let it back into the Country, while its distributors in America are hesitant to send prints out of the U.S. London's Scala Cinema showed the film almost monthly over the last ten years and their print became so chewed up that only one projectionist was capable of running it.

As for Marion, in Danny Peary's definitive book, *Cult Movie Stars* (pub. 1991 by Simon & Schuster), she is not there. The only Eaton is Shirley Eaton whom Peary canonizes for her role in a James Bond film.

So much for fame.

In fact, Marion was a dedicated and talented stage actress long before she was "discovered" by filmmakers in the mid-1970s. It began when she was 10 years old, the first day in a new grammar school in Vallejo, California and the teacher, preparing to put on a play, asks the class who wants to play the part of the Fairy Princess. Marion's hand was up in a flash. She remembers saying to herself, "My God! I'm the only actress in the room." She describes it as a voice inside herself – literally. "All of a sudden I knew who I was."

Shortly thereafter a children's theatre was established in Vallejo and *Cinderella* was one of the first productions. Marion didn't get the lead but instead played one of the wicked step-sisters. The director consoled Marion with the advice that it was easy to play Cinderella – there were lots of them – but the step-sister, now, that was a challenge!

Marion worked for several years with the children's theatre and continued acting when she entered Junior High, becoming the personal protegée of her drama teacher. In Tenth grade she joined a little theatre group, becoming, at 14, the youngest member. In the production of *Night Must Fall* she played the pregnant

Cockney maid to the outrage of some of the adults.

Majoring in Drama at San Francisco State University, where she earned a Bachelor of Arts, and at the University of the Pacific, where she earned an Associate Arts degree, Marion would go on to an active and diverse career in Bay Area stage productions that would garner more than a few rave reviews. She acted in the plays of Shakespeare, Wilder, Strindberg, Albee, Sarroyan and Williams, playing characters such as Leni Riefenstahl, Stella (*A Streetcar Named Desire*), Martha (*Who's Afraid Of Virginia Wolf?*), and the 88-year-old Lotte in Dan Turner's *Pearls Of Wisdom*.

In the mid-'70s she branched out into film and performed the rarest of roles, that of classically-trained actress in sexually-explicit movies. She would become an important figure in the flourishing San Francisco Underground film scene of the '70s, and in the '80s would earn the appreciation of key producers at Vestron Pictures where she was cast in PAINT IT BLACK and SUNDOWN.

Although little known by the movie-going public at large, Marion has contributed some of the most original, compelling and finely-tuned performances in the independent film genre and joins the likes of Mink Stole, Lung Leg and Donna Kerness in the golden glow of richly deserved subterranean celebrity.

EROTIC REALISM – PRIVATE INTIMACIES ON BIG SCREENS

It all began one evening in 1974 when Marion and a male friend drove north to Petaluma for dinner and a quiet night out. After dinner her friend suggested they take in a movie. There wasn't much else to do in Petaluma, a peaceful, rustic little country town north of San Francisco. Marion agreed.

The movie they ended up seeing was DEEP THROAT.

Marion was shocked.

Shocked mostly by the abominably bad acting. She was also put off by the "silly, circus-like" approach with which Linda Lovelace performed the act of oral sex.

Although Marion had seen porno films before, to suddenly see it "publicly" was a new and novel experience. The first pornographic feature film is generally acceded to be Bill Osco's MONA: THE VIRGIN NYMPH, made in 1970. By 1974 theatrical hardcore pornography had become "chic" and big name stars and celebrities were doing non-performing cameo roles in hardcore films that were playing in Small Town U.S.A. Although such films as MONA and BEHIND THE GREEN DOOR had come first, DEEP THROAT was Marion's – and most of America's – introduction to big screen triple-X sex as well as the first porn film to land its star on the cover of a major glossy (*Esquire*).

Marion was shocked, put-off, and... fascinated.

"The actress in me was fascinated by the fact that this was on the big screen and that you could deal with secret things. You could deal with sexuality."

"If this is being done," she thought to herself as she left the theatre, "then I could do a better job than Linda Lovelace."

Coincidently, a few weeks later she would get her chance. Dan Caldwell, a fellow actor from a Palo Alto stage production of *Othello* they had both been in, gave her a call. (Dan was also the drama teacher at the local Mill Valley highschool, Tam High.) He told her he was going to direct a feature film for some producers who'd been associated with the Mitchell Brothers (BEHIND THE GREEN DOOR) organization across the Bay in San Francisco. It was to be a film-within-a-film, a spoof on porno filmmaking that dealt with the romantic and sexual relationships of people in the process of producing a porno film. Marion thought the idea had dramatic and humorous potential. Dan invited her to audition. She did, and got the part.

SIP THE WINE, as the film was to be entitled, was envisioned as a classy, hip, unique kind of film, and while it would include sexually explicit scenes, it was not

pornography the cast and crew would be aiming for, but rather "erotic realism". That was the challenge. The producers were attempting art, not exploitation (one of the more memorable scenes in the film was shot in the now defunct San Francisco Museum of Erotic Art which housed the Kronhausen Collection). If the film had been presented to Marion as a "porno film" she would have rejected it. "It was the **challenge** that inspired me as a dramatic actress," she recalls today, "to reveal the sexual life of my character and have it **not** be pornography."

Other than the fact that it also contained explicit sex, SIP THE WINE was intended as the antithesis of what was generally construed as a "porno film". It was to be planets apart from the dreary, quickie, zero-budget porn flicks rolling off the assembly lines in San Francisco and L.A., cast as they usually were with luckless hippies, addicts and unclassifiable sleazy types. Here pains would be taken with the costumes and hair styling. Good colour film stock would be rolling through the cameras. Some glorious local scenery would be captured in the movie as well. And unlike most porn films a physically attractive cast of capable stage actors had been assembled by Caldwell. (The young leading lady was in fact an ex-drama student of his who also happened to be the daughter of the town's prominent heart surgeon, a situation which lead to a certified Mill Valley scandal.)

It was a cast of "real people" so to speak; newcomers to the world of explicit on-screen sex and nudity, a slightly naïve but intense group of local actors embarking on a challenge, an adventure in art, honesty and eroticism. Those were the times. "We were a courageous bunch," remarks Marion, "because there were **many** actors that would have nothing to do with this." They talked about it among themselves. Would they actually be able to perform at the moment of truth? As for Marion, she remembers that "when I read the script naturally I only saw the words – I didn't see the actions. I sort of said, 'yeah, well, we can skip that'... I only saw the dialogue, being a stage actress."

She found herself doubly challenged on the first day of shooting: her first time in front of movie cameras **and** her first "public" sex act. "You asked for it," she ruefully reminded herself, recalling her recent ruminations on the subject. The leading man was challenged too – his girlfriend was sitting in on the shoot. (It was probably no coincidence that Caldwell chose to shoot Marion's sex scene first, that being an old skin-flick practice. If you shot other scenes first and your star balked at the nudity or sex you were in trouble since they were already "on film".)

Marion's stage-actor friends – many of whom considered film an inferior medium to begin with – were shocked and horrified by her willing participation. They tried to talk her out of it, but to no avail.

"We had this group in San Francisco called Poverty Theatre – we put on productions, had classes and did 'internal exercises'," recalls Marion, "in which we tried to become honest with our feelings. That was one of the things that made me see the film as a way of becoming even more honest. I argued with them: 'Hey – we've been talking about honesty and baring your soul, and we come here in leotards and touch and grope one another and look directly into one another's eyes... and we **know** that the characters we create **do** have sexual feelings. Don't you see this is an opportunity to truly explore the inner life?'"

They didn't.

The movie was shot, edited and released, opening in San Francisco and then elsewhere around the Country.

SIP THE WINE elicited fairly good reviews over all. San Francisco critic, John Wasserman, called it a "breakthrough film", adding that Marion was the best actress he'd ever seen in a pornographic movie.

Despite the intentions of those involved with the film, it became known as, sold as and reviewed as a "pornographic" movie. Moreover, what might have seemed somewhat fresh and original in 1974 aged rather badly and today the film rates as obscure even among aficionados of the genre. Based on the story of a wholesome young man who comes to New York City to direct porno films (!) and ends up involved with his older and wiser female assistant (played by Marion), the film had too much clunky plot exposition for the raincoat brigade, who expected a gluttonous barrage of rude, crude and lewd sex acts. On the other hand those looking for genuine realism or art found the characters and storyline to be clichéd and uninspiring. "A soap opera" Marion deems it in retrospect.

Needless to say, the film didn't help Marion's reputation in Mill Valley (where it never played). She told her next door neighbour about it. "She was just absolutely horrified... she wouldn't speak to me – none of them would although none of them went to see the film."

JOURNEY TO THE CENTRE OF THE THUNDERSTORM: PSYCHO-SEXUAL DEMONS UNLEASHED

One of the producers of SIP THE WINE was a man named Phil Heffernan. At a post-production photo-shoot Phil told Marion about a film currently being cast in San Francisco. He encouraged Marion to audition for one of the parts that he knew she'd be perfect for – one of the female leads. Phil also planned to audition since it was his credo not to ask someone to do something he wouldn't do himself. This film would also include nudity and explicit sex.

Marion was curious but not enthusiastic. Phil persisted, offering to drive her over. She finally agreed to check it out just for the hell of it. This would be a radically different type of film than SIP THE WINE, Phil told her, directed and scripted by a couple of semi-famous renegades from San Francisco's Underground art scene. Marion had never heard of these guys: Curt McDowell and George Kuchar.

The title of the movie was to be THUNDERCRACK!. John and Charles Thomas would produce and also act in the film, drawing on funds they controlled as partial heirs to the Burger King fortune to set up their own production company.

Marion recalls the audition: "Curt had me read from the script while the camera was rolling. Then he wanted me to do an improvisation – he wanted me to imagine that I was looking through a peephole in the wall and that there was a really stimulating sexual act going on on the other side, and that it would excite me and that I would begin to masturbate."

"I simulated the scene. I had on an orange velvet blouse, no bra – I never wore a bra. I began feeling my breasts, making the sounds and expressions... I started to take my blouse off and Curt yelled **stop!** 'I want you,' he said, 'you're **it**. I'm not auditioning anybody else!'... I thought it was crazy. It was too easy. I thought maybe he'd settle for anything."

Still unsure about it all, Marion returned to Mill Valley with the script in hand. She remembers her neighbour was outside when she got home. They were finally on speaking terms again. "Guess what!!!" Marion announced to the soon-to-be-mortified woman, telling her about the new film in a burst of enthusiasm. "I was **so** naïve", laughs Marion in recollection, "and she says, 'Oh Marion! Will you **stop** getting involved in this terrible stuff!!'"

That evening Marion read the script, which had been written by George during a prolonged stay in an Oklahoma YMCA. He had used ballpoint pen to preclude erasures and the temptation of endless rewrites. The thing came to 192 pages. (Rumour later circulated that George wrote the script while high on LSD in a Nebraska thunderstorm, but Marion discounts this: "I've never known George to use drugs – I think he just gets high on violent weather and violent emotions.") George had been a film instructor at The San Francisco Art Institute since 1971 and at the point that Marion came into the picture Curt McDowell and John and Charley Thomas were students of his.

Marion found George's language to be fascinating. "It reminded me so much of Tennessee Williams. I **loved** Gert Hammond's long gorgeous speeches – I read them out loud that night. I thought, 'Oh God – **this language is beautiful!**'"

Yet she remained undecided. Curt had very matter-of-factly outlined the explicit sex acts she'd be required to do in the film; masturbation with a cucumber, a scene with another woman in a bathtub, etc. And now here it was staring up at her from the script in black and white.

"Once again," says Marion, "I approached the script as a stage actress and focused on the dialogue. I handled the sex scenes with my customary approach: denial [laughs]."

Adding to her hesitation was the fact that SIP THE WINE hadn't even hit the screen yet. What would people think of her? What would she think of herself? She was still very much in uncharted personal territory.

Yet once again she found the challenge fascinating. And Curt seemed to be a nice guy. On top of that she had fallen hopelessly in love with the dialogue of George Kuchar.

She phoned up Curt the next day to accept the part – he took the call in his bathtub. He was thrilled.

Marion was to play the role of Gert Hammond, the lonely, drunk, sexually frustrated and more than slightly insane sole occupant of "Prairie Blossom", a decrepit Midwest farm mansion. Her husband, Charlie Hammond, had been devoured by a ravaging cloud of locusts while heading home from a hard day's labour in the wheat fields. Gert saved the bloody gristle of Charlie's remains and kept it pickled in large jars in the basement. Their only son, a sexually obsessed deviant, had returned from an expedition to Borneo in search of erotica with an exaggerated case of elephantiasis of the scrotum. Gert now kept him locked in a secret room of the mansion as the proverbial family horror. "My son is no more," she ambiguously confides to her guests throughout the movie with a chilling smile, "he no longer exists".

There it was; a quintessentially American "Lonely Mansion Melodrama" in the

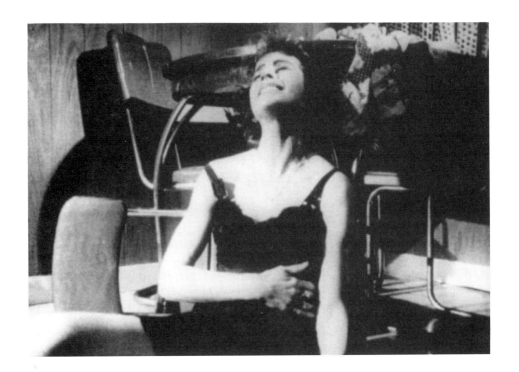

Marion Eaton as 'Gert Hammond'; *Thundercrack!*

tradition of THE OLD DARK HOUSE, HUSH, HUSH SWEET CHARLOTTE and BABY DOLL but with more of the cheesy scariness of William Castle's THE HOUSE ON HAUNTED HILL. On the other hand it was much closer in **spirit** to the Underground vulgarian masterpieces of John Waters and Paul Morrissey that were being filmed at about the same time, and with a pinch of NIGHT OF THE LIVING DEAD thrown in for good measure.

The movie hinges on the interactions of two groups of strangers that seek shelter at Prairie Blossom one dark and stormy night. Gert prepares a generous repast for her unexpected visitors while they go about fucking and sucking and jerking off and generally confronting their own psycho-sexual demons and angels in the process via George's dramatically overheated dialogue. Canned thunder incessantly crackles in the background while flies are unzipped and cheap furniture is knocked over in the midst of a series of brawls.

Phil Heffernan skilfully portrays "Chandler", the blue-blooded millionaire owner of a Texas girdle factory. (After much soul-searching Phil decided to go under the pseudonym of Mookie Blodgett on the credits roll.) Curt cast his voluptuously endowed sister, Melinda, in a key role that called for her at one point to seduce a suspected homosexual by donning a butch leather jacket and strap-on dildo. George Kuchar himself enters about midway into the film as "Bing", a travelling carnival gorilla-keeper who crashed his truck in the storm out of suicidal impulses. A host of other strange characters are involved as well.

The dramatic foundation of the film, however, is anchored almost entirely by Marion alone, established in the opening scenes of the film as Gert sits dishevelled in a black slip and bra at her kitchen table, knocking back shots of liquor and listening to weather reports on the radio. When the first stranger knocks at her door, she goes into the bathroom to vomit up the booze and her wig falls into the toilet. She simply plops it back on her head and staggers to the door mouthing platitudes of welcome. It's a stunning one-woman performance and Marion milks the monologue for all its worth as flashes of lightning illuminate the room and thunderclaps explode in the background with a frequency that Ed Wood would admire.

These opening scenes evoke a lonely, liquor-soaked dementia that rings of the spooky, the pathetic, the absurd and the simply insane, executed in a minimalist but highly effective style that hinges on the shadowy photography and Marion's skill with atmospheric dialogue rooted very much in her training for live theatre. McDowell opens the film playing straight to Marion's strength, and closes the film with a similar, very powerful Marion Eaton monologue. In a way it's a shame he didn't just film the **whole** movie with Marion alone at night in that kitchen. She could have pulled it off; creating a situation, a plot, a movie, a **world** from mere words alone and a few cheap special effects. (Ironically Marion was stoned when she filmed the now revered "Mr. Mapletree" scene at the start of the film. After she had "wrapped" her work on the film she celebrated with a **joint**, only to realize they'd forgotten to shoot that scene. She reminded Curt and they shot it right then and there in one take and then went on to party – it was also her 43rd birthday.)

Soon Prairie Blossom is invaded by strangers seeking refuge from the storm and Marion is surrounded by a willing cast of over-sexed foils. This was a set-up that would be repeated in other Kuchar/McDowell productions down the road: that of "actor among non-actors". Marion's classically tuned dramatic delivery and visual presence – abetted by the make-up work of George Kuchar – would be employed as counterpoint to the casual, clumsy or overheated techniques of the non-actors that would surround her. In THUNDERCRACK! most of the cast wore their own street clothes while Marion was lavishly made up and costumed by George. Like a pearl in the middle of hamburger. And although THUNDERCRACK! includes several fine

On the set of *Thundercrack!*: Curt McDowell

On the set of *Thundercrack!*: George Kuchar

performances, without Marion the dramatic credibility of the film would have likely dissolved – George's words reverting to mere reams of memorized dialogue, the magic language having no magic mouth to come out of.

The technique of mixing in actors with non-actors had been used before in underground film. Actress Sylvia Miles (FAREWELL, MY LOVELY, MIDNIGHT COWBOY, etc.) was surrounded to good effect by the Warhol repertory cast of non-actors in the 1972 Paul Morrissey-directed film, HEAT, where her dramatic interactions with a typically deadpan Joe Dallesandro produce intriguing results. And although the early films of John Waters were reputedly cast with his "non-actor" friends, he also in truth utilized the dynamic of "actor among non-actors". Divine and Mink Stole emerged as true actors (who went on to pursue acting careers) mixed in a pastiche of "possessed amateurs" like Edith Massey, Mary Vivian Pearce and Danny Mills.

THUNDERCRACK! was made for $9,000 and $40,000 in deferred costs and almost every scene was shot on the first take. The actors, most of whom had never been involved in a film before, let alone a porno film, were paid a flat fee of $50 a day plus donuts and coffee George brought to the set every morning. As an actor, George threw himself into the role of Bing with a foaming fury, partly because he never had time to memorize his lines (even though he'd **written** the script) and guessed, correctly, that some high-velocity momentum and hysterics could carry him over the rough spots. Curt would later reflect on the difficulties of casting THUNDERCRACK!, in that he had to find people who were bisexual, exhibitionistic and would could **act** and were willing to have sex on camera. And also, he might have hoped, stay sober. Maggie Pyle, who played Willene, the Fundamentalist wife of a famous country singer, was prone to do some drinking and in fact came to one of the last shoots so drunk that Curt had to position the cameras to film her from the back during the supper table scene. After shooting ended a good number of the cast went their separate ways and were never heard from again.

The finished product was a mash of talent and trash; some demure, charming performances interspliced with explicit gay, straight and solo sex acts, classic passages of dialogue alongside seemingly ad-libbed non-sequiturs... A Tennessee Williamsesque melodrama ramrodded with berserk sexual fantasy sequences – some hilarious and some genuinely troubling. The claustrophobia of the heavily-shadowed, minimalist sets was relieved by Mark Ellinger's lively, ever present silent-movie-style piano score and by several "dream sequences" featuring marvellous use of superimposition and filtered photography in the avant-garde/experimental mold. A 1947 Chiquita Banana cartoon commercial ("Chiquita Banana Tells A Fortune") – in colour – was included in the original version of the film but edited out of subsequent cuts.

THUNDERCRACK! was a roiling package of disparate, seemingly contradictory genre styles and dynamics and there was a definite dark side to it as well – reflective of George's attitude of "sex-as-horror" rather than Curt's view of sex as a jubilation.

It wasn't a "porn film", it wasn't an art film. It went way beyond a student film and it surely wasn't a straight horror film.

And it wasn't a hit.

It never connected with the lucrative theatrical hardcore market. Straight porno audiences were put off by the fact that it was in black-and-white. They found it too talkie, and too weird, and the fact that both gay and straight sexual acts were mixed in together was definitely not a plus – more was **not** better in this case. On the other hand many of the more progressive movie-goers who came to see this latest work from the cutting edge of the Underground were offended by Curt's loving, lingering, close-up celebration of uncensored sexuality that could be as sloppy and sticky as any of the commercial porno films playing down at the local Pussycat Cinema. For these advocates of the Underground and the avant-garde, THUNDERCRACK! had slipped over the edge from art to exploitation.

THUNDERCRACK! eventually did find its niche as a cult film on the Midnight Movie circuit where it played with some success throughout the late '70s and into the early '80s before it lapsed into obscurity, sometimes double-billing with the likes of PINK FLAMINGOS. It's hard to believe the film had ever been targeted for any other type of audience. It was a staple feature at New York City's Elgin Theatre where Midnight Movies were practically born, and played a long run at the Nuart theatre in West Los Angeles where it screened Saturdays at midnight. San Francisco's usually sympathetic Castro Theatre, however, never played the film. Marion recalls the Castro owner walking out in a huff halfway through THUNDERCRACK!, and not until November of 1993 would the grand dame of gay cinema welcome back the most radical work of the local "bad boy of the Underground" – screening the "full" original version four times as part of a Curt McDowell/George Kuchar retrospective. The film continues to crop up occasionally at Gay & Lesbian film festivals, and The Cinema Village in Manhattan "revived" it at midnight screenings on March 18th & 19th and 25th & 26th, 1994 as part of their "Unchained Images" series (curated by Johannes Schönherr) where it was ballyhooed as an "unseen" and "lost" Midnight Movie classic. In fact to a whole new generation of young film freaks in their twenties, it was exactly that, in part due to the film's unavailability on video.

WHITE ELEPHANT OVER L.A. – THUNDERCRACK! UNBOUND
Critical reaction to the film was all over the road.

John Russell Taylor, writing in *Sight And Sound*, called it "genuinely erotic and genuinely frightening." Bill Landis, author of the seminal early-'80s New York film 'zine, *Sleazoid Express*, singles out (in 12/23/80 issue of *Soho News*) George Kuchar's "hilariously overwrought dialogue" and the "highly atmospheric" photography of the film. English critic, Jack Babuscio, called it "a trash film of raw imaginative power and originality... strenuously subversive in its eroticism". "Highlighted by some of the most beautiful cinematography since the heyday of Josef Von Sternberg," praises San Francisco critic David Ehrenstein in a Curt McDowell obit. "THUNDERCRACK!," he continues, "might be described as THE OLD DARK HOUSE as Tennessee Williams and Al Capp might have re-imagined it – with an assist from the Mitchell Brothers for the sex scenes." Kevin Thomas of the *Los Angeles Times* found it to be erotica at its most hilarious: "Sex is great fun in THUNDERCRACK!, which is absolutely, definitely not for prudes."

Other critics remained unamused. In a mixed review from the December, 1980 issue of the *Monthly Film Bulletin* (U.K.), critic Cynthia Rose takes a swipe at the wretched script and opines that "the cast seems to be having a better, more stoned and way-out time than any spectator possibly could." *Variety* (April 1976) likened it to "an awful sexpo spoof that suggests Russ Meyer trying to do a Tennessee Williams subject." (An analogy of dubious merit since Russ Meyer would never do an explicit film.) *Variety* called the 150-minute running time an "ordeal", and in fact even the film's adherents find the original "complete" version – 158 minutes, actually – something of an endurance test. But an endurance test worth taking, says George today, if you want to see the picture. "If you're gonna suffer through that picture you might as well suffer through the entire thing, because it tries to make sense. If you only watch an hour and a half, you'll suffer anyway, so see the whole thing. There's a cumulative effect."

After sinking their money into the film, however, suffering was not what the Thomas Brothers had in mind as an end result, and they edited a shorter, more marketable version of the movie.

Whatever the critics thought, THUNDERCRACK! – the world's only

Underground porno horror flick – had innate drawing power. In 1977 the Seattle Film Festival ran the film at the Egyptian theatre and 600 people came to see it. Curt McDowell was by that time again broke and actually working as a janitor at the San Francisco theatre that was showing THUNDERCRACK!.

Buck Henry championed the film in his capacity as a judge at the prestigious Los Angeles Film Festival, FILMEX, and over the near-violent objections of some of his fellow judges got it accepted into the festival on a midnight slot. It would be the first

X-rated film ever shown at FILMEX.

The big L.A. première was held in Century City – a scene complete with skylights and arriving limousines. Marion and her companion, Bill Feeney, and Curt and sister Melinda drove down to L.A. in Bill's black cadillac. The drive down to L.A. was lots of fun, Marion recalls, smiling at the recollection.

Her expression of fond remembrance melts into a grimace of horror as she recalls the première itself.

"...a terrible experience for me because I was still not used to my film image, I still hadn't dealt with all my mixed feelings. I was very nervous about the whole thing and the film didn't come up until midnight.

"We'd gone out to dinner and been wined and dined, so by the time I got to the theatre I was fortified to deal with this by probably having had too much to drink. Then about 20 minutes into the film, during one of the explicit sex scenes – which was later cut out of the shorter versions – quite a large number of the audience walked out. You see, there's one scene in THUNDERCRACK! – the character's name is Roo [played by Moira Benson]... she has a masturbation scene in the lewd bedroom with a dildo, a rather large one at that. It does make people uncomfortable.

"This is the phenomenon I'm talking about in terms of actors and non-actors. I used an actor's technique to portray sexuality as 'erotic realism', but kept a line there to prevent it from being my own personal masturbation. I created a bigger-than-life masturbation so that it would be everybody's masturbation. But in this case the girl approached the scene as a reality, and so you know you are watching a woman who is being exploited. She was a very sweet girl that I liked very much. She was very young at the time, about 19, and she was not an actress. She was just doing it for the $50-a-day. Nobody knows where she is today. I've seen, at other shows, people react similarly to that scene. Curt was of course accused by people of exploitation.

"In any case, all these people walking out was really upsetting to me. I felt like I was to be damned forever. When I got back to my room I played for real the Gert scene of throwing up in the toilet bowl – all night."

This grand exodus at the FILMEX screening probably gave birth to the enduring myth that THUNDERCRACK! was the most walked-out-of movie ever made – surely something that any true Midnight Movie director ought to be boastfully proud of. Whether or not THUNDERCRACK! can lay claim to such an honour, the FILMEX screening foreshadowed the love/hate relationship audiences would have with the film. One unfailing certainty in life is that at any reasonably crowded showing of THUNDERCRACK! there will be a few walkouts – you can set your watch by it. And for any number of reasons. A November 1993 screening of the film at the Desmet theatre in Amsterdam drew a largely gay audience and produced a few early walkouts who did not go quietly into that good night – one fellow in particular railing against the appalling barrage of heterosexual pornography he'd just been subjected to. Marion herself always qualifies debate about the film by admitting, or rather insisting, that "it's not for everybody". She finds most of the criticism comes from women. "It's the women who are usually most upset or outraged, because they are fearful of being exploited. They feel I am being exploited. I myself am kind of a loner. I live by my own code and do what I believe is needed."

Back at FILMEX, Marion's mood brightened a bit the next day as a lot of positive response started to roll in too. Marion, Bill, Curt and Melinda spent the next few days enjoying the sights of Los Angeles, touring Disneyland and so forth.

THUNDERCRACK! played at the 1976 Mill Valley Film Festival, again on a midnight slot. None of Marion's stage actor friends attended. Rumours of an impending police bust added an edge of paranoia to the proceedings.

A couple of cops actually did show up. One of them told her he really liked the movie.

As noted, THUNDERCRACK! went into eclipse in the mid-'80s, victim of both the end of the "Midnight Movie" era and the more sexually uptight and reactionary mentality that would result from AIDS. Sex was no longer something to laugh about or to explore or to celebrate with the unfettered exuberance that characterized McDowell's work.

Curt McDowell himself contracted the AIDS virus. He died on June 3rd, 1987. He was 42.

"Curt was an incredibly talented artist in so many ways," remembered Marion recently. "He painted, he composed music. On his films he did everything from the photography and lighting to designing costumes, editing, make-up, props... he had to be creating all the time. When I think of that talent gone, of what he could have accomplished in later years, it's really tragic."

Before he died, Curt gave long-time companion and Roxie theatre owner, Robert Evans, possession of his films, which numbered over 30 in total. Curt hoped and assumed that once he was dead Robert would see the importance of putting time and energy into recirculating his work and giving it new life. In the meantime a large circle of friends, collaborators and hangers-on continued to meet at Curt's Mission District flat, carrying on the tradition of the Thursday night soirées he had started.

About a year and a half after Curt's death Robert discovered he also had AIDS, originally diagnosed as Lymphoma. He now put his energy into dealing with his new situation and turned away from the past – or at least certain areas of it – and shelved Curt's films. "Curt's films were the last thing Robert wanted to deal with at this point," comments Marion. Robert obsessively applied himself to the job of distributing and promoting the film VINCENT (1987), about the life and work of artist Vincent Van Gogh, and turned it into a very lucrative success. When he became too ill to work, his partner, Bill Banning, took over operation of the Roxie which he still programs today with energy and imagination.

One of the reasons for continuing the soirées after Curt's death had been to establish a ways and means of keeping his work intact and before the public. At a certain point the soirées apparently ended, although three peripheral members, a Roxie projectionist and an accountant and his wife, continued to meet in private and soon after announced that they would be the administrators of the Curt McDowell Foundation. They had Robert's cooperation and he handed over to them all of Curt's collages, drawings and voluminous scrapbooks as well as his film output, which included miscellaneous fragments, screen tests (Marion's THUNDERCRACK! audition included) and a final, reportedly ambitious, work-in-progress. The Foundation rented a storage locker and put on several Curt McDowell benefits at the Roxie where various combinations of his films were shown under the banner of raising funds to buy a headstone for the perpetually penniless filmmaker.

Robert died in 1990 and was buried with Curt at the Cyprus Lawn Cemetery in Colma. They had been married three weeks before Curt's death at a time when Curt was in the dementia stage of his illness. Marion wryly notes that it wasn't until Robert died that a headstone was purchased and that Robert got top billing. (The benefits to raise the $800 to buy the headstone went on from 1987 to 1990.) The Foundation receives proceeds from the benefits as well as income from film rentals and video sales but up-to-date information on the preservation and archiving of Curt's work is scarce since they never issued newsletters or progress reports and never made their books public. Marion voices concern about the Foundation's financial unaccountability, their lack of energy and vision in promoting Curt's work, and their notable failure as preser-vationists in preventing the destruction of the THUNDERCRACK! negative. She also scorns their failure to strike a new copy of the 35mm THUNDERCRACK! trailer that was lost in the mail, despite keeping the European booker's rental deposit of $900.00, and now there is only one copy of the trailer in existence.

On the other hand Marion is heartened by the Foundation's stated intention to donate Curt's artwork and journals to the San Francisco Public Library's permanent Gay & Lesbian Collection.

THE INDIANA STORY – MARION PLAYS MOM

On the drive back to San Francisco from FILMEX, Curt talked about how he really wanted to make a personal film about his family. These were the first vague glimmerings of a film whose long and financially troubled production would spread out over the next eight years. The film would be called SPARKLES TAVERN.

Curt, according to Marion, conceived of the film as a tribute to and a showcase for his sister, Melinda. They adored one another on a personal level, and on an artistic level this would be another attempt by Curt to capture Melinda's beauty and voluptuousness on celluloid. She had already appeared in a number of his previous films, most notably in NUDES: A SKETCHBOOK, described by San Francisco critic David Ehrenstein as "a series of cinematic portraits of Curt's friends that is one of the gentlest and most sweet-spirited erotic films ever made." Curt filmed Melinda making love with her boyfriends (there were several of them), and despite the explicit sexual content, the film is not at all "pornographic". McDowell was one of the very few filmmakers who could carry that off.

Melinda wasn't an actress but had a certain naïve and charming way with dialogue. Her soft, breathy delivery belied a knowing, sophisticated persona. Ironically once Curt began filming SPARKLES he began to think Melinda wasn't right for the role. George Kuchar, involved in the production as an actor only, tried to convince Curt – apparently succeeding – that she was **perfect** for the part, a judgement borne out by the end result.

SPARKLES TAVERN would be Curt's most sustained, personal film. He wanted to write the script himself and oversee production down to the smallest detail.

As always, money was the sticking point. Marion herself would put $10,000 into the project. It wasn't the first nor would it be the last time Marion helped out Curt financially.

Prior to the FILMEX première Marion had paid a visit to her second husband, Don Eaton. The night before Marion had watched the finished edit of THUNDERCRACK! on the moviola with Curt, and they talked about that for a while. Don was a devoted artist in his own right and had always been very supportive of Marion's decision to act in sexually explicit films. Don told her he'd like to try filmmaking himself eventually since he believed an artist should create in many mediums, not just one.

On that note they had their pleasantries and said goodbye. That night, an hour after Marion left, Don died of a coronary. (From time to time Marion has suspected that she was living a George Kuchar script instead of "real life". Shortly after Don's death came one of those moments: Marion alone down in the basement of her house talking to Don's ashes, that were soon to be scattered by his son. She'd taken the box down there since her three cats were going crazy around it upstairs. In THUNDERCRACK! Marion closes the film toasting and talking to her husband's pickled remains in one of cinema's barmiest finales.)

Marion knew she would inherit some money from Don's estate. Recalling his words that night of their last encounter, Marion promised Curt $10,000 to finance SPARKLES TAVERN on behalf of Don. On the drive home from FILMEX, as Curt talked to her about his dream film, she put two and two together and decided this would be a way for Don to make his film after the death of a dream.

Melinda McDowell

Curt launched into the script which he wrote on Acid during a trip to Yosemite National Park.

Marion was less than thrilled with this first draft. Curt wanted her to play the role of his mother. She didn't care for this part. She also found Curt's language to be inferior to George's. The script lacked the "long gorgeous monologues" she had feasted over as Gert Hammond. Yet she respected Curt's artistic individuality and never considered withholding the promised funds once the estate had been legally settled and the money released.

The Thomas Brothers, who were now working on a never-to-be-completed film about Wilhelm Reich, also offered to invest in SPARKLES TAVERN if Curt would drop the hardcore sex scenes from it and deliver a more marketable R-rated film. They were having a devil of a time distributing the X-rated THUNDERCRACK!

Curt was saddened: he'd so dearly wanted to make a XXX fuck-and-suck film, it was his heart's fondest desire. But he finally agreed. SPARKLES TAVERN in its final form would contain no explicit sex (even if the **implications** of the story were X-rated and then some). The film earned an R rating. George maintains that Curt lost interest in the project because it was devoid of hardcore pornography.

The Thomas Brothers never did invest.

At about this juncture, while waiting for Don's estate to be settled, Marion got a call from famous San Francisco porno producer, Alex DeRezny. DeRezny, along with the Mitchell Brothers, had pioneered American hardcore porno cinema and already had to his credit hardcore blockbusters such as CENSORSHIP IN DENMARK and A HISTORY OF THE BLUE MOVIE.

Marion agreed to meet with him at his office. He immediately offered her a starring role in an upcoming film. "It did mean money," Marion recalls. "He was very, very persuasive. He described himself as climbing up the ladder and being big, and he'd make me a star and so on and so forth."

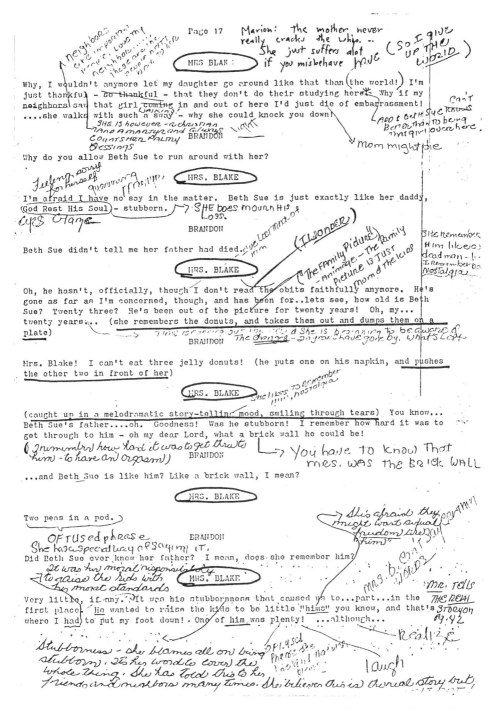

Page 17

(handwritten top margin) neighbors are important, neighbors are right, prove, love, tm these are right

Marion: the mother never really cracks the whip... She just suffers alot if you misbehave *(handwritten)* (So I give up the world!)

MRS. BLAKE

Why, I wouldn't anymore let my daughter go around like that than (the world!) I'm just thankful - so thankful - that they don't do their studying here! Why if my neighbors saw that girl coming in and out of here I'd just die of embarrassment! ....she walks with such a sway - why she could knock you down!

(handwritten) walking / SHE IS however - a Christian / and A martyr and always / counts her palmy / Blessings

(handwritten right) Can't / Add & Beth Sue knows / Better than to being / That girl over here.

(handwritten) mom might die

Why do you allow Beth Sue to run around with her?

MRS. BLAKE

(handwritten) Feeling sorry for herself / quavering / (maudlin)

I'm afraid I have no say in the matter. Beth Sue is just exactly like her daddy, (God Rest His Soul) - stubborn. *(handwritten)* SHE does mourn his / Loss. / eyes aflame

BRANDON

Beth Sue didn't tell me her father had died. *(handwritten)* (sue loved him) (I WONDER)

MRS. BLAKE

(handwritten) The Family Picture - The Family / image is just / picture / mom & the kids

(handwritten right) She remember / Him like as / dead man - / I remember too / Nostalgia

Oh, he hasn't, officially, though I don't read the obits faithfully anymore. He's gone as far as I'm concerned, though, and has been for..lets see, how old is Beth Sue? Twenty three? He's been out of the picture for twenty years! Oh, my... twenty years... (she remembers the donuts, and takes them out and dumps them on a plate) *(handwritten)* Time is running out... and she is beginning to be aware of / The oranges - 20 years have gone by. What's left

BRANDON

Mrs. Blake! I can't eat three jelly donuts! (he puts one on his napkin, and pushes the other two in front of her)

MRS. BLAKE *(handwritten)* She likes to remember / him, nostalgia

(caught up in a melodramatic story-telling mood, smiling through tears) You know... Beth Sue's father....oh. Goodness! Was he stubborn! I remember how hard it was to get through to him - oh my dear Lord, what a brick wall he could be!

(handwritten) (I remember how hard it was to get thru to / him - to have an orgasm))

BRANDON *(handwritten)* → You have to know that / mrs. was the Brick Wall

...and Beth Sue is like him? Like a brick wall, I mean?

MRS. BLAKE

(handwritten) → She's afraid they pay / might want equal / freedom like you "him"

Two peas in a pod. *(handwritten)* OFTused phrase / She has a special way of saying it.

BRANDON

Did Beth Sue ever know her father? I mean, does she remember him? *(handwritten)* It was her moral responsibility / to raise the kids with / her moral standards

(handwritten) mrs. B says.. mr. tells

MRS. BLAKE

Very little, if any. It was his stubbornness that caused us to...part...in the first place. He wanted to raise the kids to be little "hims" you know, and that's where I had to put my foot down! One of him was plenty! ...although... *(handwritten)* The real / story on / pg.42 / Realize

(handwritten bottom) Stubborness - she blames all on being / stubborn). It's her word to cover the / whole thing. She has told this to her / friends and neighbors many times. She believes this is the real story but, *(handwritten)* OF used / phrase she / laugh

Script page: *Sparkles Tavern*

Marion explained her commitment to Curt, telling DeRezny about SPARKLES TAVERN, her role in it and her intention to fund production with the $10,000. DeRezny scoffed at the notion. He told her it was impossible to shoot this filmscript for $10,000. Why lose $10,000 when you can **make** $10,000 he pressed, arguing on. Finally Marion took her leave, telling him she'd simply made a promise to a friend and couldn't back down from it now. "He was very right about the money, though," Marion recalls today with some chagrin, "I was very naïve." Marion drove from DeRezny's office over to the Cliff House for lunch where by sheer coincidence she ran into Curt who was lugging the completed script of SPARKLES TAVERN, which he promptly gave her. This karmic encounter convinced her she'd made the right decision. Eventually the $10,000 from Don's estate was freed up and production on SPARKLES moved forward. Curt relocated into a large loft on Golden Gate Avenue east of Van Ness, in the Tenderloin district. There he would build the set interiors while Melinda lived at the other end of the loft, in a tent with her boyfriend. Curt lavished great amounts of time and detail on the sets, creating a realistic kitchen, a living-room and a night club cabaret complete with stage. Actual framed family photos from the McDowell house in Indiana adorned the coffee table and flower-papered walls of the cosy living-room. Curt obsessively crafted the interiors of a facsimile of a homey midwestern household here in the middle of San Francisco's most sordid ghetto.

Marion, Melinda and George would again appear in main roles, and, like THUNDERCRACK!, this would be a black-and-white feature film with a running time in excess of two hours. There the similarities would end. SPARKLES TAVERN would be a more serious, personal, down-to-earth drama. The simple fact that Curt wrote the script guaranteed it to be a very different film since, despite their personal ties and filmmaking collaborations, George and Curt applied distinctly individual sensibilities to their cinema.

Although SPARKLES TAVERN received a "mere" R-rating, there would be some blazingly vulgar and spirited performances, and various scenes and settings would ooze with McDowell's genuine and heartfelt love of smut.

George recalls that the actors in SPARKLES TAVERN gave it their utmost as there was a feeling on the set that this movie might go big and open doors to them on some higher level. Among the supporting cast, Connie Mercede who plays Brenda, a jealous white-trash dancer, is especially outstanding – equal parts Yvette Mimieux and Mink Stole. Jerry Terranova, who played the Curt McDowell character, Buster Blake, was also exceptional. Curt wasn't looking for "good actors" but rather for actors who had some spiritual or emotional quality in common with the film characters he sculpted in minutest detail. In a sense he didn't want the actors to perform his lines but to **live** his lines in this reconstituted reality he laboured obsessively to create, and the more personally or intimately he knew the actors the better able he was to implant in their screen characters the core of a truth and soul. In fact George, Marion and Melinda, while playing fictional, or even mystical, characters in SPARKLES TAVERN, are also very much playing themselves in the story. The film was very much a personal contract between Curt and the actors, especially the main players. One senses he wasn't trying so much to create plausible fiction or "realism" as he was trying to re-order reality itself to find answers and meaning, to find or define love. In retrospect SPARKLES TAVERN seems to be a seance as much as a movie. Curt wanted a happy ending. If he couldn't have it in life he would make a movie of life and put it at the end of the movie.

Melinda was cast as Sparkles, a dolled-up showgirl in a sleazy cabaret-tavern-whorehouse managed and emceed by her brother, Buster. At the conclusion of each stage show Sparkles leads the small chorus line in song. She can't sing worth a damn but everyone knows it ain't her singing voice that brings the guys around. After each performance the girls – and Buster – repair back to the "suck stalls" to dispense assembly line blow-jobs to the roughneck cowboy patrons through glory holes.

Jerry Teranova, Marion Eaton, George Kuchar; *Sparkles Tavern*

Mom, kept in the dark about her children by flimsy deceptions, worries about Sparkles while comforted by the innocent neighbour boy, Brandon, who genuinely loves her daughter. Marion's portrayal as the worried, repressed, doting old-fashioned mom exhibits an almost brutal realism that Curt had never attempted in his shorter, experimental films. Brandon tries to shield Mom from the unsavoury reality of Sparkles Tavern, named after its star attraction. Fantasy intrudes in the form of a stranger, played by George, who peddles bizarre sing-song remedies for personal troubles that actually work.

It was figuratively the story of Curt and Melinda's life in decadent San Francisco, with Sparkles Tavern metaphorically representing the city and the carnal corruptions and temptations afforded in heaps. In a way the film plays on everyone's worst fear: that your mom is going to find out what you've **really** been up to since you left home.

Like THUNDERCRACK!, SPARKLES TAVERN blends seemingly disparate genre styles. It's part soap-opera, part musical burlesque review and part underground smut film. The look of the film encompasses the comic impressionism of the hand-painted sets and backdrops Curt created for the cabaret, as well as the meticulously mundane accoutrements with which he outfitted the home interiors. Curt could blend these filmic styles and looks together like nobody else to create a film that from a written synopsis would seem a genetic impossibility. But in fact he pulled it off with characteristic panache.

But even after you've seen it you're not sure what it **is**.

It certainly wasn't a "Midnight Movie". In 1984 Marion received a letter from the acquisitions department of New Line Cinema stating that THUNDERCRACK! had often double-billed with New Line's own PINK FLAMINGOS and that New Line was eager to add McDowell's new film, SPARKLES TAVERN, to their roster of midnight offerings. Things never went any farther than that, most likely because, (1) the Midnight Movie craze was nearly over, with video about to plunge a stake into its faintly beating heart, and (2) SPARKLES TAVERN, in its final 2 hours and 10 minute edit, and with its delicate, dialogue-laden characterizations and lack of explicit sex, special effects or overt grotesqueries, was the antithesis of a midnight movie.

Most of the principal photography was done over two months in 1976, although it would be 8 years before the picture was ready for exhibition – tagging it misleadingly as a 1984 film. Things couldn't have changed more in those 8 years.

The struggles to finance SPARKLES TAVERN were endless. Marion contributed several thousand dollars beyond the initial ten thousand, and on top of that cajoled her boyfriend of the time into contributing funds in exchange for screen credit as "Executive Producer" – hence diverting money from his spiralling freebase cocaine habit into better uses.

There were also numerous fund-raising fandangos with purportedly interested patrons attending wine-and-cheese receptions where footage was screened and pitches were made. For one reason or another the prospective investors never proffered the promised bucks.

Finally in 1982 Curt got a $11,000 grant from the National Endowment of the Arts for finishing funds, and two years later the film was finished – or at least reportedly so.

SPARKLES TAVERN premièred at the 1984 Seattle Film Festival. The film was still technically "in progress". Curt and Marion arrived at the Seattle airport with suitcases full of film and about $4 each in their pockets. Since the soundtrack hadn't yet been "married" to the print, the film had to play on synchronized A and B rolls on a duel-system interlock projector. Such a projector was obtained but the splices just wouldn't feed through it. It was, simply, a disaster – and in front of a packed house no less. After frustrating false starts the audience had to go home. Curt and Marion had spent their way through their eight bucks and a fan gave them $5 to get home on. They spent that on a bottle of cheap wine, a loaf of bread and some salami and repaired back to Curt's hotel room to party and toast the debacle. Curt photographed their beggar's banquet, incorporating the pictures into one of his patented collage scrapbooks, which, along with all the others, the Curt McDowell Foundation now possesses.

The film's next engagement was two weeks away, booked to play at the Castro theatre as part of the San Francisco Gay and Lesbian Film Festival. The palatial and cavernous Castro would no doubt be packed for the show. Marion upbraided Curt that he **had** to get the rolls to a lab and get an acceptable show print. They were both flat broke at the time but Marion figured that if they went to the Castro the day before the show and told them they had no money to get the print out of the lab that the Castro would have to pay for it. And that's how it worked... although actually the Roxie paid for it.

The San Francisco première was a success and attracted the interest of the programmer for the Mill Valley Film Festival who booked it into a midnight slot there. Marion, then living in San Francisco in the Castro district, returned with Curt to see the show. Again, none of her actor friends came. SPARKLES TAVERN also played at the New York Gay and Lesbian Film Festival and had several other screenings around the country at festivals and universities. Marion distributed the film herself and by her own admission was not as thorough and professional about it as she could have been. For one thing she doesn't use a typewriter, let alone a computer. All her communications are in meditative longhand, even her Will. Then again she is first and foremost an actor, not a filmmaker or film distributor.

In October of 1992 SPARKLES TAVERN returned to Seattle for a proper run at the Pike Street Cinema. Seattle critic Frederic Kahler welcomed the film back to town at long last, calling it "a lusty, bizarre, sexually-dripping marvel of the emotional dangers in a dysfunctional family crippled with secrets and lost passions". Marion returned in person to Seattle in July of 1993 when the same Pike Street cinema presented a definitive Mike and George Kuchar retrospective guest-curated by Johannes Schönherr. Mike and George appeared in person to introduce their films, and Marion was present to introduce THUNDERCRACK! and SPARKLES TAVERN. She also had other reasons for presenting the films at the Seattle retrospective, those being: (1) to bring SPARKLES TAVERN back to town for a **successful** show, and (2) to reclaim a print of THUNDERCRACK! from The Foundation to replace the mint copy she had given to Robert Evans some years previous. The Foundation never contested the fact that SPARKLES TAVERN was her film, but they were enraged when she informed them that she was keeping the print of THUNDERCRACK! that had played in Seattle and they promptly threatened to sue her. Marion, on the other hand, felt that Curt's work should be more actively distributed and promoted, and that her contacts with film show organizers in Europe and America could facilitate this. It was also, simply, a case of her taking back her own image. Nobody in the Foundation had the slightest real connection with the film and there she was up on the screen baring her soul and various regions of her naked flesh in a daring and controversial work of film art that had caused her much emotional turmoil in the past. Acting in a Curt McDowell film had always involved a personal contract. Curt was dead but the movie lived and the contract remained. Marion had always believed in the film and "stayed with it" while other actors who had participated in it had disappeared or disowned it. The Foundation still controlled 2 or 3 prints of the movie; if Marion, broke as she was, could also make some money off this print, she wasn't about to scorn the dough. (Not that there **is** much money to be made on one print of such a politically-incorrect, oddball item whose booking potential is greatly diminished due to the near-extinction today of the independent repertory cinema. Video, obviously, is where the real money is.) Finally, Marion felt justified legally in reclaiming the print via the fact that she possesses a handwritten and signed letter from Curt stating that she should have full control over three films that could not have been made without her: TABOO, THUNDERCRACK! and SPARKLES TAVERN. As of this writing no formal legal action has been initiated between Marion and The Foundation, but the situation nonetheless raises a host of interesting questions that bear broadly upon issues such as AIDS and the handling of the creative legacies of its victims.

At the time of SPARKLES TAVERN's release in 1984, Curt's irreverent, playful approach to all matters sexual was strictly out of style. The AIDS crisis would impel a more serious, almost political approach to sex. And while SPARKLES TAVERN lacked the explicit sex of THUNDERCRACK!, it had a radiantly explicit **spirit** and a decidedly politically-incorrect bent. The '70s already seemed a long time gone. The film had arrived in a time capsule. After a brief round of spot shows and festival appearances the film was mothballed. Marion gave The Foundation the answer print and information about the film lab in Memphis, Tennessee where the print had been struck and where the negative now lay in storage. She had in the meantime moved to a small cottage in Mill Valley. She was broke and the cottage didn't even have a phone, so she figured The Foundation could look after the film best. In late September of 1993 she turned up the address of the lab and passed it along to a friend who wrote to them in the hope of having the negative shipped back to Marion. The lab wrote back with some shocking news: the negative had been destroyed sometime around 1990. They had tried to contact concerned parties in San Francisco several times to return the negative but the only address they had there was out-of-date and no forwarding address had been filed. Their policy was to destroy all film unclaimed after a 5 year period, and so, finally, the negative was destroyed, leaving only 2 prints in existence: a showable "slop" print and the timed "A" print that the Foundation returned to Marion and which at the time of this writing resides in Europe. The European distributor refuses to rent it out and gamble on the crap-shoot of careless postal clerks and projectionists. The film has never been transferred to video. Its very existence today is precarious.

One of Curt's best known films was LOADS, a popular short at Gay film festivals. Curt shot it on the sly, after hours while living in the Golden Gate Avenue loft and working on SPARKLES TAVERN. LOADS profiles men Curt paid to come up to the loft and masturbate or perform sex acts with Curt. The film captured the grainy black-and-white "dirty" porno look he favoured. "He had a wonderful sense of smut cinema," George would say of Curt in a 1988 interview. "He loved zooming, his movies always had a lot of zoom shots and they were kind of over-exposed – he loved the raw-looking stuff because he was turned on by pornography. He incorporated all pornographic movie techniques into his pictures. That was his calling in life."

Marion didn't know Curt was making LOADS at the time and surmises with an expression of horror that Curt must have been paying these tricks with her money because as usual he was broke at the time. She also speculates that Curt's unhappiness at having to jettison explicit sex from SPARKLES TAVERN had driven him to simultaneously create one of his most explicit films ever. LOADS was too much for a lot of people, including, at first, Marion. And including John Waters as well. "I was shocked by LOADS!" declared the supposedly shock-proof Waters in a 1988 interview.

ON GRAFFITI, SHAKESPEARE AND USING PAYPHONES IN THE RAIN
Marion played an important part in another Curt McDowell film in 1982: the 45-minute TABOO – THE SINGLE AND THE LP. McDowell described the black-and-white film as a "cubistic narrative" inspired by seven pieces of graffiti he came across in various men's rooms. The film ends with grisly, unflinching footage from an actual autopsy. "I just wish I knew what this film meant," Curt commented to a critic at the première. San Francisco critic Ellen Trabilcy described the film as "a rhythmic jumble of sights, sounds and sensations". Marion views TABOO as a "pure" Curt McDowell film in its experimental, avant-garde approach. The strong narrative line of SPARKLES TAVERN had in fact been a radical departure for McDowell.

Marion also acted in several of George Kuchar's class films and personal productions, among them, A REASON TO LIVE (1976), BLIPS (1979) and the magnum opus of the class films, SYMPHONY FOR A SINNER (1979). "SYMPHONY was planned as our big, full-scale colour production", recalls George of the film that New York critic, J. Hoberman would rank as one of the ten best films of the entire year. Stan Brakhage praised it as the "ultimate class picture", while John Waters was in envy of the lurid colour look and suggested George do the photography on his next film – it was the look he had craved for DESPERATE LIVING he said.

George wrote Marion's part and gave it to her to prepare for a week in advance, and the film plays pointedly on the dynamic of "actor among non-actors" discussed previously. Curt created her costume and make-up and they took a cab to the class.

Marion appeared in another class film shot around 1986. She was broke and needed the $50 the Art Institute paid as a guest-artist fee. This was more of a "show up and act" gig, and lacking dialogue, George told her to just recite some Shakespeare. And she does so with equanimity while laying and falling about with a cast of students. The scene is basically a non sequitur in motion that somehow works. George reports that student cast was in awe of Marion; here was a **real** actress! Marion

Marion Eaton; *A Reason To Live*

also acted in Mike Kuchar's film, FABLE FOR A NEW AGE, in 1984.

Since 1986 Marion has lived in a small cottage on back acreage of what remains of Mill Valley's first farm, now bordered on one side by a 7-11. In the upstairs cottage next to Marion lives Charlie Deal, famous in Rock & Roll circles for the guitars he constructs out of toilet seats. Tool sheds, vine-covered trellises, garden plots and a rabbit house crowd the grounds. Occupying the small front house until his death at 97 on December 29th, 1993, was Henry, the eccentric gentleman who was born there. Henry specialized in constructing little tin animals and spirit figures which populated the overgrown grounds and hung in the boughs of the trees, many of them named and dated by Marion. Henry also liked to paint: he painted his shoes, his belt, his tools, the tin figurines... the upshot is a bizarre, carnivalesque atmosphere something akin to Art Brut meets Disneyland. The spread was called "Goldieland" after Henry's pet rabbit, but that one accidentally strangled and then he got a black rabbit so they tried out "Blackieland". Henry had a phone in his house and took incoming calls for Marion by rattling a cow bell on a line in the back yard to get her attention (and jangle her nerves into the bargain). To call out long distance she used a pay phone down the street, sometimes in the rain. (Henry was a stickler about the phone bill!) Marion helped Henry cultivate several garden beds of vegetables through seven springs. He claimed he never got cucumbers to grow so good as when "the girl" came to live there.

In 1988 Marion got a bit part in a Vestron Pictures production entitled PAINT IT BLACK, directed by Tim Hunter (RIVER'S EDGE, etc.), a long-time Marion Eaton/ George Kuchar fan. On the strength of her role in PAINT IT BLACK, Marion got a role in another Vestron picture: SUNDOWN – REVENGE OF THE VAMPIRES, directed by Anthony Hickox. She was flown out to Moab, Utah to film on location and had her own make-up trailer – a new experience to be sure. Joe Bob Briggs gives SUNDOWN three stars and says check it out.

In the spring of 1992 Marion flew to Frankfurt, Germany to begin a film tour that would take her to Vienna, Munich, Berlin, Amsterdam, a score of smaller Dutch cities, and to London where she appeared live on stage to introduce THUNDERCRACK! to a full house of her long-time fans. She took trains through Europe unescorted and carried the 16mm prints of THUNDERCRACK! and TABOO in her knapsack. She wryly remarks that the warm and positive memories of Curt she nurtured throughout the initial stages of the tour gave way to vile invective the heavier the prints got to lug around. "God Damn him!..." (3 hours worth of 16mm film is not light.) And she knows he's laughing about it now, wherever he is.

Back in Mill Valley, Marion continued working short-term jobs as a nursing as-sistant and was 24-hour bedside companion and nurse to Henry in the last week of his life. In the months that followed Henry's death, Marion remained at the cottage to clean up the house and put loose ends in order for Henry's son. It was when she found herself polishing up a 3-D picture of the Virgin Mary that lights up when you plug it in that she realized it was definitely time to move on.

Over the last few years she's spent considerable time and effort reading and memorizing the works of her favourite author, Edna St. Vincent Millay. She plans to create a one-woman theatre production around the poetry of Millay and return to her first love – the stage. Once again she finds herself saying, "Oh God, this language is beautiful!" Her latest screen role is in Dan Ireland's THE WHOLE WIDE WORLD, the real-life tale of author Robert E. Howard.

The November 1993 Kuchar/McDowell retrospective at the Castro drew big crowds for every show. Marion never made it but George went. He mailed her a short note soon after: "Everything looked grand on the big screen. It was a real treat. I hadn't seen THUNDERCRACK! in so long and I want to tell you what a marvellous and memorable performance you gave. Truly a gem. The film is quite startling, especially now, in the '90s."

FILMOGRAPHY

The following lists are not exhaustive in every case, but every effort has been made to make them as complete and up to date as possible.

JOHN WATERS

Hag In A Black Leather Jacket (1964)
Roman Candles (1966)
Eat Your Make-Up (1968)
Mondo Trasho (1969)
The Diane Linkletter Story (1970)
Multiple Maniacs (1970)
Pink Flamingos (1972)
Female Trouble (1974)
Desperate Living (1977)
Polyester (1981)
Hairspray (1988)
Crybaby (1990)
Serial Mom (1993)

GEORGE & MIKE KUCHAR

The Wet Destruction Of The Atlantic Empire (1954)
Screwball (1957)
The Naked And The Nude (1957)
The Slasher (1958)
The Thief And The Stripper (1959)
A Tub Named Desire (1960)
I Was A Teenage Rumpot (1960)
Pussy On A Hot Tin Roof (1961)
Born Of The Wind (1961)
A Woman Distressed (1962)
A Town Called Tempest (1962)
Night Of The Bomb (1962)
Lust For Ecstasy (1963)
The Confessions Of Babette (1963)
Tootsies In Autumn (1963)
Anita Needs Me (1963)
The Lovers Of Eternity (1963)

GEORGE KUCHAR

Corruption Of The Damned (1965)
Hold Me While I'm Naked (1966)
Leisure (1966)
Mosholu Holiday (1966)
Color Me Shameless (1967)
Eclipse Of The Sun Virgin (1967)
The Lady From Sands Point (1967)
Knocturne (1968)
Unstrap Me (1968)
House Of The White People (1968)

Encyclopedia Of The Blessed (1968)
The Mammal Palace (1969)
Pagan Rhapsody (1970)
Portrait Of Ramona (1971)
The Sunshine Sisters (1972)
The Devil's Cleavage (1973)
Back To Nature (1976)
A Reason To Live (1976)
La Casa De Chorizo (1977)
Ky Kapers (1977)
Wild Night In El Reno (1977)
Forever And Always (1978)
Mongreloid (1978)
Blips (1979)
Aqueerius (1980)
The Nocturnal Immaculation (1980)
Yolando (1981)
Cattle Mutilations (1983)
Mom (1983)
Untitled Musical (1984)
The X-People (1984)
Ascension Of The Demonoids (1985)

Produced at San Francisco Art Institute:

Destination Damnation (1972)
Carnal Bipeds (1973)
I Married A Heathen (1974)
The Desperate And The Deep (1975)
I, An Actress (1977)
The Asphalt Ribbon (1977)
One Night A Week (1978)
Prescrition In Blue (1978)
The Power Of The Press (1979)
Remember Tomorrow (1979)
Symphony For A Sinner (1979)
How To Chose A Wife (1980)
The Woman And The Dress (1980)
Ochokpug (1980)
Boulevard Kishka (1981)
The Oneers (1982)
Ms. Hyde (1983)
Club Vatican (1984)
The Legend Of Thelma White (1985)
Motel Capri (1986)
La Noche D'Amour (1986)
PRC Musical (1986)

Insanitorium (1987)
Summer Of No Return (1988)
La Verbotene Voyage (1989)

MIKE KUCHAR

The Pervert (1963)
Born Of The Wind (1964)
Sins Of The Fleshapoids (1965)
Green Desire (1966)
The Secret Of Wendel Samson (1966)
Fragments (1967)
The Craven Sluck (formerly titled *Madonna*, 1967)
Variations (1968)
Cycles (1968)
Tales Of The Bronx (1969)
Chronicles (1969)
Abode Of The Snow (1970)
Aqua Circus (1971)
Didgeridoo (1972)
Faraway Places (1972)
Death Quest Of The Ju-Ju Cults (1976)
Dwarf Star (1977)
Fable For A New Age (1984)
Tone Poem (1984)
Seascape (1984)

Produced at San Francisco Art Institute:

The Masque Of Valhalla (1972)
The Wings Of Muru (1973)
Blood Sucker (1975)
The Passions: A Psycho-Drama (1977)
Isle Of The Sleeping Souls (1979)
Circe (1984)

Produced at the Collective For Living Cinema's
Dramatic Narrative Class:

Scream Of The Damned (1987)

CURT McDOWELL

Films as director and as actor:

A Visit To Indiana (1970)
Confessions (1971)
The Devil's Cleavage (1973)
Baggy Depot (1974)
True Blue And Dreamy (1974)
Lunch (1974)
Nudes – A Sketchbook (1975/76)
Thundercrack! (1975)
Fly Me To The Moon (1975)
Tasteless Trilogy (mid-'70s)
Siamese Twin Pinheads (mid-'70s)

Ronnie (mid-'70s)
Pornografollies (mid-'70s)
Peed Into The Wind (mid-'70s)
Wieners And Buns Musical (1976)
Sparkles Tavern (1976/84)
Loads (1976)
Taboo – The Single & LP (1981)

MARION EATON

Film appearances:

Sip The Wine (1974)
Thundercrack! (1975)
A Reason To Live (1976)
Sparkles Tavern (1976)
Undertow (1977)
Symphony For A Sinner (1979)
Blips (1979)
Taboo (1981)
Fable For A New Age (1984)
The Presence Of The Goddess (1984)
Miracle On Neptrune Street (1984)
Paint It Black (1988)
Sundown (1991)
The Whole Wide World (1995)

INDEX OF FILM & VIDEO

Page number in bold indicates an illustration. Video productions appear in italics. See also filmography and footnote page 184 for productions not mentioned in the main text.